THE COMPLETE
PERFORMANCE
HORSE

THE COMPLETE PERFORMANCE
HORSE

Feeding • Fitness • Lameness
Preventive medicine

Colin Vogel

David and Charles

PICTURE ACKNOWLEDGEMENTS

Author pp2, 6, 8, 13, 14, 21, 22, 23(2), 24, 25, 27, 30, 31, 38, 57, 62, 66, 69, 74, 77, 106, 127(4), 138, 139, 151, 152, 152, 155, 158, 160(2), 161, 162, 164, 165, 167(2), 175, 180(2), 183, 186, 188, 189, 190(2), 192(top), 194(2), 197, 203, 204, 207, 211, 216, 219, 221, 223
Pfizer Limited p26(4)
Kit Houghton pp32, 33(2), 34(2), 35(2), 42, 50–1, 58, 59, 79 (top), 91, 92, 93, 98–9, 110–11, 122, 129, 130–1, 135, 146–7, 176, 178–9, 234
Derek Croucher p44
Bob Langrish pp63, 65
Mary and Philip Bromiley p79 (btm)

Line illustrations all by Chartwell Illustrators except:
Author pp10, 70, 177, 182, 183, 184, 185, 189 (btm right), 194, 205, 211, 214, 233; Hayward Art Group p46; Eva Melhuish pp102, 103 (left), 154 (btm right); Drum p189 (top)

A DAVID & CHARLES BOOK
Copyright © David & Charles Limited 1996, 2006

David & Charles is an F+W Publications Inc. company
4700 East Galbraith Road
Cincinnati, OH 45236

First published in the UK in 1996
Reprinted 2004
First paperback edition 2006

Text copyright © Colin J. Vogel 1996, 2006

A catalogue record for this book is available from the British Library.

ISBN-13: 978-0-7153-2307-6
ISBN-10: 0-7153-2307-5

Printed in Italy by Milano Stampa - A.G.G.
for David & Charles
Brunel House   Newton Abbot   Devon

Visit our website at www.davidandcharles.co.uk

David & Charles books are available from all good bookshops; alternatively you can contact our Orderline on 0870 9908222 or write to us at FREEPOST EX2 110, D&C Direct, Newton Abbot, TQ12 4ZZ (no stamp required UK only); US customers call 800-289-0963 and Canadian customers call 800-840-5220.

PREVENTIVE MEDICINE

CONTENTS

INFECTIOUS & CONTAGIOUS DISEASES

When is an Infectious Disease Contagious?

The distinction between infectious and contagious disease is actually quite an arbitrary one. An infectious disease is simply a disease which can spread from one horse to another. This means that it is caused by a living organism, which has to survive the transfer if it is to survive itself. Equine influenza is an infectious disease: if one horse in a group develops the disease, other horses will also probably become infected. In contrast to this, although a couple of horses grazing the same field may both develop acorn poisoning, that is not an infectious disease; it arose independently in each horse rather than going from one to another, and it is not caused by a living organism.

All contagious diseases are also infectious, the distinction being that a contagious disease can only pass from one horse to another as a result of direct contact between the two horses. In this case the organism responsible cannot really survive away from the horse. There are relatively few contagious diseases of the horse, ie diseases where we can categorically say that if a horse has the disease it must have had direct physical contact with another infected horse. An example would be lice, which cannot survive away from the horse, and which spread by direct contact. Of course, man upsets such classifications: for example, transfer lice from one horse to another by grooming one horse and then immediately going on to groom another with the same grooming kit.

How Parasites, Fungi, Bacteria and Viruses cause Disease

Although everyone nowadays has heard of parasites, fungi, bacteria and viruses, relatively few people understand exactly what they are. A **parasite** is a living creature which lives on or inside another living creature, and derives its food from that host; it takes everything, but gives nothing back in return. **Fungi** are plant-like parasites. Each cell is a self-contained organism in its own right, but they often form filaments of cells attached to each other. In the case of one common fungal infection of horses, ringworm, the fungal cells form a collar around hairs, weakening them and causing them to break off. Fungal cells multiply by dividing and forming new cells, but when adverse conditions come along, they form spores, which have special protective coats and are really a form of seedpod to spread the fungus to another host.

Bacteria are microscopic single-celled organisms which multiply by simply dividing into two, a process called binary fission.

1   A horse showing skin lesions typical of ringworm

In ideal conditions they can do this every forty minutes or so. This may not sound much of a threat when it is one bacteria becoming two, but when we are considering ten million bacteria becoming twenty million within the hour, then it is rapid multiplication indeed. There are many families of bacteria, each one with a family name *eg Streptococcus*, and a specific name, *eg equi*, thus *Streptococcus equi*.

Not all bacteria are harmful, of course. The horse relies on the bacteria living in its colon to break down and digest all the cellulose in the plant material it eats; they convert this to simple sugars and amino acids, which can then be absorbed through the gut wall. Without these bacteria the horse would be no more able to live off grass than we can. When an organism gives a positive benefit back in return for its shelter and food, it is said to be a **commensal**.

It is important to realise that only bacteria are killed by the drugs which we call antibiotics. In theory, all bacteria are susceptible to the drugs, but specific bacteria tend to be able to resist specific antibiotics, either partially or completely. There is no such thing as a stronger or a weaker antibiotic: in any given situation there are only effective and ineffective drugs.

Viruses are even smaller than bacteria. Basically they are tiny parcels of DNA or RNA, the genetic material found in the nuclei of each cell in our body. Because viruses do not really have any protective coats, they are all relatively susceptible to environmental conditions such as heat and drying. They can reproduce extremely rapidly in the cells of the horse's body, and antibiotics have no effect against them. Indeed there are no drugs which will kill viruses without damaging the body tissues as well. As everyone knows, we still await cures for the common cold and for AIDS, two viral diseases of man. Equine herpes virus (EHV) would be the horse's equivalent of the common cold.

Skin Diseases

It is worth considering the various ways in which infectious disease can affect the competition horse by reducing its performance. Infectious skin diseases have very little effect on performance but they are very noticeable, and so all the other owners at the competition cannot fail to be aware that your horse has an infectious disease (Fig 1). Occasionally skin lesions become rubbed by tack and so become raw and painful, but in most cases the danger looks worse that it is. However, one feature of skin diseases is that they can often survive away from the horse for some time. After all, they are exposed to most environmental factors on the horse's skin anyway. Fungal spores from ringworm, for example, can survive in a stable for years sometimes.

There are a number of infectious diseases which, although they are not a skin disease as such, do affect the skin in a way that limits performance. Some viruses, such as Equine viral arteritis (EVA), cause the accumulation of oedema or tissue fluid underneath the skin. When there is oedema of the legs this will affect performance, quite apart from how rotten the horse feels as a result of the infection; it must be like exercising with the legs bandaged. Strangles, on the other hand, causes abscesses which burst through the skin even though the skin is not the main site of the infection.

Infections affecting the Legs

There are few infectious diseases which specifically infect the horse's legs and so reduce its locomotor efficiency. Lymphangitis is often associated with infection. The whole leg becomes swollen due to the accumulation of fluid under the skin when the drainage of tissue fluid becomes blocked (Fig 2, p.8). Most viral and bacterial infections will make the horse feel lethargic when they spread through the body, and it will not do itself justice in such a situation; it is therefore best to acknowledge this from the start. If a horse has a raised body temperature, its muscles will not work properly because the chemical reactions which result in muscle contraction are very sensitive to temperature. Viruses in particular will infect a horse's whole body without causing a high temperature or any obvious clinical symptoms – though when it is worked, its performance is much reduced. How many times do racehorse trainers attribute their lack of success to the effects of 'a virus'? There are, however, certain ways of telling whether the horse has a virus infection or not.

Infections of the Nervous System

There are two infectious diseases which affect the horse's nervous system and also affect its performance. **Tetanus** is certainly the best known of

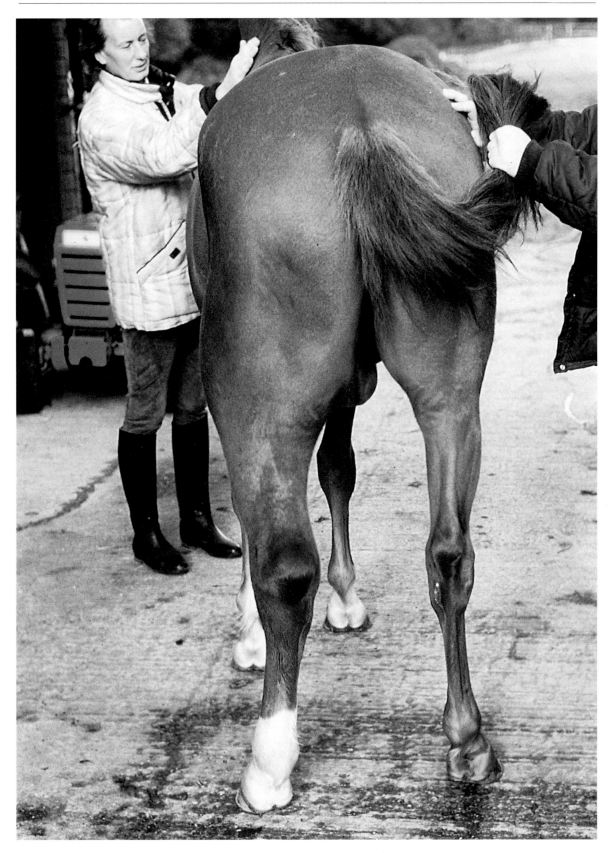

2 Lymphangitis: the rear hindleg clearly shows the characteristic swelling (see p.7)

these. It causes abnormal contractions of muscles, and so certainly prevents any performance. Another bacterium from the same clostridial family causes **botulism**, where the muscles become paralysed. These are serious diseases which can kill a horse. They develop quite quickly, so there is not usually any time when the horse's performance is affected but without the owner knowing why. There are also some viruses which specifically affect the brain, such as Eastern equine encephalomyelitis, which occurs in the USA.

Infections of the Respiratory System

These have a tremendous effect on the horse's performance, and most of them are caused by viruses. Indeed, when a trainer excuses poor performance as being due to the horse having 'a virus', he usually means a respiratory virus. Respiratory infections spread very rapidly because they are droplet-spread: the tiny water droplets in

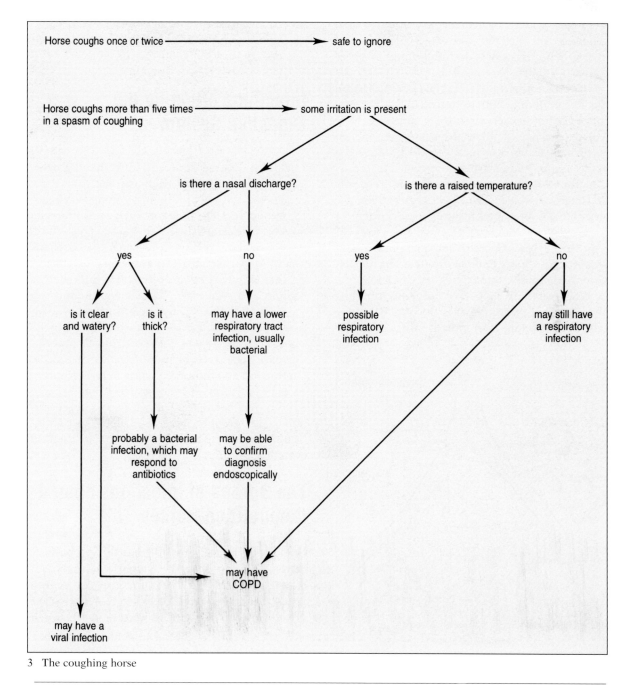

3   The coughing horse

the atmosphere are light enough to be carried for a hundred yards or more in the breeze, and each droplet can contain one or more virus particles. Nor are they any respectors of property, passing easily from one stable to another. Respiratory infections trigger off coughing in the horse, and each cough produces a very large number of infected droplets. Because they are light enough to float in the air, they are also light enough and small enough to be sucked right down into the lungs by another horse, there to establish a new infection.

Owners often expect vets to stop a horse coughing. Although there are drugs which may do this, it is not in itself a desirable thing to do. A cough is a defensive mechanism. If we stop the horse coughing up mucus from its lower airways, the accumulating mucus may have a serious effect. Owners are very sensitive to coughing. They will ignore a persistent nasal discharge or reduced performance, but may call the vet because the horse coughs four or five times a day. It is important to realise that some horses are more prone to cough as a defensive mechanism than are other horses. As a simplification horses either use swallowing or coughing as their main way of removing excess mucus from their larynx and pharynx. So a horse can have quite a serious respiratory disease but not cough very much.

When we think about the common symptoms of respiratory infections, it is obvious why they affect performance so much. Mucus in the nostrils, trachea and lungs reduces the cross-sectional area of the airways, so the horse can breathe in less air (Fig 4). If the lymph nodes around the horse's neck do their job and trap the infectious agent, they will swell up and possibly put pressure on the larynx as well. Finally at the site of absorption of oxygen into the bloodstream, there should only be one cell between the air and the blood; but during respiratory infections there will be mucus as well. The inflamed lung tissue will also be swollen and thicker than normal, and with a thicker barrier between the air and the blood, less oxygen will be transferred. Because oxygen is used in energy production, that means less energy is available for performance.

Infections affecting the Digestive System

Luckily the horse does not suffer from gastro-intestinal infections as often as some species do. It does not fall prey to food poisoning very readily, although if an infection such as Salmonella does become established in the horse, it may cause diarrhoea and this can have serious repercussions regarding performance because diarrhoea means the loss of both fluid and electrolyte salts such as sodium and potassium. Muscle contraction can only occur if the right concentrations of electrolytes are present in the tissue fluid bathing the muscle cells, so loss of both fluid and electrolytes means a reduction in the efficiency of muscle contraction and thus a reduction in performance. At the same time, if a horse which has become dehydrated because of diarrhoea is forced to undertake strenuous exercise, it will lose more fluid in sweat, and this will make the situation even more serious.

The Spread of Infections among Competition Horses

In the wild, horses stay in quite stable groups or herds. There are some individuals which remain outside the herd, but a herd member comes into contact with few, if any, foreigners. When an infectious disease is introduced into the herd, it will spread very rapidly because the members are in such close contact with each other. However, after the disease has done its worst, the remaining

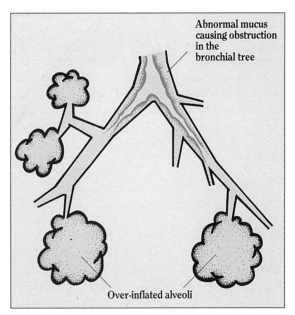

Abnormal mucus causing obstruction in the bronchial tree

Over-inflated alveoli

4 Mucus-reducing area of bronchi

horses will be resistant to further attacks of the same disease for some time.

The life of the competition horse is very different. The stable yard of horses is the equivalent of the herd, and diseases will spread rapidly around that yard; during that time performance will deteriorate. The difference lies in how the disease spreads from yard to yard. Thus every time a horse goes to a competition, it is potentially exposed to infection. That infection may or may not be able to establish itself in or on the horse, depending on the level of its immunity against that disease. What is more important is that the horse can act as a passive transfer agent, and infections brought back to the stable yard in or on a horse can easily pass direct to the other horses. Even handlers, tack and transport can act as the carrying agent.

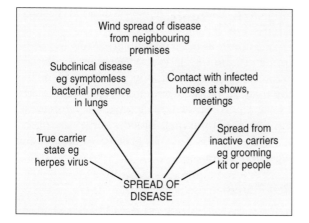

5 The spread of disease

After the introduction of a disease into a yard, immunity develops against further infection with the same disease. This immunity gradually decreases, although should the same disease be introduced a second time, there will still be some level of protection. So there are a number of diseases which are said to be endemic in a particular horse population, meaning that the disease is always present to a greater or lesser extent, but because of the existence of immunity it does not always result in clinical disease. What the transport of horses over long distances to competitions has done, however, is to provide numerous opportunities for 'foreign' strains of disease to be brought back to the stable yard. A strain which is endemic in one area will be foreign in another, and as I have already indicated, it is when a foreign infection is first introduced into a group of horses that you get the most severe symptoms of the disease.

The international movement of competition horses poses a particular threat. In the UK the introduction of a virulent strain of equine influenza into the country by a show jumper in 1979, and the introduction of EVA by a stallion in 1994, are two examples of the serious consequences which the international movement of horses can have. In an effort to prevent such consequences, governments may place restrictions on the importation of horses (including the re-importation of horses after competitions); such controls are usually based on the testing for specific diseases, and the quarantining of horses prior to import. Each country will decide its own priorities for disease control, depending on the particular threat they see to be posed by the diseases endemic in the other country. There are two aspects of testing which can pose problems. The first is its scientific reliability. Regrettably there have been occasions where a horse was given a clean certificate by a laboratory in the country of origin, even though it was suffering from the disease. In the case of a horse visiting another country and wanting to return to its country of origin, this would only happen accidentally due to poor laboratory standards. As regards a horse being purchased abroad, there have been suggestions that disease clearance has been 'bought'.

The other problem with testing is that it cannot tell the difference between immunity due to infection, and that which is due to vaccination. As we get cleverer, we are being able to make vaccines against more and more diseases. At the same time, as the value of competition horses is so high we naturally wish to protect them as fully as possible against as many diseases as possible. However, if you vaccinate a horse against EVA in the UK and take it to a country such as Poland where the disease does occur, when you come to bring that horse back to the UK there will be problems, even though you might have thought that you had taken a wise precaution. We want to keep the disease out of the country and so will only allow horses in if they have a negative blood test for EVA – but of course your horse, being vaccinated, will give a positive result and so will not be allowed back into the country. It may be that in the future we will be able to develop tests that do differentiate between natural and vaccinal immunity, but until that time it is a wise precaution before vaccinating a horse against anything except the ubiquitous flu, tetanus and herpes to have a blood sample taken and tested at a laboratory recognised by the state veterinary service. In the future you then have proof that it is the vaccination given at the same time as the test which has caused any raised immunity levels, rather than natural infection. A number of countries which ban the import of horses with EVA have already indicated that they will allow the importation of horses from the UK which had a clear blood test taken at the time of the first vaccination against the disease.

Sometimes countries set very unreasonable import requirements, possibly merely as a way of limiting imports that might compare too favourably with native-bred horses. The worst example of this was when the USA insisted that any female horses being imported had their clitoris surgically removed as a precaution against the introduction of contagious equine metritis (CEM). Obviously most people would consider it unethical to remove part of a horse's body just to satisfy an official whim which had little scientific justification.

We usually think of government import requirements as being very rigid, but the Barcelona Olympic Games showed that this is not always the case. During the period prior to the Games, Spain had African horse sickness (AHS) in a couple of southern provinces. Because of this, most non-African countries would not allow any horse to be imported from Spain. This is the way such restrictions had always been imposed – they applied to the whole country. However, nobody would then have sent horses to the Olympic Games, a situation which would have been very embarrassing. The solution was to abandon the national border and to restrict imports from just a part of Spain. Surprisingly, this did not include Barcelona, so the equestrian classes at the Olympics went ahead!

Preventing the Spread of Disease

■ Quarantine

Years ago the only way by which we could prevent the spread of disease was to stop the movement of animals, and this is still a very effective method. The code of practice for the control of CEM and other diseases still says that if an outbreak of disease occurs on a stud farm, no animals should leave the stud until the situation has been controlled. An alternative to a complete ban on movement is to allow movement in conjunction with a period of quarantine. People sometimes interchange the words 'quarantine' and 'isolation': they do have similar meanings, but 'quarantine' is really a period of isolation imposed on you *by others*, and sometimes supervised by them.

The period of quarantine usually occurs in the country of origin, before the horse is moved. This makes sense, because then if the disease does occur at the quarantine centre and 'escapes' into the surrounding country, it does not matter. African horse sickness (AHS) is a good example of this because it is spread by a biting midge, which obviously can fly in and out of the quarantine station. If horses were quarantined on arrival in a country where AHS did not occur and the disease escaped, then it could kill the completely susceptible horses around and establish itself in that new country.

The duration of quarantine naturally depends on the disease which you are seeking to control. In many cases countries impose a blanket thirty-day quarantine requirement, because there are few, if any diseases which have an incubation period longer than that. Blood samples are often taken during this time, and they also have to be negative if the horse is to be allowed to move on.

■ Isolation

Isolation simply means to separate the horse from any other horses. It is not enough to have a stable just round the corner from the others and call this an isolation box: there must be a separation of 200 to 300 metres/yards if viruses are not to spread between the two sites. Even then it would be wise to have the isolation unit downwind from the main yard. In areas of high horse populations, care must be taken that separating an isolation unit from one stable yard does not put it close to someone else's yard.

The ideal is for any horse in isolation to be looked after by a different person to the other horses, using different tack, and feeding from a separate food store, so that there is no contact between the isolated horse and the others. If this is not possible, the groom should have a complete change of clothes and footwear at the isolation unit.

Of course the greater the risk, the stricter the isolation should be. Bringing a horse that has been away at a competition back into a stable just around the corner from the others may be all that is justified in view of the low risk of disease spread, but if there was a high incidence of equine flu around the country it would not be sufficient isolation to provide reliable protection. Time is another consideration: most viruses that we are concerned about have an incubation period of three to ten days, so at least ten days' isolation would be required.

■ Disinfection

Even apparently healthy horses may be carrying diseases to which they have immunity but which may infect other horses; for this reason, whenever a stable is to be used for a new horse it should first be disinfected. Even a visiting horse using a stable for a couple of hours brings a certain risk, and should result in the disinfection of that stable rather than just mucking it out. Horse boxes and trailers especially should be disinfected before being used for a different horse, and in some countries it may well be illegal for commercial transporters not to do this.

Disinfectants kill bacteria and suchlike by direct contact; thus if the disease organism is protected by a covering of dried faeces, for example, it will survive. Some disinfectants, such as those based on hypochlorite, are inactive in the presence of such organic material anyway. So the stable must be cleaned before it is disinfected, and any disinfection will only be as effective as the cleaning allows.

There is a wide range of disinfectants to choose from. Some may have been approved by the Ministry of Agriculture for use in disinfecting farms where notifiable diseases have occurred, and this gives rise to all kinds of advertising claims. It is worth remembering that most disinfectants will kill bacteria and viruses if applied to a clean surface for a long enough time at the recommended dilution, and allowed to dry *in situ*. Indeed, even the drying effect of water evaporating after the cleaning will kill a significant number of infectious agents. Many people expect cold alone to kill off infections, and rely on the frosts of winter to reduce their overall level. In fact most infections, and bacteria especially, are more readily killed by heat than by cold, and you should never rely on either hot or cold weather to do the job of cleaning and disinfection.

Another point which is often forgotten is that the stable walls extend right up to the roof. There is no point in just cleaning and disinfecting the floor or the bottom couple of feet of wall; infectious organisms are often airborne, and can become trapped in cobwebs or lie safely on the tops of mangers. Incidentally, a vacuum cleaner can be the most effective way to get rid of cobwebs high up the walls. Steam cleaning or pressure-hosing (Fig 6) will be easier than getting up stepladders and scrubbing by hand.

6 Steam cleaning: easier than scrubbing by hand

THE IMMUNE SYSTEM

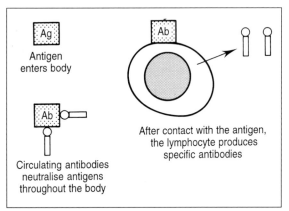

7 The horse's immune system is based on the antigen/antibody reaction

Antigen enters body

Circulating antibodies neutralise antigens throughout the body

After contact with the antigen, the lymphocyte produces specific antibodies

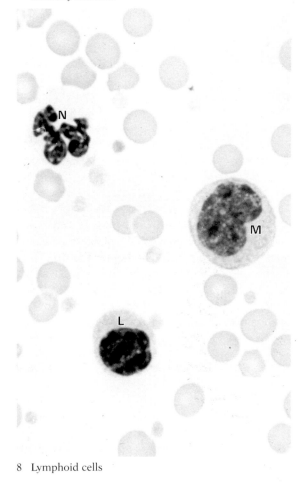

8 Lymphoid cells

Before considering the diseases against which vaccination is possible, it is first necessary to understand how the horse's immune system works. It is based on the antigen/antibody reaction (Fig 7). An antigen is a foreign molecule, usually a protein, which can trigger off an immune reaction in the horse. Antibodies are specific proteins produced by the horse which react with specific antigens to neutralise their effects. There are several different types of antibody, or immunoglobulin (Ig). IgG is the type of antibody which provides most of the protection against specific disease, although IgM provides the initial protection after vaccination. IgA is a rather less specific antibody which provides protection against invasion of the body surfaces such as the lining of the respiratory system. Finally there is IgE which triggers histamine release and which is therefore rather less beneficial.

Although horses can produce antibodies to protect themselves from six weeks onwards, we do not normally vaccinate foals before twelve weeks of age. This is because during the first twelve to eighteen hours of its life the foal absorbs large quantities of IgG from its mother's colostrum, or first milk; any vaccines given whilst that maternal antibody is present will be destroyed and so ineffective. By vaccinating at twelve weeks of age we compromise between our desire to protect the foal as early as possible, and the risk that any antibodies from its dam have not yet worn out.

The immune system is based on the lymphoid cells found in the horse's lymph nodes, spleen, bone marrow and so on (Fig 8); each type of cell has its own specific role. So there are large cells called macrophages whose role is to swallow up or engulf any foreign particles, whether disease organisms or not. Pus is basically a 'soup' of dead macrophages and bacteria. The most important cells from the disease-protection point of view are the lymphocytes. These cells circulate in the blood but also spend time in the lymphoid tissues mentioned earlier.

As macrophages digest the antigens present in

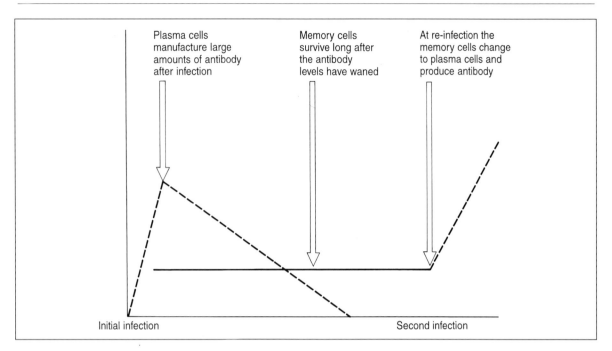

Plasma cells manufacture large amounts of antibody after infection

Memory cells survive long after the antibody levels have waned

At re-infection the memory cells change to plasma cells and produce antibody

Initial infection

Second infection

9   The effect of natural and vaccine stimulation of the immune system

a bacterium or virus they secrete a substance which attracts T-helper lymphocytes. These then become sensitised to that specific antigen and start to look for B-lymphocytes which are capable of producing antibody against that particular type of antigen. When it finds B- lymphocytes it secretes a substance which transforms them into memory cells and plasma cells.

The plasma cells then start to manufacture massive amounts of specific antibody in the lymph nodes and so on. The memory cells are long-lived cells that for months or years afterwards will be able to recognise the antigen if it appears again. They then quickly change into plasma cells and produce large quantities of antibody in what is called a secondary or anamnestic response. It is this response which is utilised in many vaccines (Fig 9). The first dose of vaccine provides antigen which stimulates the production of a certain amount of antibody and also some memory cells. The second dose of vaccine causes those memory cells to transform and produce high levels of antibody which are hopefully capable of protecting the horse against infection. In time those antibody levels will decline because no more antibody is being produced. However, a booster vaccination given at an appropriate time will stimulate memory cells to produce further antibodies.

Some viruses stimulate a reaction called a cell-mediated immune reaction. The T-helper lymphocytes sensitise other lymphocytes called cytotoxic T-lymphocytes to attack viral antigens in the invaded cell's wall, thus destroying the whole virus-invaded cell. The important point about this form of immunity is that no antibodies are produced and so we have no means of detecting its existence.

Detection of the mere existence of antibodies does not of itself guarantee that a horse is likely to be able to withstand an infection because there have to be significant numbers of antibodies present. We measure the quantity of antibodies indirectly by a figure called the antibody titre, which looks like a fraction: 1/320. It represents the ability of the antibodies in a blood sample to neutralise the antigen even when the blood sample has been diluted 320 times. The higher the titre, the more antibody there is present and hopefully the stronger the immune response would be (Fig 10).

Stress can have an important effect on the horse's immune system because it causes the release of a hormone called cortisol. Although a powerful anti-inflammatory agent, cortisol has the unfortunate side effect of inhibiting the immune system, which is why synthetic derivatives of cortisol are used to try and reduce organ rejection after transplant surgery. So if a stressed horse is exposed to infection it will be easier for that infection to establish itself in the horse. It has also been shown that if stress is mimicked by injecting large

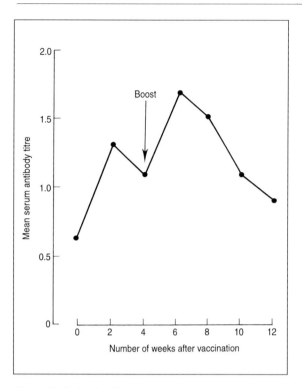

10 Antibody levels after vaccination

amounts of corticosteroids, the synthetic cortisol, then apparently healthy horses may start secreting herpes virus because the dormant virus in the bone marrow and so on has been reactivated.

The antidote to stress is routine, and the basic stable management routine should be followed meticulously whether abroad or at home, at a show or at an event. Into this framework we can introduce the stress of competition. Of course with familiarity a stress ceases to produce a stress reaction, so an occasional competition may in fact be relatively more stressful than a regular routine of competition.

Examples of factors which can be kept constant even during overseas competitions are:
● timing of meals
● source of roughage and concentrate feed
● groom
● pattern and timing of exercise
● build up/warm up on the day of competition

Limitations of Vaccination

When we vaccinate a horse we assume that the vaccine will stimulate an adequate immune response. This will never be the case in 100 per cent of horses, however, and there will always be a few horses which produce little or no response. Nor is it really fair to say that the vaccine has failed if such horses subsequently become infected with the disease because it is, after all, the horse itself which has failed. Failure to respond to vaccination usually reflects the fact that the horse's immune system has been temporarily reduced by stress or is having to cope with an existing challenge. Moreover there are a few horses which are immunologically incompetent and unable to produce antibodies at all. We do not normally check horses after vaccination to make sure that they have produced sufficient antibodies, and even if we did, the antibody titre may not give the whole story. It does not reflect any cell-mediated immunity against viruses, and it may not reflect the ability of memory cells to produce antibody if infection were to occur.

Vaccine Types

There are three main types of vaccine. We may take a living disease organism and change it in such a way that it can still infect the horse and stimulate antibody production but cannot produce disease. This is called a **live attenuated vaccine**. Live vaccines have the advantage that only one dose of vaccine is needed because the organism lives on like a natural infection, and acts as its own second vaccination. A disadvantage of live vaccines is that they may escape from the vaccinated horse and infect other in-contact horses. This may be undesirable because if the vaccine has any side effects these other horses (perhaps not even owned by the same person) will also show these side effects. Furthermore, the other horses will now show positive in any test to detect the disease, and may therefore be ineligible for import/export if a country requires freedom from that disease. Finally there is always the risk that the attenuated vaccine organism may regain some of its disease-producing properties. So although live vaccines may be very effective at producing rapid immunity, in practical circumstances we prefer to avoid using them if there is an alternative that is just as effective.

Dead vaccines contain either the whole or part of the disease-causing organism but the bacteria or viruses are first killed chemically (Fig 11). As such there is no shedding of living organisms from vaccinated horses to their companions, nor is there any risk of even mild symptoms of the

	Dose needed to stimulate protection	Side Effects	Spread to other horses
Live vaccine	Usually only one dose	May actually cause mild disease	Vaccine strain can spread to other horses. May revert to disease strain
Dead vaccine	2 – 3 doses	Occasional reaction to adjuvants (chemical carriers in the vaccine)	No effect on other horses

11 Comparison of live and dead vaccines

disease being produced after vaccination. Dead vaccines do have the disadvantage that they require two doses of vaccine to stimulate an anamnestic response, the time interval between the initial two doses varying from one vaccine to another. Manufacturers use sophisticated production techniques to ensure that the antigens from the disease organism that actually trigger off the most protective antibody production are exposed to the horse's immune system. In some cases only those immune-stimulating complexes (ISCOMs) are included in the vaccine, the rest of the organism being discarded.

The third type of vaccine is called a **toxoid**. In this case none of the actual disease organism is present, and the stimulation of the immune system is carried out by toxin released by the organism and subsequently made safe. Toxoids are only used where the major symptoms of disease are caused by toxins; they have similar advantages and disadvantages to inactivated dead vaccines. Toxoids must be differentiated from antitoxins, in that these are actual antibodies against the toxin, which have been harvested from healthy horses. Antitoxins only last for a short time (about three weeks) in the horse before they are destroyed. They are used to fight current disease rather than to provide protection against future infection.

The ability of vaccines to stimulate immunity can be markedly increased by incorporating a substance called an *adjuvant*. These can be looked upon as irritants which 'wake up' the immune system as well as holding the vaccine particles safely in one place rather than spread out and open to destruction. The more effective the adjuvant, the more likely it is to cause an inflammatory reaction around the vaccination site. Modern adjuvants may enable a vaccine to achieve the impossible, namely to produce an immunity which lasts longer than it would do after even mild clinical diseases. However, there is often a basic incompatibility in that the more effective the adjuvanted vaccine is, the more likely we are to see a swelling at the vaccine site which may last several weeks. If manufacturers design a vaccine which causes no reaction, even in fine-skinned horses, then we may find that it only stimulates low or short-lasting levels of immunity.

Side Effects of Vaccination

Since the decision by some regulatory bodies to introduce compulsory vaccination against equine influenza for all competitors, there have been a variety of claims from owners and trainers that this has affected their horse's performance. However, inactivated vaccines can only affect a horse in two ways: they may cause a reaction around the injection site, as already described; and they may also stimulate the immune system throughout the body. They cannot of themselves produce any direct symptoms of the disease. So if a horse which has recently been vaccinated against equine flu starts coughing, that cannot be directly due to the vaccination. A survey of vaccinated racehorses has shown that, statistically, recently vaccinated horses are no more likely to develop problems than non-vaccinated horses; it is just that owners make the connection when the two events happen within a week or two of each other.

Nevertheless, although inactivated vaccines will not directly cause symptoms of disease, a horse which has had its immune system challenged in this way and then been stressed by very strenuous exercise may not reach its maximum performance potential. The *Rules of Racing* prohibit horses from racing within ten days of receiving a vaccination because large bets may be affected by a favoured horse failing to perform as well as it has previously. It is never a good idea to vaccinate a horse within fourteen days of a competition if it can possibly be avoided. Some vaccines have in the past carried a recommendation that the horse should not be given fast work at all for a period after vaccination even though there was never any scientific evidence to suggest that this was necessary. It did, however, raise all sorts of doubts in people's minds, and more recent vaccines do not usually carry such advice.

If a disease epidemic occurs there is usually a rush to vaccinate horses if a vaccine exists. It must be realised, however, that maximum protection (which of course may or may not be effective protection in all cases) will not be achieved until after the anamnestic response; and in the case of inactivated vaccines this means about ten days after the second dose of the vaccine. The result is a time lag of around six weeks between the first vaccination and maximum protection, and during that time the epidemic will often have run its course anyway. Vaccination is something which needs to be considered and implemented away from such a panic situation if its full benefits are to be achieved.

Major Strains of Equine Influenza Virus

Origin	Year Isolated	Type
Prague	56	A Equi 1
Newmarket	77	A Equi 1
Miami	63	A Equi 2
Fontainebleau	79	A Equi 2
Solvalla	79	A Equi 2
Brentwood	79	A Equi 2
Kentucky	81	A Equi 2
Sussex	89	A Equi 2
Suffolk	89	A Equi 2

12 The major strains of equine influenza virus, with their origin and date

In some diseases such as equine flu and African horse sickness there may be several antigenetically distinct strains of the disease organism causing problems in different places and at different times (Fig 12). A vaccine prepared specifically against one strain will stimulate less (and sometimes no) immunity against another strain. At any one time and any one place there is usually only one disease strain causing problems, and it is important that vaccine manufacturers and vets

ensure that horses are vaccinated against that strain and not against old strains which only occur rarely in the field. Vaccine manufacturers are not always keen to admit this, because they may not be prepared to invest the considerable sums of money needed to update their vaccine. Moreover competition horses have another problem in that they frequently travel to other countries, and even other continents, where their vaccination package may no longer provide full protection. And it is not enough to rely on the hope that the horses they meet at overseas competitions will be free from disease – several major outbreaks of disease have in the past been traced to this very situation.

As a general rule, if a vaccine manufacturer claims that a strain of virus in their vaccine cross-reacts with a strain producing actual clinical disease, that is not as desirable as having a vaccine which includes that disease-producing strain. It is also often true that the year that the virus strain is identified is more important than the place where it is isolated. So a virus strain from the same year as the disease-producing strain is likely to produce a better vaccine than a strain from earlier years.

Although modern adjuvants enable vaccines to stimulate better immunity, they are also much more likely to stimulate localised reactions in the area around the vaccine site. Such reactions are not abscesses and are not the result of the vet using a dirty needle; they are reactions to a foreign substance. Hot, raised swellings can develop within hours of the vaccination, but in time such reactions usually disappear completely. It has been suggested that phenylbutazone, or bute, may be given to relieve pain in severe cases. However, just because a horse has a reaction to one dose of a vaccine does not mean that it will react to further doses of the same vaccine. Also, it can safely be given its normal work as far as any possible stiffness will allow.

Named Diseases

■ Tetanus

Tetanus is a bacterial disease which is caused by *Clostridium tetani*. The bacteria enter via a wound in the skin or a break in the lining of the gut wall and if they end up in a site which has a low oxygen level, they will multiply and release toxin into the bloodstream which affects nerves anywhere in the body. Muscles supplied by affected nerves go into a spasm. The alternative name for the disease, lockjaw, reflects how the horse may be unable to eat or drink because its jaws are locked together. Death is due to spasm of the respiratory muscles.

Vaccination is with a toxoid vaccine. Two doses are given 4–6 weeks apart, followed by booster vaccination every 1–2 years. Tetanus antitoxin is also available to provide instant protection lasting up to three weeks. It is not safe to rely on giving antitoxin when needed because the entry wound may be undetectable, for example via the intestines. Vaccination is carried out because of the high mortality rate with the disease, even with antibiotic treatment and large doses of antitoxin.

■ Equine Influenza

There are a number of distinct strains of equine influenza virus, named after the place where they were first isolated, and divided into strains Equi/1 (of which the Prague 56 strain was the first isolated) and Equi/2 (of which the Miami 63 strain was the first isolated). Thankfully there are far fewer strains of equine flu than of human flu, and vaccination is therefore more successful. There is no real difference in the symptoms of the various strains of virus. Affected horses cough and have a nasal discharge which may be watery at first but then becomes more purulent. They have a raised temperature although this may not last very long, become lethargic and go off their food. Young foals are very susceptible and may die from the disease. In some cases the heart muscles may be affected and unless a sufficient period of rest (at least six weeks) is given after infection this may result in serious heart problems later.

Vaccination is carried out using an inactivated vaccine. Many regulatory bodies make vaccination compulsory for competitors although there may well be a discrepancy between their minimum vaccination requirements and those actually recommended by the vaccine manufacturers. The usual official requirement is for two initial doses separated by 21–90 days, with a first booster 150–210 days later and annual boosters thereafter. No leeway is allowed beyond those dates. The manufacturers often recommend a further six-monthly booster before switching to annual boosters.

It is very important to use a vaccine which protects against the strains of virus likely to be met in the field, and responsible manufacturers do alter the constituents of their vaccines from time to time. Suffolk 89 is the dominant disease strain at the time of writing, and so a vaccine providing proven protection against this strain should be used. Cross-protection from one strain to another is often poor and cannot be relied upon.

Vaccination is carried out because the disease is extremely infectious and can quickly spread to epidemic proportions. When it does so, all equine activities over a large area may have to be cancelled. Vaccination may not be 100 per cent effective at preventing infection, but it greatly reduces its effect. Some vaccines are more effective than others at preventing the spread of the virus to other horses.

■ Equine Herpes Virus

There is a whole family of herpes viruses. We are mainly concerned with types 1 and 4, both of which are basically respiratory viruses, causing a cough and nasal discharge. Although they usually cause a raised temperature, this may have already returned to normal by the time clinical symptoms appear. The EHV1 virus may cause abortion storms if it infects groups of pregnant mares. In a small percentage of cases EHV can also cause neurological symptoms, in particular ataxia, and the horse may even become recumbent and unable to stand.

There are a number of different vaccines available against equine herpes virus, aimed at protecting against either the respiratory or the abortion form of the disease. Most of the vaccines are inactivated vaccines, although live vaccine is available in some countries to control abortion storms. Immunity to natural EHV infections is relatively short-lived, and vaccine protection will not usually last a whole year. Six-monthly boosters are therefore required after an initial two doses of inactivated vaccine aimed at the respiratory disease. Vaccination against abortion usually needs to be correlated with specific stages of pregnancy.

Vaccination is carried out because EHV is the commonest cause of viral respiratory disease and causes corresponding problems for competition horses. The virus may become latent, or hidden, in an infected horse and suddenly become active again at a later date. The result is an apparently spontaneous disease without the need for contact with clinically affected horses or for an incubation period. The stress of training or competition may stimulate such a reactivation of viral activity.

■ Equine Viral Arteritis (EVA)

As its name suggests, the EVA virus damages blood-vessel walls. We can see the effect of this in infected horses because they develop raised patches of oedema over the body where tissue fluid has leaked out into the subcutaneous tissues. The horse has a raised temperature and shows respiratory symptoms. However, perhaps the greatest significance of this disease is that it can cause abortion.

The EVA virus can spread via droplets in the air but more important is the fact that it is a venereal disease, spread via the stallion's semen. It can even be spread to mares inseminated artificially because the majority of infected stallions remain shedders of the virus into their semen even though they recover clinically. This enables the disease to spread very successfully. It may be that the only way to detect these carrier stallions is to test-mate them with mares which have never had the disease and see if the mares show any evidence of infection.

Vaccination against EVA is possible, but before it is implemented owners should be aware that the antibodies it will stimulate the horse to produce will be more or less indistinguishable from those present in naturally infected animals. If at any stage in the future it is desired to transport the vaccinated horse to a country where EVA does not exist, and where there are controls to prevent its importation, then the vaccinated horse will fail those tests. Some countries will allow the importation of horses with antibodies against EVA if the owner can provide proof that the horse has been vaccinated but was negative for EVA at the time of the first vaccination. Because antibodies are not a reliable indication of a stallion's status, entire stallions may need to be test-mated in quarantine or even castrated before importation.

■ Rabies

Rabies is an important disease because the virus can affect all mammals, including man. The UK and a number of other countries which are free from the disease operate a long-term quarantine system for dogs and cats being imported, because when these animals are infected with the disease they can become aggressive and blindly bite anything that comes within reach (the 'mad dog' that man has feared for so long). Infected horses, on the other hand, do not become aggressive and do not pass the disease on to man; in effect, they provide a dead end for a chain of infected animals so there are not usually any quarantine restrictions or any testing for rabies when horses are imported. It is worth pointing out that it is always the importing country that imposes restrictions on the movement of animals, not the exporting country, even though some of the measures such as blood testing or quarantine have to take place in the exporting country.

Vaccination is possible against rabies using an inactivated vaccine with annual boosters. The long incubation period of rabies means that some apparent failures of vaccination will occur when already infected animals are vaccinated. In the UK, vaccination of any species of animal is only allowed if that animal is about to be exported.

■ Strangles

Strangles is a bacterial disease caused by *Streptococcus equi*; it results in the development of large abscesses full of foul-smelling pus in the horse's lymph nodes. When the lymph nodes around the throat or under the jaw are affected we can see marked swellings (Fig 13) but when the internal lymph node along the digestive tract is affected there will be nothing visible (**bastard strangles**). The abscesses may result in the horse having difficulty breathing because they obstruct its airway. Eventually they burst, leaving large discharging craters. If, as is often the case, the lymph nodes of the pharynx at the back of the mouth are affected then the horse will have a pusy nasal discharge when they burst. Affected horses are lethargic and run a high temperature.

Strangles occurs most commonly when young horses are brought together, for example at sales, but it can affect horses of any age. Immunity after clinical disease is good, however, and long lasting; this immunity may be due to circulating antibodies which can easily be measured but it can also be entirely due to surface antibodies, which cannot easily be detected. As a result there are horses which do not have any circulating antibodies but which are nonetheless immune to the disease. In most cases strangles is spread by the discharges. However, in some cases horses which have no history of recent contact with such a clinical case suddenly develop the disease. This is thought to be due to the activation of previously dormant bacteria which the horse has carried for months or even years but without developing any immunity to them.

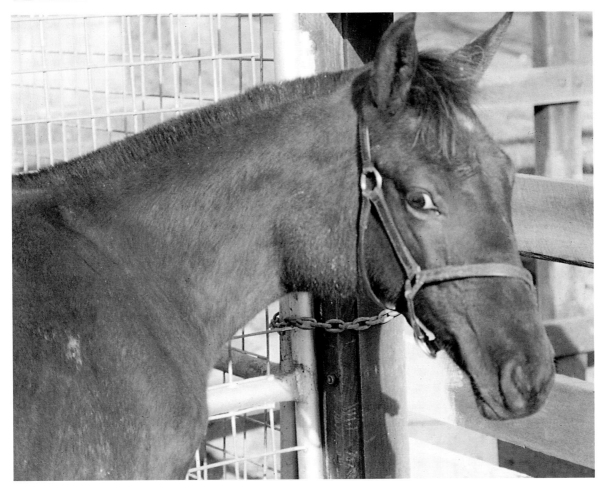

13 Swelling in the throat typical of strangles

The reason why vaccines have so far been rather ineffective against strangles is that they do not stimulate the surface immunity. Recent research has indicated that it is possible to stimulate this immunity, and if this can be carried through to commercial vaccine production then it should be possible to reduce dramatically the incidence of strangles.

There has been debate for many years over the treatment of strangles, and time and time again the dictum is put forward that antibiotics should not be used until the abscesses have burst open. However, there is no real scientific evidence for this view – indeed theoretically, all the horses in a yard should have a course of penicillin as soon as possible in order to stop subclinical or carrier cases developing.

■ Bacterial Respiratory Disease

Recent research in racing yards has shown that as many as 60 per cent of the outbreaks of respiratory disease blamed on viruses such as herpes or influenza are in fact caused by bacteria. The important result of this finding is that it is worth treating such horses with a proper course of antibiotic because the bacteria are likely to respond. During the past twenty years or so the experts have been telling us that the horse with a bit of a cough or a runny nose should not be given antibiotics because such cases were always due to a virus, and antibiotics have no effect on viruses.

■ Other Localised Diseases

The diseases discussed above are not the only ones against which vaccines are available; more localised diseases such as African horse sickness and various viral encephalitic diseases also have vaccine developed against them. The diseases covered illustrate the main vaccine types and the problems associated with their use.

External Parasites

Skin diseases may not be terribly serious from the point of view of a horse's performance but they are very obvious to even a casual spectator. As such they can cause a horse to miss competitions just as often as can lameness. There is often debate as to whether a skin disease pulls the horse down in its general body condition, or whether it is that horses in rather poor condition succumb to skin diseases more readily *ie* which came first: the chicken or the egg? Faced with an overwhelming infection, even the most shiny-coated, healthy horse will succumb. However, when the level of infection is low, horses in poor condition are more likely to develop clinical symptoms of skin disease than are healthy horses.

ITCHY CONDITIONS	NON-ITCHY CONDITIONS
Lice Mange mites Sweet itch	Ringworm Mud fever / rain scald Warbles Warts and tumours

14 Louse eggs on hair

■ Lice

Infestations with lice are quite interesting in horses. The life cycle of the louse – which may be either *Damalinia equi* (the biting louse) or *Haematopinus asini* (the sucking louse) – is relatively straightforward. It lays its tiny, creamy-coloured eggs and sticks them to the hairs of the horse's coat (Fig 14); after a while they hatch. The growing lice feed on either surface skin material which they bite off, or tissue fluids which they suck, and when they are mature they lay eggs. In other words, they spend the whole of their life on the horse. The clinical history of a horse infested with lice is as follows: during the cold winter months it starts to rub and bite its skin. This breaks off hairs and may be so uncontrolled that it results in superficial skin damage. When the weather warms up and the horse changes its winter coat, the symptoms disappear. In other words, lice live on the horse all the year round but they only cause clinical symptoms during cold weather.

Although lice cannot survive off their host for any great length of time, they can be transported from one horse to another through contact by, say, a horse rubbing against a place where an infested animal has just rubbed. More frequently we spread the infestation via grooming kit or tack. In the wild, spread would be by direct physical contact between horses. Because lice infestations are asymptomatic for so much of the time, we are rarely able to say exactly when and how a horse became infested.

SYMPTOMS

The symptoms of lice infestation are of an intense itching over the face, neck or shoulder, usually starting during the winter or in the early spring (see Fig 15). The horse has patchy bald areas, but the hair has been rubbed off rather than just fallen out. Closer examination may reveal the light-coloured eggs, tightly stuck onto the hair; the fact that no lice can be seen running around on the skin does not mean that there are none there.

TREATMENT

The treatment of lice obviously has to be directed at the horse's skin; there is little point in treating the whole loosebox but then ignoring the horse. BHC was a very effective drug for killing lice, but unfortunately it has now been withdrawn in many countries. At the time of writing pyrethrins are the alternative, and pyrethrin shampoos are available. Grooming kit and so on should be treated with either a solution of pyrethrin, or a very powerful disinfectant, or with boiling water. Ivermectin, which is widely used as a wormer, also kills horse lice but it is eliminated from the horse's body so quickly that it cannot be relied on to kill them completely. All other things being equal though, it is the obvious wormer to use in this situation.

■ Mange Mites

Lice are more likely to cause irritation by their activity in a thick winter coat than in a clipped coat and the same goes (to some extent) for both chorioptic and psoroptic mange mites (see Fig 16). These tiny parasites live in, rather than on the skin because they can burrow into the top skin layers. The irritation can cause the horse distress, and again it rubs the affected areas. Chorioptic mange usually affects the lower limbs, whereas psoroptic mange usually affects the mane and tail.

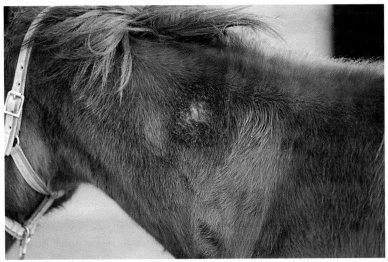

15 The effects of lice on the condition of the hair and skin are considerable

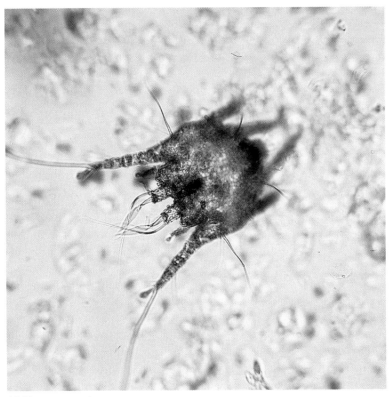

16 The mange mite

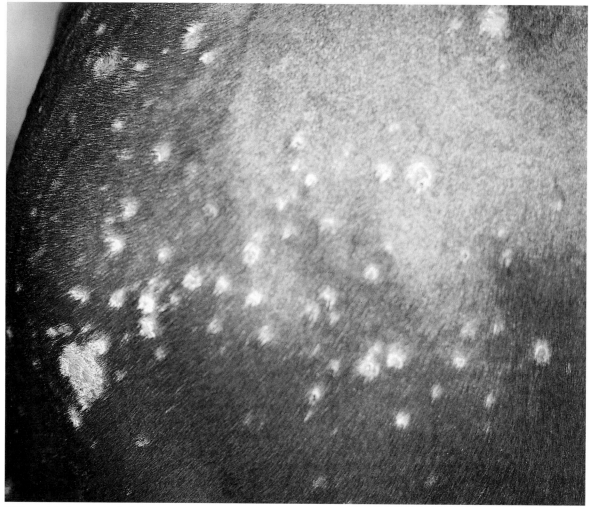

17 Round lesions typical of ringworm

There are some parasitic worms which live in the skin, either in adult form or as larvae. Adult *Onchocerca* worms live in the tendons of the neck or legs, but the immature *microfilariae* live in the skin along the ventral midline of the body. The parasite has to spend some time in an intermediate host, a biting midge, before returning to the horse.

SYMPTOMS

These mites can cause symptoms all the year round. They are so contagious and troublesome that in the days when we relied on horses completely for all our transport they were made notifiable diseases. This means that if such a disease is diagnosed or suspected, the State Veterinary Service must be notified so that they can oversee treatment.

TREATMENT

Treatment is exactly the same as for lice although often the burrowing habit protects the mites and makes treatment very difficult. Clipping the affected area helps to ensure that the shampoo does penetrate right down to the skin.

■ Ringworm

RECOGNITION

Probably the commonest skin problem that affects the competition horse is ringworm. Classically this causes ring-shaped lesions on the skin (Fig 17), but it is certainly nothing to do with worms: ringworm is caused by fungi. There are two families of fungi which can infect horses, dermatophyton and trichophyton; they infect both the skin and the hairs. The round bald patches which everyone looks for are due to the fungus so weakening the base of

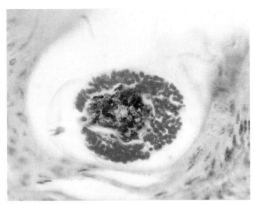

18 Ringworm fungus on a hair shaft

the hair shafts that the hairs break off (Fig 18). Ringworm is not usually irritating and so the horse does not rub itself raw, although the skin of affected areas often looks rather dry and scaly. It is important to realise that the lesions can be any shape and size: owners often ignore the possibility of ringworm just because the lesions are not the classic circles. In severe cases a large proportion of the body can be affected. Such horses do tend to be in rather poor condition.

CONTAGION

Ringworm poses a number of problems: first, it can sometimes affect people. Second, it is obvious to everyone that your horse is affected, and it remains obvious for a considerable time because it takes a long time for the hair to regrow completely. So there may be a long period when the horse is apparently infectious to other horses but has actually been successfully treated. Some regulatory authorities allow horses to compete even with ringworm lesions as long as they have completed a course of treatment. This attitude recognises both the efficacy of modern treatment and the unfairness of banning non-infectious horses.

Third, the ringworm fungi produce spores which are very resistant to environmental conditions, and which can survive for months or years before causing infections in the same or other horses. Spores do not necessarily become active straightaway after they are deposited on the horse's skin, and so the incubation period for ringworm can be very long – months rather than days. This makes it difficult to say when and where the horse became infected. Spores can survive in the stable, the horsebox or even on fencing and can cause infection in later months or years. Undoubtedly some of the apparent failures of ringworm treatments are really due to rapid re-infection associated with large numbers of spores in the horse's environment.

TREATMENT

Treatment for ringworm has a number of aspects. As the fungi infect the skin, it is possible to use specific antibiotics – for example griseofulvin – so as to kill them. A seven-day course of such an antibiotic given as paste or in the food is usually sufficient. Unfortunately the drug cannot be used for pregnant mares. Because the fungus is also superficially on top of the skin and on the hairs, it is also possible to treat ringworm topically with shampoos and/or sprays; the antibiotics natamycin or enilconazole may be used in this way. In the past some incredible remedies have been used, such as sump oil mixed

with soot, although any effect these had will have been because they prevented spread by sealing in the infection rather than by killing the fungi. Whatever treatment is used, owners must be prepared for new lesions to appear after it has started; these represent areas where the hairs are already so weakened that they break off.

The horse's environment should also be treated. Tack and grooming kit must be dealt with, to reduce the risk of spread of the disease. Strong disinfectants such as 1 per cent caustic soda or 0.25 per cent sodium hypochlorite can be used as an alternative to the antibiotics already mentioned, but they are toxic and must be handled with care.

■ Flies

The warble fly, Hypoderma, can cause problems for horses even though it is basically a cattle parasite. It lands on the horse's leg and lays its eggs. After these hatch, the larvae migrate through the horse's body until they end up under the skin of the back. Here another problem arises. Unlike cattle, which are the natural host of the warble fly and where almost all the larvae emerge through holes they make in the skin of the back, a high proportion of the warble larvae in the horse just remain swellings on the back, neither emerging nor disappearing. These swellings can be painful, and when they occur in the saddle area they are particularly troublesome. It may be necessary to remove them surgically, resulting in lost competition time. Thankfully attempts to eradicate warbles in cattle have almost eliminated them in horses as well.

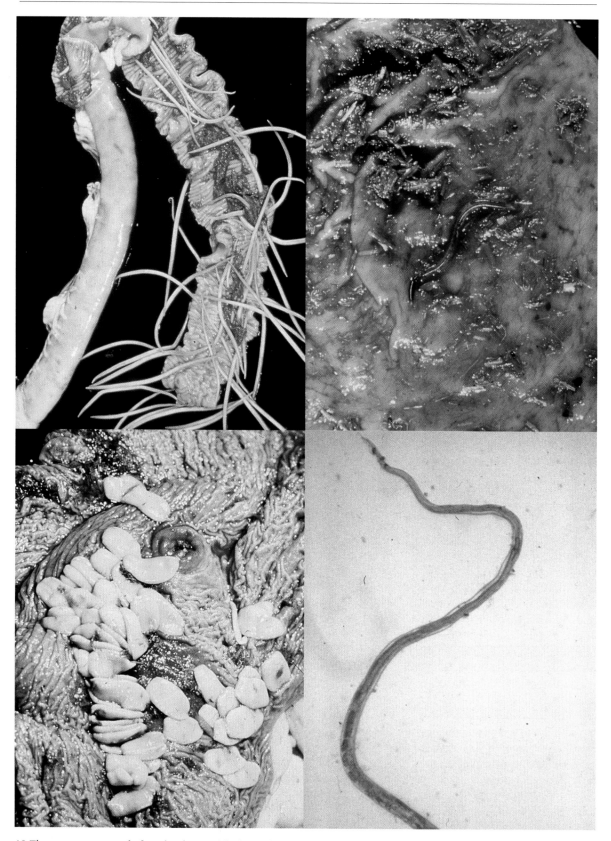

19 The worms commonly found in horses (clockwise from top left) ascarids; strongyloides (large strongyles); trichostrongylus (small strongyles); tapeworms

Internal Parasites

The gastro-intestinal parasites of the horse are usually referred to as worms, although they may not always look like the standard earthworm (Fig 19). They vary in their life cycles, the sites where they live inside the horse, and the problems they cause. The basic story is usually that the horse picks up the parasite whilst grazing; with a few specialist exceptions, horses do not pick up worm infestations if they are stabled all the time. This does not mean that worms are not a problem to competition horses, however, because these may be given an hour or so out at grass even if they are stabled most of the time.

The parasite passes through perhaps four larval stages before it becomes an adult which can lay eggs and start the process all over again. When devising methods to control worms, the emphasis should be on reducing the numbers of worm eggs which are passed onto the pasture ready to cause further problems, rather than just on the straightforward removal of adult worms from the digestive tract.

■ Ascarids

Parascaris equorum, the ascarid worm, is a young horse's problem. Adult horses become immune to it and so it relies heavily on its eggs surviving out on the pasture over the winter in order to infest the next generation of foals. Because it is quite a large worm, up to 50cm (20in) in size, high numbers of worms present in the foal's intestines can physically block the movement of food along the intestine. Contrary to many owners' perception of the threat worms pose to their horse, this is not a common problem with other types of worm.

Ascarids migrate through the liver and lungs before ending up in the intestines. The horse may have all the typical symptoms of a respiratory infection and it is obviously important not to mistake this 'summer cold', as it is sometimes known, for one of the respiratory virus infections which are also prevalent at this age. Counting the number of worm eggs in the horse's droppings will confirm whether or not an active ascarid infection is present.

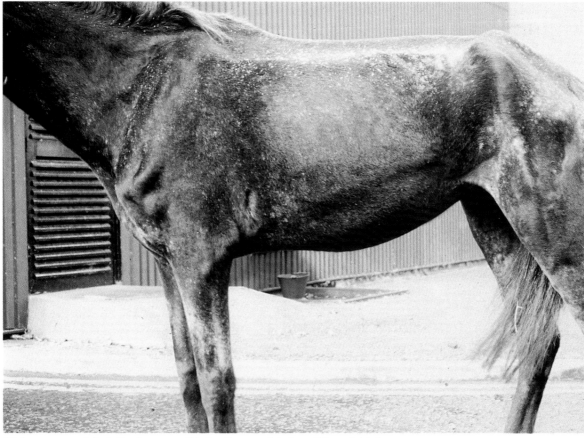

20 Severe worm infestation is responsible for the emaciated condition of this horse

■ Large Strongyles

The significance of the various worms changes as our patterns of management and treatment change. *Strongylus vulgaris* used to be the major problem because of its involvement in colic. The worm larvae pass through the bowel wall into the blood vessels which supply each loop of bowel, and then move along the blood vessel until they reach its origin at the hub of that blood supply (Fig 21). Here they sit for perhaps three months before migrating back to the bowel to become adult and start laying eggs. The problem is that the waiting larvae can damage the blood-vessel wall and thus cause a blood clot, or thrombus, to form. This cuts off the blood supply to that section of bowel with resulting pain and eventually possible death of that short section of bowel.

The development of a drug called ivermectin which, unlike the other anthelmintics (wormers), kills the migrating *S. vulgaris* larvae, has drastically reduced both the incidence of the worm and the severity of clinical symptoms. There is even some evidence that after treatment the blood supply will re-establish itself. The practical effect has been a worldwide decrease in the incidence of *S. vulgaris* and a corresponding decrease in the number of worm-related colics.

■ Are Cyathostomes Important?

The small strongyles, or Cyathostomes, pose a problem for different reasons. They have a relatively simple life cycle (Fig 22), the larvae usually spending only a short time in the wall of the bowel before emerging as adult worms. However, the clinical significance of the parasite is increasing because it is becoming resistant to a major group of wormers, the benzimidazoles, the use of which can lull owners into a false sense of security: whilst the owner is confident that the situation is under control, the number of worms is in fact escalating. Small strongyles can also pose a different problem. Under certain conditions, especially in the autumn, the worms become dormant, or encysted, in the bowel wall. They are much less easily killed in this situation, so their numbers accumulate. Eventually the brake on further development is removed, and very large numbers of worms emerge from hiding at once. This causes serious damage to the bowel wall, and the resulting diarrhoea can be fatal in quite a short time.

Small strongyles are undoubtedly the major worm problem of the present time. So chronic weight loss and poor condition are the worm-derived symptoms rather than colic, although the sudden appearance of diarrhoea may be more life-threatening.

■ Are Tapeworms Significant?

Another change in recent years has been the gradual accumulation of evidence that tapeworms cause problems in the horse. These parasites are relatively common and in most cases cause no clinical symptoms whatsoever, despite their large size. There is, however, evidence that when horses develop an impaction centred on that section of the bowel where the caecum joins the small intestine, then these horses are far more likely to have tapeworms present at the same place. Some experts consider this too flimsy a degree of evidence on which to justify a specific worming programme, but owners of expensive horses or horses whose competition programme cannot accommodate occasional periods of ill-health may well decide that they would rather be safe than sorry.

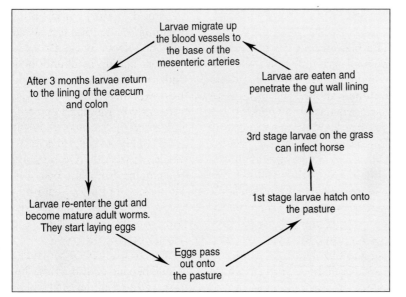

21 The life cycle of *Strongylus vulgaris*

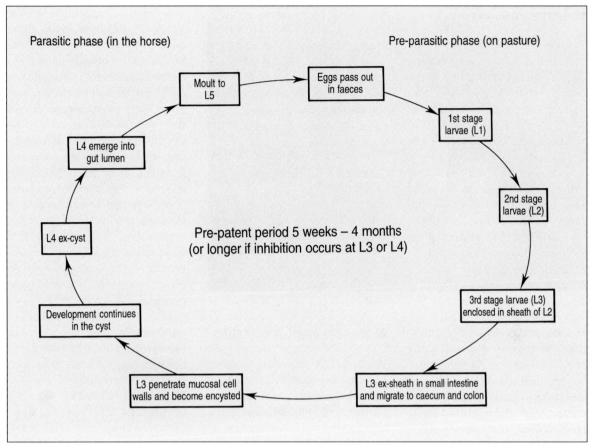

Parasitic phase (in the horse) Pre-parasitic phase (on pasture)

Moult to L5 → Eggs pass out in faeces

L4 emerge into gut lumen

1st stage larvae (L1)

L4 ex-cyst

2nd stage larvae (L2)

Development continues in the cyst

Pre-patent period 5 weeks – 4 months (or longer if inhibition occurs at L3 or L4)

3rd stage larvae (L3) enclosed in sheath of L2

L3 penetrate mucosal cell walls and become encysted

L3 ex-sheath in small intestine and migrate to caecum and colon

22 The life cycle of the small redworm

■ Bot Flies

Another slightly controversial parasite is the horse bot. This is not a worm at all, but the larval stage of a fly which attaches its eggs to the hairs of the horse's legs (Fig 23). The horse licks the hairs and takes in the larvae, which end up in the stomach looking rather like grubs. Here they stay over the winter, before being passed out in the spring and hatching into flies. Some experts would say that bots don't cause any problems either, other than when they are present in very large numbers. Of course we cannot tell when this is the case, so competition horse owners will probably be advised to take preventive action and dose accordingly.

Designing a Worming Programme

The planning of a worm treatment programme must take into consideration all the points outlined above. The basis is to use a wormer that will keep the pasture level of worm eggs as low as possible. At the present time, two drugs are available which are active against the wide spectrum of common adult worms without any drug-resistance problems: these are ivermectin and pyrantel. The benzimidazole drugs – and that includes all those wormers whose active ingredient ends in the suffix -ndazole – now have resis-

tance problems in many countries. When they are used their effect should be monitored by having faecal worm-egg counts measured before and after worming. If the total egg count does not drop markedly then their use should be abandoned. Under no circumstances should the wormer be changed frequently in the hope that this will avoid resistance; it is far more likely to encourage it. Needless to say, there is no point in changing from one benzimidazole compound to another, because if the worms are resistant to one then they are resistant to the others.

The frequency of worming should depend on the drug being used, rather than on the owner's memory or the size of his wallet.

23 Bot eggs on legs

If a benzimidazole compound is used then the horse should probably be wormed every four weeks; if pyrantel is used then worming should probably be carried out every six to eight weeks; and with ivermectin, every eight to ten weeks should be sufficient. If tapeworms are to be controlled, then a double dose of pyrantel should be given around September time. If bots are the target then a dose of ivermectin should be given in November/ December.

■ Management Techniques

The use of expensive worm preparations is not the only way to reduce the worm burden: pasture and stable management also have an important role to play (Fig 24). Worm larvae tend to crawl up to the top of grass stems in the hope of being eaten, so topping the grass, either mechanically or by grazing with another species of animal, for example cattle or sheep, will reduce worm larval intake. It

also helps to limit the deterioration of the grazing into 'lawns' which are grazed very intensively, and 'roughs' where the horse only really passes faeces and which, therefore, develop very high concentrations of worms (Fig 25). There are no chemicals which will kill worm eggs or larvae out on the grass. Ideally, of course, droppings should be removed from the pasture regularly and frequently, thus removing the parasites before they even hatched. Harrowing the grazing spreads out and breaks open the droppings, exposing them to the potentially lethal effects of drying, although horses should not be allowed to graze the area for some time after harrowing because it temporarily increases the risk of infestation.

Management of the horse or horses can significantly affect the worm risk. For example, if the horses on a pasture are not all wormed at the same time, the risk is increased. Ideally horses would be wormed and then moved to 'clean' pasture, that is pasture not previously grazed that year. If this were possible the number of worm treatments

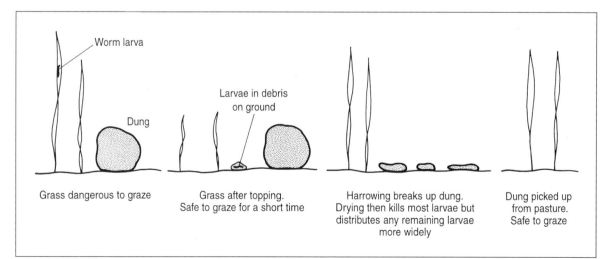

Grass dangerous to graze   Grass after topping. Safe to graze for a short time   Harrowing breaks up dung. Drying then kills most larvae but distributes any remaining larvae more widely   Dung picked up from pasture. Safe to graze

Worm larva   Larvae in debris on ground   Dung

24 Ways of managing pasture to control worm infestation

25 The horse's grazing habit leaves areas of well grazed grass known as 'lawns', and areas of coarse, rank growth –
'roughs' – the 'lavatory' areas

could be reduced because the number of larvae on the pasture would be so low that it would take a long time for numbers to build up to serious levels. Grazing only a few horses on a large area means that the worm numbers per square yard are relatively low. On the other hand, if the horses are more intensively grazed but are moved frequently, then they are removed from the risk as soon as it has arisen. Even if worm-clear pasture is not available, resting it for six to eight weeks will allow worm numbers to decrease somewhat by natural wastage.

Horses are sometimes provided with a companion to keep them company whilst travelling away to competitions. A sheep or a goat does not increase the worm risk, indeed they slightly reduce it because they will eat and destroy some worm larvae. If, however, the companion is a donkey then that does pose a risk because donkeys are the natural host of a lungworm, *Dictyocaulus arnfieldi*, which can also adversely affect horses. The lungworm does not usually cause symptoms in the donkey, whereas in the horse it causes a cough. It is reassuring, however, that the widespread use of ivermectin has markedly reduced the incidence of this parasite, because unlike other wormers it kills lungworms at its normal dose rate. Particular care needs to be taken to ensure that the donkey is wormed with ivermectin every time the horse is wormed.

GENERAL CONSIDERATIONS FOR POSITIVE HEALTH

Buying a Performance Horse

One of the best ways to prevent problems is to buy a sound horse in the first place, and in this respect 'sound' means more than just the opposite of lame: it means that the horse does not have any abnormality which will interfere with its usefulness or is likely to do so in the future. The competitor may think that he or she has found such a paragon of equine virtues, but is it really a wooden horse, masking all sorts of problems? The sensible way to find out is to ask a veterinary surgeon to 'vet' it.

The exact form of the pre-purchase examination, and the certificate produced at the end of it, varies from country to country. Some certificates have dozens of specific questions which the examining vet must answer; some countries place great store on the number of x-ray plates which accompany the report. The aim, however, is always the same: to detect any abnormalities that are present, and then to offer an opinion as to whether these will interfere with the proposed use or not. Note that it is an *opinion*, not a guarantee, and the vet is not necessarily to blame if later experience shows that the opinion was wrong.

In the UK the form of the examination has been laid down by the British Veterinary Association and the Royal College of Veterinary Surgeons, and is as follows:

Stage One:—The horse is examined at rest in a

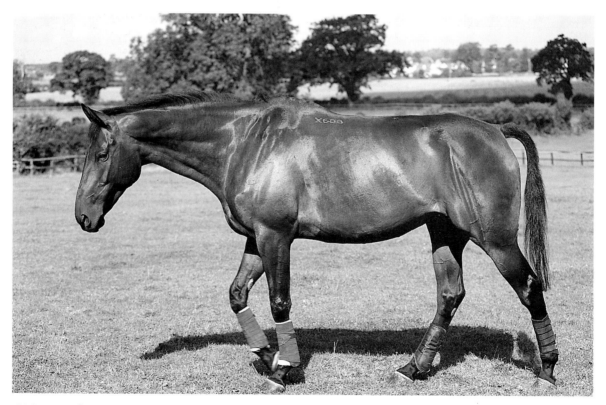

26 Some conformation questions are debatable. It could be argued, for example, that this top eventer has too long a back and too pronounced a 'hunter's bump' – where the back meets the hindquarters at an angle. The latter has been said to predispose a horse to sacro-iliac problems

stable; moreover it is important that it has not had exercise within the hour preceding the start of the examination. All parts of the horse are examined by sight and feel, whilst a stethoscope is used to listen to the heart and respiratory system. Examination of the feet usually includes the use of hoof testers.

Stage Two:—The horse is observed whilst walking and trotting in hand, and it is important that this is carried out on a hard level surface. It is turned in tight circles and made to go backwards for a few strides. Flexion tests may be carried out on the hind legs or on all four legs.

Stage Three:—The horse is given fast ridden work. If this (or any other) stage of the examination is restricted in any way, then this must be mentioned in the subsequent report. The exercise needs to be sufficient to make the horse tired. The vet listens carefully as the horse gallops past for any abnormal inspiratory noises, and at the end listens to the heart and lungs again.

Stage Four:—The horse is then returned to the stable and left for at least twenty minutes, to give it a chance to stiffen up. An ophthalmoscopic examination is carried out, and the horse's identification details are often noted at this stage.

Stage Five:—The horse is trotted up in hand again.

In the past, vets were sometimes prepared just to examine a horse's heart, lungs and eyes at rest, but modern consumer legislation means that if they advise the purchaser to buy the horse and it turns out to have a defect such as lameness, then they are deemed to be negligent, even though the horse was not ever trotted up. So the only way you will get a proper written opinion from a vet on a horse's suitability for purchase is if a full examination has been carried out.

This examination is similar all over the world, although the results are presented in various forms and reported in different ways.

27 A straight, or upright shoulder is a less efficient shock absorber than a sloping shoulder. The front leg does not have a joint linking it with the rest of the skeleton so the shoulder muscles have to absorb all the shock of landing

28 A straight hock or stifle is also less efficient at absorbing shock. The result is extra wear and tear on these joints

The timing of the vetting is quite important. There is absolutely no point in having a horse vetted *after* you have bought it because then you have no redress against the previous owner if the vet finds anything major wrong with it; nor is it safe to rely on being able to stop the cheque before the vendor can cash it. Also, the examination should not be carried out before you have ridden the horse: it should *confirm* your decision to buy the horse, not make it. There is no point in buying a sound horse that does not suit you, just as it is

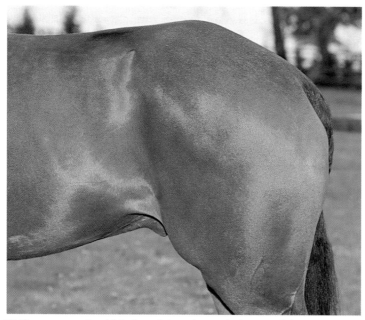

29 The acute angle which the pelvis makes with the rest of the spine – known as a 'goose rump' – places increased strain on the sacro-iliac joints

hock? If a sound, unblemished horse has x-ray changes, do they have any significance? But if you are not going to turn down a horse with x-ray changes, why bother taking the x-rays in the first place.

Sometimes insurance companies request specific x-rays for high value horses. If this is the case I would suggest that the x-rays are sent, without comment, to the company with a completed proposal form. Do not complete the purchase, however, until you hear that the proposal form has been accepted. Increasingly, owners complete the insurance arrangements before they finalise the purchase, because insurers may place exclusions on 'problems' even in horses which your own vet has passed.

The real role of other techniques such as radiography, endoscopy and ultrasonography is to elucidate a query, such as whether a bony lump affects a joint or not. Your vet may have the choice between rejecting a horse for purchase because he did not know the significance of the lump, or x-raying it

really not advisable to buy an unsound horse just because it *does* suit you.

The choice of vet to carry out the examination is entirely yours. Bear in mind that if you are buying a horse in a different part of the country, it is not always a good idea to ask the vendor whom he would suggest to vet the horse, because it is not in his interest to recommend the vet who will be most thorough: and I have known vendors recommend vets who do relatively little horse work, whilst omitting to mention very experienced horse vets in the area. Ask your vet at home if he will recommend someone in the area.

When you contact the vet you should be prepared to describe the horse you are buying – its age, sex, breed and so on, and what kind of work it will be expected to do. Be realistic, and tell him the hardest kind of work you envisage, not just what it will be doing in the first couple of weeks. The vet's advice may hinge on this point, and his written advice will certainly be restricted to the types of work you tell him about at the time of the examination.

You should also have a view about whether you require certain specialist procedures carried out. Most vets are against the idea of routinely x-raying various bits of the horse at the time of purchase. Firstly there is the problem of what to x-ray. If you x-ray the foot, then why not the fetlock? If you X-ray the knee, then why not the

30 Don't forget to look underneath the feet as well. Flat feet, such as this, are not in themselves a problem but in conjunction with a long toe and a short heel they expose the foot to a lot of jarring

and making a decision based on facts. Specific types of horses may warrant special techniques. If you are buying a 17hh heavyweight hunter it might be advisable to endoscope it whether you can hear it making a noise on inspiration or not, because the incidence of laryngeal paralysis in such horses is high.

You should discuss with your vet whether to take a blood sample or not. The idea is to take and store a blood sample which, if the horse happens to go lame shortly after purchase, can then be analysed for the presence of painkillers. In many circumstances merely asking the vendor if you can take such a sample will show you whether he or she has anything to hide – but there are still occasions when they try and beat the system.

So what should a vetting produce? It should provide, on the certificate and in any oral report, a list of any significant abnormalities; sometimes this is a long list because things such as splints are all identified, even though their presence is not going to affect the decision whether to recommend purchase or not. The report should also include a definite statement of advice as to whether the horse is suitable for purchase for specific activities.

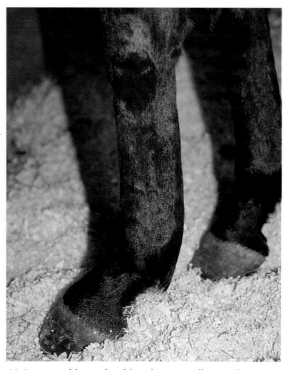

32 Some problems should make you walk straight away from a horse, for example a bowed tendon. Unless you really don't want to go faster than a trot, don't buy trouble like this. There is a great difference between bringing a horse you already own back to competition fitness after major injury, and buying a supposedly recovered horse with an obvious problem. In the former instance, it is a shame for the horse: in the latter you are left feeling foolish because you made the wrong decision and wasted your money

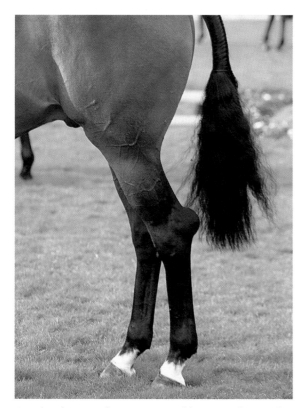

31 When buying a horse, some problems are obvious, for example a capped hock. This is only a superficial blemish and will not affect the horse's performance

All this should be on an official form that states that the examination was carried out in accordance with the RCVS/BVA memorandum.

There are limitations to the examination. It can only detect symptoms that are present, which means that if a horse has an allergic condition such as sweet itch, COPD or headshaking, this may not be detected if the triggering factors are not present – there is no way of detecting the allergy other than from clinical symptoms. That is why I always suggest that, if the horse is bedded on shavings or kept out in the field, clients ask for a *written* warranty that it is not allergic to the fungal spores on hay and straw.

The vetting procedure does not make any claims for the future, it deals only with the situation on one specific day, and the fact that a horse is sound this week does not mean that it will not go lame in a couple of week's time. If, unfortunately, it does so, then although hidden changes may have been present at the time of the vetting, a vet cannot be held negligent for failing to spot the problem as long as no clinical symptoms were evident. We do not use crystal balls, we only look at the evidence available. It is a statistical fact that navicular disease, and possibly other lamenesses, commonly first show clinical symptoms 6–8 weeks after a change of ownership. However, no amount of trotting up or x-raying will detect all of these in horses at the pre-purchase examination. The most significant factor in the development of the lameness is probably the extra work which the new owner has given his purchase. Such a development does not mean that the vetting was pointless. It was obviously better to detect most of the problems rather than none at all.

The high prices paid for competition horses means that they are usually insured on purchase – but it can be embarrassing if the insurance company refuses to accept the risk when you have already paid the cheque after having the horse vetted. This can happen, though, because the insurance company is looking at the risk from a different point of view from the prospective owner. In most cases equine insurance companies either accept a risk at a normal premium or they refuse to cover the risk. They do not say 'we will insure this horse against the risk of its developing navicular disease despite the changes visible on these x-rays, but the premium will be twice the normal premium'. So wherever possible, delay completing the purchase until the insurers have confirmed whether they would exclude any parts of the horse.

Whenever possible, purchase a horse that is in work rather than one which is just turned out at grass. Lamenesses are far more likely to show in a horse which is in full work than in one which has been rested for a month or so. It is also better to buy a horse which is being stabled for at least part of the day. Allergic respiratory diseases may require a period of exposure to the stable before symptoms become detectable. If there are no symptoms because the horse is turned out, the vet will be unable to detect the disease.

Finally, accept the vet's opinion. There is no point in paying a vet to examine a horse and then buying it despite his advice not to do so. Moreover, do not allow the vendor to persuade you that the vet was hyper-critical. People selling horses often lose their sense of right and wrong, and will say practically anything to convince a potential buyer to purchase the horse.

Equine Insurance

Just as it is important to take steps to prevent disease, it is also important to take steps to make sure that one can afford to pay for any veterinary treatment if problems do occur. Equine insurance can provide cover for veterinary fees and/or mortality and/or permanent loss of use. It is important to understand the limitations of any cover proposed, however, and to remember that its cost is directly proportional both to the sum that the insurance company will have to pay, and to the likelihood of its having to pay it.

■ Veterinary Fees Insurance

Veterinary fees insurance is relatively straightforward. At the time of writing the standard cover is for £2,000 per condition. This will cover the cost of most treatments, although repeated surgery – for example, two abdominal operations for colic – might well result in bills exceeding that amount. The owner must notify the insurance company as soon as the horse is taken ill, but the choice of treatment is made by the owner's vet, not by the insurance company. There is a tendency for insurers to put a time limit on treatments as well as a cost limit, so they will only pay for treatment that is incurred within twelve months of the condition occurring. If this is the case it is important that the treating vet is informed. The length of time allowed to elapse between treatments is often quite arbitrary and it is very frustrating if a long period of rest, for example, results in further treatment being outside the twelve months' limit. Vets' fees cover for existing problems is not affected by any exclusions made when a policy is renewed. So if a horse sprains its tendon a month before its insurance policy is due for renewal, treatment is covered for twelve months even though the renewed policy will often specifically exclude cover for sprains of that tendon.

■ Mortality Insurance

Mortality insurance not only covers the horse's death, it also covers the risk of its immediate slaughter being necessary because it is in excessive pain which cannot be relieved and for which there is no prospect of a cure. In the latter situation the insurance company's agreement must be sought whenever possible before the horse is put down. The main point about this type of cover is that the horse must require immediate slaughter: if a condition has been treated for months without success then it is unlikely that the horse can be said to require immediate slaughter.

The policy is therefore concerned with situations where the excessive pain cannot be relieved. A particular situation here is the horse which sprains a tendon badly during a competition. It will be in severe pain, but over several weeks the pain will subside and more or less disappear, so such a horse would not warrant euthanasia under the insurance policy. On the other hand if the flexor tendons were completely ruptured then that may well warrant euthanasia under the policy, because the injury will not stabilise and subside. Another situation is the horse which is in great pain without painkillers but where that pain can be substantially reduced by the use of such drugs. Euthanasia of such a horse may well not be covered by the policy unless the painkillers themselves start to cause serious side effects and have to be withdrawn. If treatment is likely to resolve a condition then the insurers can insist that it is carried out, whether or not the horse is covered for the cost of veterinary fees. So if a horse breaks a cannon bone and surgery is possible, then the owner may have to have it carried out even if he has to pay the cost out of his own pocket because he did not have any vets' fees cover.

■ Loss of Use Insurance

Loss of use cover usually specifies the particular equine activities which are included, and the higher the risk of injury, the higher the premium. The horse is covered against being able to take part in the activity, not against maintaining a particular level of performance. So the fact that a horse's jumping ability was reduced would not justify a claim, whereas if it was no longer able to jump at all then a claim might be justified. In many cases a loss of use claim has to be made because the horse requires permanent medication which is banned under the rules of a particular competition. It is always the case that any loss of use must be permanent: thus if a horse misses one season's competition that does not justify a claim, but if it will never be able to compete again then this may well constitute valid grounds for a claim.

Veterinary Attendance at Equine Events

Competitors usually expect that vets will be in attendance at any major equine event, and such attendance falls into two quite different categories. They might be present in a regulatory function, on behalf of the national or international body under whose rules the competition is being held; or they may be present in order to provide treatment for any injured animals, at the request of the competition's local organisers. The two functions are quite separate.

In racing the Jockey Club vet is concerned with the integrity of racing. He checks the identity of horses with their official passports to make sure that horses of greater or lesser ability are not substituted in the race for the horse named in the entry. He is also responsible for carrying out any sampling for routine dope control. Finally he has a welfare role, inspecting horses if it is suggested that a jockey has used the whip too much or too hard, for example. The racecourse owners will also appoint treatment vets, who will provide prompt treatment for any horse which injures itself. In countries where the horses are stabled and trained at the racetrack a resident vet will obviously perform this function. Owners have to pay the vet for any treatment they receive.

In major non-racing competitions a similar division will exist. The FEI, or International Equestrian Federation, will appoint a veterinary delegate to the Grand Jury which provides on-the-spot control of the event, whereas the local organisers will provide the treatment vets. Veterinary delegates should be informed of any drugs given to a competitor's horse during the competition, and it is part of their role to advise the Grand Jury whether the competitor should still be allowed to continue in the competition, or whether the horse should be withdrawn because it will have gained a potential advantage. In practice owners often don't declare the fact that their horse has been treated, and either withdraw it themselves or take a chance that it will not be dope-tested. The authorities have only themselves to blame for this situation because they have not shown any flexibility in the past – every time such treatment was reported, the horse was officially withdrawn or dope-tested, even when the treatment consisted of a drug such as an antibiotic which had no performance-enhancing effect. The result has had bad

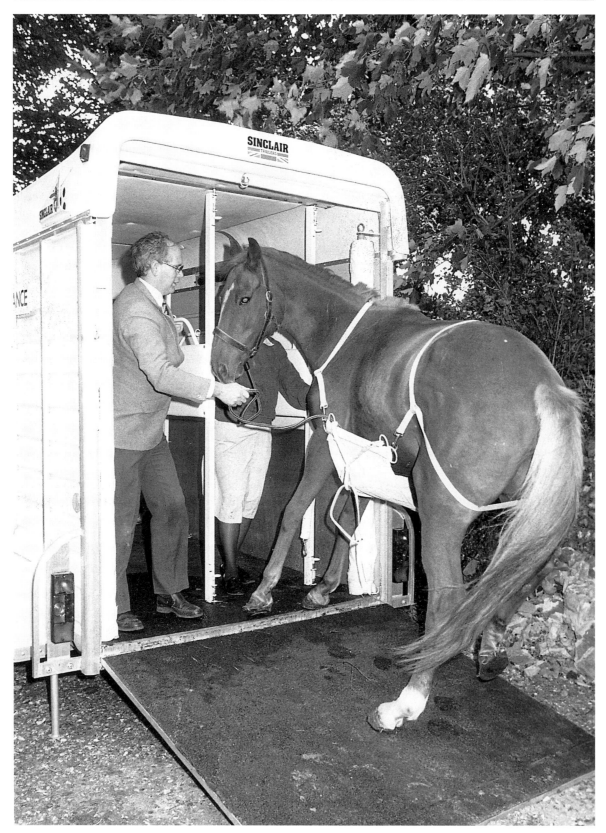

33 Major equestrian events should have an equine ambulance on site in case horses which have been injured need transporting in a support sling to a veterinary clinic for further treatment

welfare implications because horses have been denied painkillers when they have experienced colic, or been denied a local anaesthetic when they needed a few stitches in a wound, in order to keep open the option of continuing in the competition. Perhaps worse still, horses have been competed with unstitched wounds solely for the same reason. Thankfully there are signs of a more flexible attitude developing in this area, but the question of what action is taken is still a lottery in many respects.

When owners take their horses to a competition they should find out what veterinary cover is available because this will vary even between events of comparable stature. The fact that the event programme lists an honorary veterinary surgeon does not mean that a vet will be present throughout the competition. During a one day horse trial, for example, the rules stipulate that a vet must be present whilst the cross-country section is taking place, but there might not be a vet present during the early stages of the dressage section. It is worth pointing out again that in many cases the responsibility for payment for any treatment your horse requires is yours alone. Very few competitions pay a normal fee to the vet to cover both his total attendance time and the drugs used – and the latter can amount to a considerable sum nowadays, of course.

Vets on duty at equine events expect to deal with emergencies such as a wound or colic. They do not expect to be asked to look at a lameness which has existed for the past four weeks, and indeed they may refuse to do so. In particular they are not equipped to carry out specialist diagnostic procedures such as endoscopy or radiography. These need time, peace and quiet if they are to be performed properly. This has caused problems in the past when trainers have asked vets to endoscope a horse immediately after racing in order to see whether there is internal bleeding which might account for its reduced performance. Whilst this might be easy to organise in countries where horses are stabled at the track, on British racecourses it requires organising a stable, a separate vet, the equipment and a source of electricity. Obviously this requires a degree of prior organisation.

The most fraught situation is when a horse is so seriously injured that euthanasia has to be considered. In this situation the vet's responsibility is to the horse rather than to anyone else, so he must resist any pressure to move it just so that the course is clear for the competition to continue; anyone moving a horse when this might make its situation worse would be liable to prosecution on a cruelty charge. Occasionally a situation arises where the vet considers that euthanasia must be carried out but the owner is not present or will not agree. Under UK law a policeman has the power to order the euthanasia of an injured horse, and if he does so the vet must carry out the order. More frequently, owners of insured horses request the immediate destruction of horses where the vet is not convinced that this is necessary for the animal's sake. Of course a vet will probably be willing to put the horse down, but not prepared to sign a declaration saying that this was necessary because the horse was in severe pain which could not be relieved and from which there was no likelihood of recovery. Owners may well be asked to sign a consent form which clarifies the reason why euthanasia is going to be carried out.

The act of euthanasia itself can be carried out either by shooting the horse, or by means of intravenous injection. Shooting is instant and as far as one can tell, painless, but it is noisy, and to a degree messy, and this can upset people. Whilst other horses may be startled temporarily by the noise, they cannot connect the noise with the death of this other horse. On the other hand, administering an intravenous injection takes longer both to perform and to take effect than shooting, and the horse is certainly aware that something is happening during this time. However, there is no noise, and people are less likely to be upset. When a fractious horse requires euthanasia, shooting with a free bullet requires care and a wide, 'safe' surrounding area – but equally, if an injection is preferred, it can be very difficult to inject the whole dose of drug into such a fractious horse, and if it receives only part of the dose it may become even more difficult to control. Leave the method of euthanasia to the vet who has to perform it. He has the experience to know how best to carry it out quickly and safely in any given circumstance.

If a horse does require veterinary attention at an event it is important to obtain the name and address of the vet concerned. You should also ask for a written description of any drugs given so you can pass this information on to your own vet on your return home and thus ensure continuity of treatment. It is not in the horse's interest for follow-up treatment to be delayed because the vet who gave the initial treatment cannot be traced. Even if no follow-up treatment is necessary, you need to know what drugs have been given in case they require you to abandon plans to compete elsewhere because of the rules on prohibited substances.

Dental Care

By and large horses are not troubled by tooth decay during their competitive life. The main dental problems are associated with pain resulting from teeth damaging the tongue or the inside of the cheeks; the molar, or cheek teeth are particularly involved. Unlike our teeth, those of the horse erupt continuously, each pushing further out through the gums throughout its life until eventually there is not enough of the tooth left in the gums to anchor it securely and it falls out (Fig 34). This continuous eruption is matched by a corresponding amount of wear on the grinding surface, but problems arise when wear does not keep pace with eruption. In particular in the horse the upper molars are wider than the lower molars. This means that there is usually little difficulty in wearing down the lower molars, but even wear across the whole grinding surface of the upper molars often fails to occur. The result is that the outer edge of the upper molars appears to 'grow' longer than the inner edge and the grinding surface becomes angled (Fig 35); from time to time that outer edge becomes so sharp that it damages the inside of the cheek and causes ulceration. The pain and discomfort is particularly noticeable when the horse is ridden because the bridle presses the cheek against the teeth. Any sign that a horse is starting to fight the bit, or not respond as well to it as it has done in the past, may indicate dental problems. In some dressage horses the first sign of a problem is just a lowered competition score.

The other main symptom of dental disease is a failure to eat properly because of discomfort when chewing. This can be the result of sharp points along the molars, or because pronounced hooks have developed on the front or back teeth which restrict chewing movements, or similarly a wave pattern along the molars which also affects grinding efficiency.

■ Tooth Rasping

The answer to all these problems is to remove all the sharp points and to flatten the grinding surfaces by means of a file called a tooth rasp. In my opinion the only way that this can be done properly is if the jaws are held apart by a mouth gag; otherwise it is not possible to move the rasp freely between the upper and lower jaws, and the back teeth tend to remain untouched. All horses

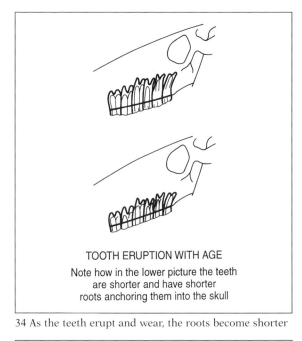

TOOTH ERUPTION WITH AGE
Note how in the lower picture the teeth are shorter and have shorter roots anchoring them into the skull

34 As the teeth erupt and wear, the roots become shorter

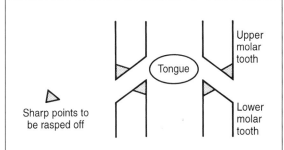

35 Cross-section of the upper and lower molars showing sharp edges

should have their teeth checked at least once a year for possible problems, and competition horses, where control from the bit can be so important, may well benefit from more frequent checks. Some horses have a slight abnormality of jaw movement during chewing that tends to form sharp points more readily than others. Besides the beneficial effect on performance, rasping the teeth also helps to prevent impaction colic, which can be the result of failure to digest fibrous material which was imperfectly chewed.

■ Wolf Teeth in the Horse

Some horses have present a relatively small tooth immediately in front of the main molars. This small tooth is called a wolf tooth and it does not have a proper root securely fixed in the jaw bone. The result is that the bit can cause small amounts of movement in the wolf tooth, and this is naturally resented by the horse. In most cases it is difficult to tell whether a wolf tooth is causing problems or not, although if they are present they should always be suspect should a horse develop a bit problem. If there is any doubt I consider that they should be removed. The more precise the work the horse is required to perform, the more sensible it is to remove any wolf teeth as a preventive measure.

Shoeing

Mention has already been made of the importance of maintaining a correct hoof/pastern axis and foot balance for all horses. This requires regular farriery, with the horse's feet being checked every 4–6 weeks whether it is in work or not. It is wrong to leave a longer period between farriery check-ups just because the horse is not actually competing or is not shod; the hooves will grow at more or less the same rate no matter what the horse is doing.

Farriery is a very skilled craft – but this should not mean that horse owners cannot learn to distinguish whether a horse's feet have been properly trimmed and shod or not. It is perhaps unfortunate that the great shortage of farriers in modern times allows them the luxury of being able to take umbrage (and sometimes to take off altogether) if they think that their work is being criticised. It is important to work with your farrier, to let him see the horse's feet often enough to keep them properly trimmed, and as a result to build up a relationship which allows you both to discuss what is happening.

There is general agreement that the commonest fault in modern horses with regard to shoeing is the development of a long toe but short heel. This results in shearing forces on the sensitive laminae down the front of the feet and extra percussion on the heel region, which is where sensitive structures such as the navicular bone are situated. It also puts more tension on the flexor tendons down the back of the leg. There are several ways in which a farrier can deal with this situation but only one results in a real improvement (Fig 36): when the foot is properly trimmed, the weight of the horse lies in the centre of the foot rather than towards the heels.

When we make the decision to shoe a horse we take on completely the responsibility for the shape

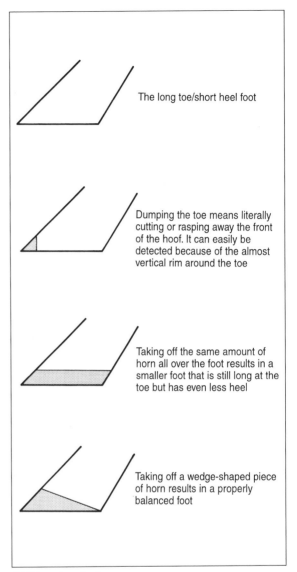

The long toe/short heel foot

Dumping the toe means literally cutting or rasping away the front of the hoof. It can easily be detected because of the almost vertical rim around the toe

Taking off the same amount of horn all over the foot results in a smaller foot that is still long at the toe but has even less heel

Taking off a wedge-shaped piece of horn results in a properly balanced foot

36 Trimming the foot

of its feet. The hooves of a shod horse receive no wear at all, and if the foot is incorrectly balanced when the shoe is put on, it will be incorrectly balanced when the shoe is taken off; it will just have grown longer. We sometimes talk about the importance of making the shoes fit the feet rather than the feet fit the shoes, but if the feet are not correct to start with then this does not apply. For example if a foot is slightly smaller in one dimension than it ought to be, the correct thing to do is to use a shoe which is slightly larger in that dimension than the foot, because the hoof will tend to spread to fit the shoe.

Controversy has long raged over whether it is best to shoe a horse hot or cold. Supporters of hot shoeing point out that the shoe can be made to

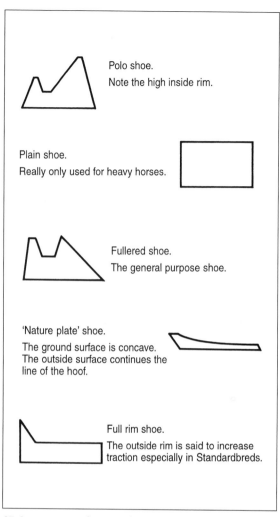

Polo shoe.
Note the high inside rim.

Plain shoe.
Really only used for heavy horses.

Fullered shoe.
The general purpose shoe.

'Nature plate' shoe.
The ground surface is concave.
The outside surface continues the
line of the hoof.

Full rim shoe.
The outside rim is said to increase
traction especially in Standardbreds.

37 Cross-sectional views of some different types of horse-shoe

fit more accurately when it is hot, but supporters of cold shoeing deny this. Only rarely do we have the luxury of the third option, which is hand-made shoes. My main concern is that it is possible to shoe a horse more quickly cold than hot, and the farriers who shoe a horse in seven minutes flat (and they do exist) all shoe cold. This attitude of mind is not as conducive to the studied, careful moulding of iron to hoof as when they are working with the more 'plastic' medium of hot metal. A good farrier will shoe horses well whether he shoes hot or cold, but a bad farrier may be worse shoeing cold than he would be shoeing hot.

The cross-sectional design of the metal used for the shoes can vary (Fig 37). We should be shoeing to provide protection for the hoof and a degree of grip, not to produce shoes which won't wear out. In the racing world horses spend 90 per cent of their time in normal shoes but are then shod with very light racing plates for the race itself. Although this certainly saves a bit of weight during the race, the frequent changes of shoe do result in a weakening of the hoof wall. I am surprised that dressage horse owners have not resorted to a similar routine to encourage a more exaggerated action when a horse performs a test with lighter feet.

One of the advantages of being present when your horse is shod is that you see for yourself whether any nails are misdirected and enter the sensitive part of the foot. This can result in lameness afterwards, which is often just at the time of the competition. Nail bind, when the nails are pressing on the sensitive tissues but have not penetrated it, often results in temporary lameness after shoeing. Ideally the farrier's visits should be arranged so that the horse has about 3–4 days afterwards before a competition, during which time it can adapt to the effects of the hoof trimming and the shoeing. It is often said that after shoeing a horse has 1–2 weeks when its feet are properly balanced, 2 weeks when they are acceptable and then 1–2 weeks when they are too long. The ideal would be to compete during those initial few weeks of the shoeing cycle.

We must not forget that shoes are an artificial addition to a horse's feet, and that studs, calkins and pads are artificial additions to shoes that almost invariably make the feet worse. Studs may provide an increased amount of grip, but they also result in a second percussive force every time the foot hits the ground, one for the stud hitting the ground and one when the stud sinks in and the surface of the shoe hits the ground. On hard surfaces studs dramatically reduce contact between the shoe and the ground, besides which they ensure that the foot is at an artificial angle. Thus when studs are used, they should be removed as soon as possible after the competition.

Pads are usually worn over the sole in order to protect sensitive or thin soles. They may do so, but they will also encourage flattening of the sole and frog.

It is possible to improve drastically the action of a lame horse by remedial shoeing, but this is a specialised field, and is not included in the basic farriery training. I would therefore urge caution before adopting remedial shoeing, except on veterinary advice. Make sure that the farrier has the further qualifications which ensure that he has been properly trained. Another circumstance where experience is important is in the field of glue-on shoes. Some farriers have more success at keeping these shoes on than others – although the more often they use such shoes, the better they tend to become at their application (Fig 38).

Just as man has for centuries searched for a way to turn base metals into gold, so he has searched for ways to make his horse's hooves grow stronger or more quickly. In fact he has not made spectacular progress in either search. It does seem to be accepted that no amount of ointments applied around the coronet will affect hoof growth. Blistering, for example, is painful, nor does it increase the rate of horn production – yet it is quite possible that supplementing certain substances in the diet can, in some cases, result in stronger horn. An amino acid called DL methionine has been identified as an essential part of the

links between individual tubules of horn, and it is likely that over a long period of time, supplementation with methionine does improve horn quality. Lack of the vitamin biotin has been similarly implicated in poor quality horn. These two substances can be fed in pure form or, more usually and more expensively, in a special supplement.

Surprisingly there has been very little proper research carried out in this field. The work that has been done has involved small numbers of horses and has not been repeated by other workers. More research is urgently needed, not least because of the extravagant claims made by some supplement manufacturers. Meanwhile, money spent on good farriery is probably a better investment than what can amount to a considerable sum of money spent on such supplements.

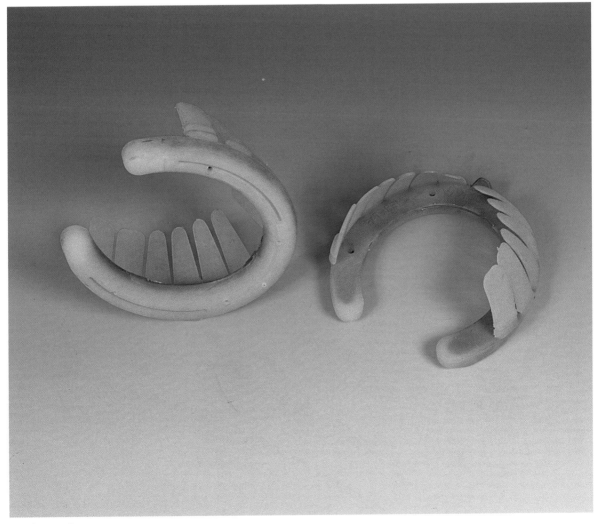

38 Glue-on shoes

The First-Aid Kit

By virtue of the very nature of the work they do both in training and in competition, the horses which are the subject of this book are more likely to require first aid than a horse which leads a less active life, and the contents and availability of a first-aid kit are therefore particularly important. The following general considerations regarding first-aid kits should certainly be observed:

1) **They must be readily available twenty-four hours a day.**

   Locking the first-aid kit up in the tack room, for example, means that anyone who is not actually carrying a key at the crucial time will have to waste precious minutes gaining access to the kit, rather than giving first aid.

2) **Their contents must be regularly reviewed and up-dated.**

   Everyone tends to use things from the first-aid kit and then forgets to replace them –then when an emergency occurs the cupboard is bare. Also, most drugs now have an expiry date, and although it may seem like madness to throw away a nearly full container of antibiotic dusting powder just because it is past its expiry date, we should not take the risk that it has lost some of its efficacy. So check the expiry dates once a month.

3) **Everyone concerned must know how to use their contents.**

   It is not enough for one person in a yard to know about first aid. Time spent searching for that person is time wasted that could save life. All those concerned with the horse should be familiar with the items in the kit and how to use them.

A distinction must be made between a first-aid kit and a medicine cupboard. The former has an ongoing role, the latter contains drugs currently in use to treat existing problems. When the problem has

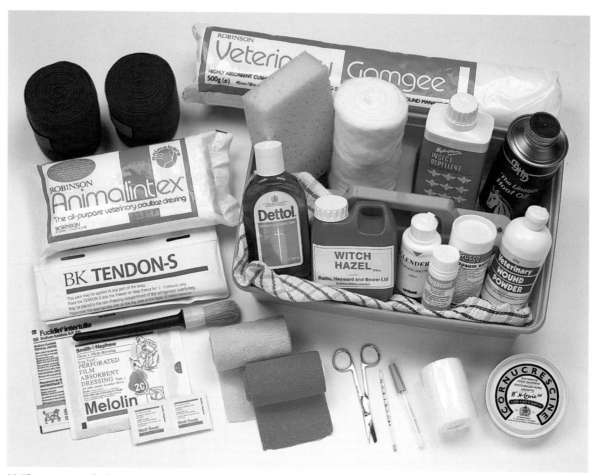

39 The contents of a first-aid kit: these should be readily available and regularly up-dated

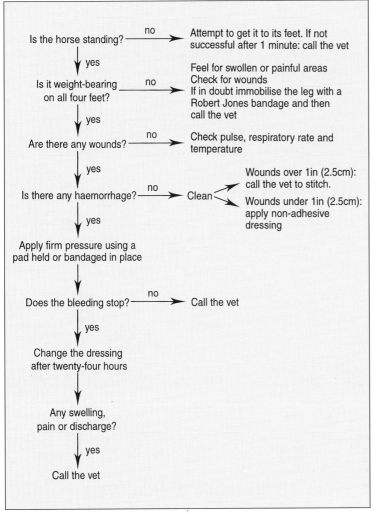

40 Emergency first aid

been dealt with or the treatment otherwise ceased, then any remaining drugs should be disposed of. Having a box of bute handy 'just in case' is a dangerous practice because it tempts people to mask symptoms when they are inconvenient. Drugs prescribed for one horse should not still be around to enable another horse to receive home treatment!

The suggested minimum contents of a first-aid kit are shown in Fig 39. The idea is not that you should be able to perform major surgery, but that you should be able to carry out *first* aid. There are a few procedures with which all those who look after horses should be familiar:

1) Controlling bleeding.

Pressure stops bleeding. Wiping away the blood or washing the wound will encourage the bleeding to continue. The first step in controlling bleeding is to prepare a pad of an appropriate size and thickness. Gamgee is a suitable material. Put a non-stick wound dressing (or dressings) over the wound, place the pad on top and bandage in place as firmly as possible. If it is not possible to bandage the area – for example, a wound on the chest wall – then someone must hold the pad firmly in place. The severity of the bleeding does not affect how it is treated: whether it is a spurting artery or a small oozing cut, the treatment is basically the same.

2) Immobilising the leg.

This is best achieved by means of a Robert Jones bandage. The basic principle is that at least four layers of tightly compacted gamgee are applied to the leg from top to toe.

3) Cleaning a wound.

Plain water will clean a wound just as efficiently as an antiseptic because cleaning is all about the physical removal of dirt and debris. Clean a wound from the centre outwards, and don't return to the wound itself with a dirty swab. Gamgee makes a suitable swab. If the wound is bleeding it is more important to stop the bleeding than it is to remove every last speck of contamination. As mentioned earlier, washing a wound can both prevent clotting and disturb existing clots, so it is possible to clean too much.

Antiseptic aerosols or dusting powder are preferable to cream or ointment when it comes to dealing with any wound infection. Note that these only need to be applied in a thin film to be effective; a thick layer of powder in particular can result in damp, exhausted powder being in contact with the wound, and the infection being protected from the beneficial effects of drying by the thick crust of powder which covers it. A thin layer replaced every couple of hours is better than a thick layer left untouched all day.

Generally, wounds which are more than one inch (2.5cm) long should be stitched by the vet.

place where artery
passes over inside of jaw
bone and can be felt as a pulse

41 Taking the horse's pulse

4) Taking the temperature and pulse.

The thermometer should be checked to make sure that it reads below 100°F (37.75°C) before being inserted up to at least half its length in the horse's rectum and held in place for a minute. It is worth making sure that everyone concerned can read the thermometer, because the mercury line can be difficult to see. A horse's normal temperature is 101–101.5°F (38.4–38.75°C), and a temperature of 102°F (38.9°C) is cause for concern.

Taking the pulse does not require any special equipment, but it does require practice. The fingers are placed lightly over an artery that can be felt crossing the bottom border of the horse's jaw (Fig 41). It is not necessary to count for a full minute: count for 15 or 30 seconds and multiply the result by four or two respectively. The normal pulse rate is 40–50 per minute. With experience the quality of the pulse can also be evaluated, whether it is strong or weak.

Prevention of Disease: The Overall Plan

Disease prevention is something which needs to be worked at: it doesn't just happen. It really is worthwhile devising an overall plan for the whole year and writing this up on a year planner so that nothing is forgotten.

■ Shoeing

Start by noting when the horse will need shoeing; some farriers can cope with regular appointments, others need constant reminders and requests. In the latter situation even the reminder phone call can be logged on the planner. Also, don't forget to warn the farrier if a lameness problem develops which means that the horse cannot be shod on its appointed day. Six-weekly shoeing is a reasonable compromise, but there are people who advise shoeing every four weeks.

■ Worming

Worming dates should be incorporated into the plan next. Bear in mind that all horses on the premises should be wormed on the same day, so other people may need to be involved. Worming should be carried out every ten weeks if using ivermectin, and every six to eight weeks if using pyrantel. The planned dates should be such that worming is carried out immediately prior to any anticipated paddock rest; this is because regular worming is all about preventing worm egg build-up on the pasture. Delaying worming until after the period of paddock rest allows both worm build-up in the horse (which can be dealt with by further worming) and egg build-up on the pasture (which can't be dealt with). The worming which occurs in November or December should be ivermectin anyway, to control bots. A tapeworm dose may also be incorporated into the plan.

■ Vaccinations

The planner should obviously show when any vaccinations are due. Competition organisers are very strict about the equine flu vaccination rules, and if the vaccination is given even a day late then the whole course will have to start all over again. So having checked with the vet when the next dose is due, it might be advisable either to mark it on the planner a week early, or to put an extra warning one to two weeks beforehand to ring the vet. Owners should not expect to ring the vet on the morning of the last possible day and insist that a horse is vaccinated that same day; although it might be important to them, they cannot expect the vet to cancel other appointments for what is, in veterinary terms, a non-urgent visit.

■ Insurance Renewal

Although insurance companies normally send out reminders when policies are due for renewal it is worth noting the renewal date on the planner. Check that the premium really has been paid if it is paid by standing order or other automatic payment. Filling in the renewal application form which is sent out in advance does not mean that you have entered into a binding contract with the insurers. Receipt of the premium by the insurance company starts the policy period, so if payment is late there may be a number of days when the horse is not covered by insurance.

■ Recording Blood Samples

If routine blood samples are being taken to check on the blood cell numbers and to provide true 'normal' levels of blood enzymes, then these must also be entered on the planner. Remember always to arrange for blood samples to be taken at the same time of day, and be sure that the horse has done no strenuous work on the previous day.

FITNESS

MOTORS TROPHY

CONTENTS

DEFINING FITNESS

Fitness can be defined in different ways. Sometimes people consider a horse is fit if it is in full work, doing a couple of hours of exercise every day. In other words, the amount of work is more important than its effect. Other people are more concerned with the visual appearance of the horse – á lean horse would be considered fit. I would define a fit horse as one which is able to carry out a specific activity to the limit of its genetic ability without the onset of fatigue.

It is important to realise quite how specific fitness is. There is no such thing as a fit horse, only a horse which is fit for sprinting, or for a fifty-mile endurance ride, or for show jumping. In a later chapter we will see how different activities need different training techniques to achieve fitness.

Mental Fitness

Fitness has a mental component as well as a physical one. One example of this is the showjumper: just as a piano player practises to be able to play fast passages up and down the scale accurately, so a horse needs to practise sending the messages along the nerves that co-ordinate jumping. A sedated horse will not jump as well as an unsedated horse: it will be just as fit physically, but its mental or nervous fitness has been blocked. Dressage horses are more concerned with mental fitness than physical attributes, and the hours a day that they spend training are not really concerned with delaying the onset of fatigue; they are all about persuading the horse to surrender its free will voluntarily and to carry out particular movements precisely as the owner wishes. There are some horses whose temperament will be a limiting factor in their physical fitness because they waste energy fighting against the rider, and keep their body in permanent readiness for fight or fright. These horses have not really been fully domesticated; they have a wild streak which does not trust men to control them.

Physical Fitness

Fitness has a genetic component. Racehorse owners have bred horses for specific distance races for centuries. Some people claim that the lack of any significant improvement in racing speeds over the past century, compared with the human athletic field where there is no specific breeding for performance, indicates that breeding has little effect. Certainly the most successful racehorses are not always the best bred ones. Other people say that the lack of improvement is precisely because breeding has already brought the horse near to its maximum possible genetic ability. Whereas originally only racehorses were ever bred for performance, competitors in almost all disciplines now place increasing emphasis on the breeding of their horses.

■ The Role of Aerobic and Anaerobic Metabolism

The concept of aerobic and anaerobic metabolism is crucial to physical fitness. Both of these types of metabolism are concerned with the restoration of ATP (adenosine tri phosphate) from ADP (adenosine di phosphate), ready to be broken down again to release movement energy, rather than the direct production of that movement energy (Fig 1). In aerobic metabolism both carbohydrate and fat can be broken down completely in the presence of oxygen to carbon dioxide and water (Fig 2). These are basically non-toxic substances, so such aerobic metabolism is quite safe: the horse's body already has the ability to remove carbon dioxide using haemoglobin, and the tissues are bathed in water anyway.

When oxygen is not readily available because of muscle bulk or because of lack of training, for example, glucose is broken down to lactate instead (Fig 3); the energy released enables ADP molecules to be restored to ATP molecules, but much less efficiently. This is anaerobic metabolism. If the lactate is not removed as quickly as it is

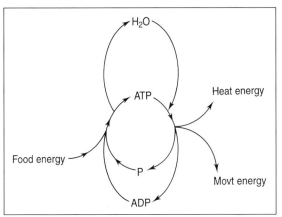

1 The simple ATP cycle showing the consumption and production of energy

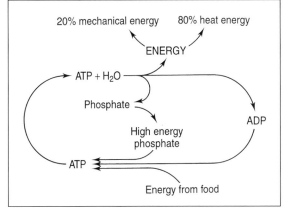

2 The aerobic metabolism cycle

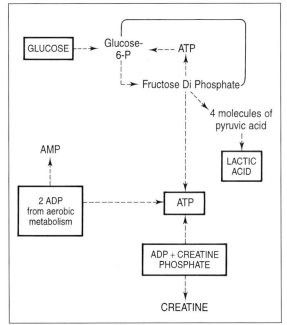

3 In anaerobic metabolism glucose is broken down to lactate, and the energy release enables ADP molecules to be restored to ATP molecules

formed, the tissues become acidic and this in itself further reduces their ability to restore ATP. The chemical reactions that enable muscles to contract don't operate as well in acidic conditions either and they become fatigued.

It may help to consider aerobic metabolism to be a long-term, continuous process, and anaerobic metabolism to be a short-term, potentially toxic process. Both are very dependent on the circulatory system, one to bring in the oxygen and the other to remove the lactate. Accumulated lactate is a problem because it is acidic. It has been suggested that as a horse becomes fitter some alkaline substances in the muscle act as a chemical buffer to neutralise that acidity, and there is good evidence to indicate that a horse's ability to perform really strenuous exercise is directly linked to its ability to buffer the acidity that exists. Training increases the buffering capacity, so a fit horse can withstand more lactate in its muscle than an unfit horse.

During light work very little anaerobic metabolism is involved in muscle activity. However, there comes a certain speed or a certain severity of work where the horse has to switch to anaerobic metabolism because aerobic metabolism is failing. The speed at which this occurs varies with the horse's fitness: the fitter the horse, the faster the galloping speed at which this change occurs. Oxygen availability is obviously a crucial factor in determining the changeover point. Fitness affects this by increasing lung ventilation or by increasing the circulation of blood by the heart, although it probably has little role in increasing the haemoglobin present to bring the oxygen.

The horse's oxygen intake is usually measured in millilitres of oxygen per kilograms of bodyweight per minute. The maximum amount of oxygen that a horse can use is referred to as the VO_2 max, and it has considerable significance with regard to fitness. As the amount of work the horse performs increases, so does the amount of oxygen it uses. This can be measured quite easily by working a horse on a treadmill wearing a mask that supplies air down one tube and removes wasted gases down another tube (Figs 4a and 4b). There comes a point where instead of increasing further, the oxygen consumption levels off and stays more or less constant despite further work. That level is the VO_2 max, and the level of exercise which a horse can perform before the VO_2 is reached depends on its fitness as well as its genetic make-up; thus increasing its fitness delays the point at which VO_2 max is reached, decreasing its

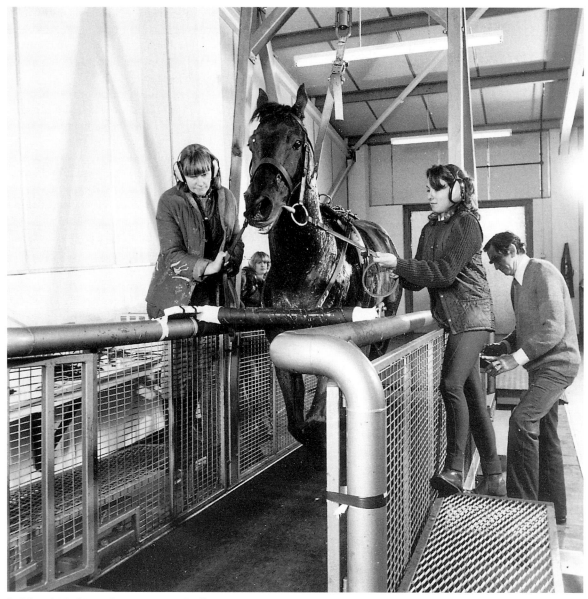

4a (above) Working a horse on a treadmill
4b (opposite) Mask for use on a treadmill to measure oxygen consumption

fitness speeds it up. The actual oxygen consumption at VO_2 max is likely to be around 140ml/kg/min, which is a 3,500 per cent increase on oxygen consumption at rest!

■ Linking Appearance and Fitness

There is a link between appearance and fitness, but it can be a misleading one. Horses used for sprinting need power from their muscles. They don't have extra muscle fibres but they do have large and powerful fibres, the idea being that because most of the energy for sprinting is obtained anaerobically, the distance between the centre of the muscle fibre and any blood vessels outside the fibre can be relatively great. So sprinters have large, bulky muscle masses, and the fitter they are, the bulkier these are likely to be. However, horses used for long-distance riding need stamina from their muscles. Because long-term energy production has to be aerobic, the distance between the centre of the muscle fibre and the blood vessels removing the waste gases has to be relatively short. Therefore unlike the sprinter, endurance horses have wiry frames with relatively little muscle mass.

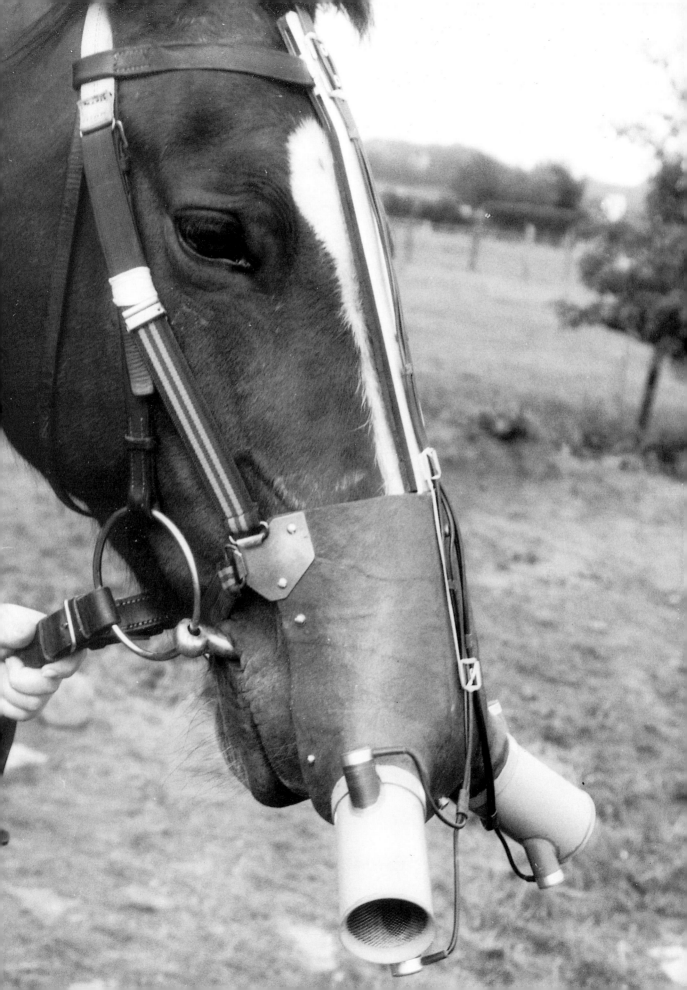

The Limits on Performance

There is always a limit to what fitness and training can achieve in the way of performance. That limit is the individual horse's inherent maximum performance. It is determined by factors such as the type of muscle fibre the horse is born with, the relative size of its heart and its conformation (Figs 5a and 5b). A fit horse will hopefully reach that genetic potential: an unfit horse never will. That is not to say that the unfit horse will not beat the fit horse; if its genetic potential is much greater than that of the fit horse, it may well be able to do so. Some owners find it very frustrating that they put a great deal of time and effort into getting their horse fit, only to find that their arch enemy gets *their* horse out of a field the day before the competition and yet beats them. That does not mean that fitness isn't important, it just means that some horses are better than others!

The Effects of Fitness

Fitness is not only about the ability to gallop a fraction faster than another horse; some of the changes that contribute to fitness occur at quite moderate exercise levels. A good example to illustrate this is the change in the actual volume of circulating blood that occurs. This increases by around 25 per cent within two weeks of the horse starting moderate exercise, and most of that increase happens in the first week. What's more, the concentration of red blood cells in that blood stays the same, so the oxygen-carrying capacity of the blood also increases by the same amount. Such a short time-scale is too soon for new red blood cells to have been manufactured, so presumably the horse uses its splenic reserves to provide the cells and then replaces the reserves over the next four to eight weeks (it takes approximately thirty days to manufacture an equine red blood cell from start

5a Endurance horses, like marathon runners, are usually thin and wiry

5b Sprinters have very well developed muscles

to maturity). The increase in oxygen-carrying capacity contributes to the effects of training on the VO_2 max.

■ The Heart and Fitness

The need for the horse's heart to be given sufficient work during training to raise heart rates significantly has already been mentioned. It should exceed 200 beats/minute. Most of the evidence indicates that fitness is also accompanied by an increase in stroke volume: that is, the amount of blood which is pumped out of the heart at each contraction of the heart muscles. The value of this in increasing oxygen availability to the tissues is obvious. There is some uncertainty over whether this increase in stroke volume occurs in response to fast work or even to moderate work.

6 Muscle fibre types and their roles			
	Type I slow-twitch fibre	Type II fast-twitch high-oxidative fibre	Type II fast-twitch low-oxidative fibre
Speed of contraction	slow	fast	fast
Maximum tension developed	+	+++	+++
Oxidative capacity	+++	++	+
Capillary blood supply	+++	++	+
Enzymes for glucose breakdown	++	+++	+++
Enzymes for fatty acid breakdown	+++	++	+
Ability to withstand fatigue	+++	++	+

6   Muscle fibre types and their roles

■ The Skeleton and Fitness

The bones of the skeleton are not the inactive scaffolding that some people imagine, but respond to exercise and increase in fitness: exercise produces an increase in their tensile strength, the effect being triggered off by very short bursts of strenuous activity – even less than a minute may be enough. It is as well also to remember that with rest the opposite occurs and bone loses some of its tensile strength. Bone also remodels in response to exercise. It produces more bone where the stress is greatest, and to avoid unnecessary weight and bulk reduces the amount of bone where stress is less. One of the roles of training is to show the bones where the stress will be greatest, and so allow that area to be strengthened, without producing so much stress that injury results. An example of this is sore shins in young racehorses. The bone on the front of the cannon bone becomes painful and the horse becomes lame when given too much work or too much jarring from hard surfaces too soon. But with time and a reduction in workload it will settle down and produce bone which is hard enough to withstand racing. If, however, the stress continues unabated then stress fractures will occur.

■ The Muscles and Fitness

The type of fitness which a horse can achieve depends to some extent on the types of muscle fibre it is born with. Muscle fibres can be classified as type I fibre, which contract, or twitch, slowly; or as type II fibres, which can contract or twitch quickly. The type II fibres can also be divided again into type IIA and type IIB. The latter can contract fastest of all, but they are only ever used when maximum power is required. If a horse is going to be a successful sprinter it obviously needs mostly type II muscle fibres. If it is going to be an endurance horse it needs mostly type I fibres, with all shades of activities between these extremes (Fig 6).

The percentage of different fibre types present in a horse's muscles is not affected by training. Thus we cannot make a good endurance horse into a good sprinter just by altering its training because the basic fibre percentages are fixed genetically at birth. The extreme example of this is the Quarter Horse, which has been bred for sprinting over a short distance (a quarter of a mile) and which as a breed has almost 100 per cent fast-twitch, or type II, fibres.

Muscle fibres also vary in their ability to produce energy aerobically or anaerobically. The slow-twitch fibres can use oxygen and produce energy aerobically. Some of the fast-twitch fibres can do the same, but others cannot and have to resort far more readily to anaerobic metabolism. This ability to use oxygen and function aerobically can be altered by training and is a function of fitness. Conversely a resting horse loses that ability.

The percentage of the fibres in a muscle which actually contract varies with the exercise being performed, from perhaps 10 per cent when the horse is walking to 100 per cent when it is galloping flat out. One suggestion is that training carried out at the walk would only therefore involve a low percentage of the muscle fibres, and when more had to be recruited they would be found wanting. With a fit horse there are enough conditioned fibres available for that particular activity.

FATIGUE

Defining Fatigue

Fatigue is in some ways the opposite of fitness, although it, too, can mean different things to different people. The basic definition is that fatigue is the state where the horse's ability to perform a specific type of work deteriorates because of the amount of work that has already been performed. Fatigue is tiredness, but tiredness sometimes only implies muscle weakness, whereas there is also actually an element of pain in fatigue which stops the muscles contracting. Fatigue is a safety warning: its real role is to stop severe exhaustion occurring, because that might result in long-term damage to the muscles; fatigue itself is a short-term situation.

■ The Role of Lactic Acid

- Fatigue is all about the accumulation of lactic acid within the muscle fibres during strenuous exercise, an accumulation which, as has been mentioned, is basically painful.
- Fatigue can also occur during prolonged, less strenuous exercise, due to the exhaustion of the muscle-glycogen stores which fuel the muscle contractions.
- Fatigue can occur for circulatory reasons: dehydration following excessive sweating leads to reduced blood flow to the muscles; this decreases the oxygen available for aerobic metabolism and also reduces the amount of lactic acid washed safely away in anaerobic metabolism.
- Finally fatigue can occur because lameness has resulted in abnormal stresses being placed on specific parts of the locomotor system, stresses which they are not able to withstand.

A build-up of lactic acid is most likely to occur during bursts of maximum effort, when all the muscle fibres are working. At lower exercise levels the horse will rotate the muscle fibres used, allowing each one to recover before it is used again. The fibres which are only used at faster speeds are the most sensitive to the build-up of lactic acid because they have only a very limited aerobic capability; the large amounts of adenosine tri phosphate (ATP) they need to provide the energy for movement have to be replenished anaerobically. The supplies of phophocreatine used for this are soon exhausted and lactic acid ends up being produced in such large amounts that it can no longer be removed by the circulation. The acidity, or pH, of the cell then drops and it cannot contract properly.

The build-up of lactic acid affects both the power output and the speed of contraction of the muscle as a whole. It is the cause of the fading or slowing that so often occurs at the end of a race. Indeed it has been suggested that horses rarely accelerate during the last furlong, and that what actually happens is that most horses slow down; the fitter horse that continues at more or less the same speed is therefore made to look as if it is accelerating.

■ Pain and Fatigue

Fatigue is often associated with pain. Human athletes sometimes refer to 'the wall', or to a pain barrier which they have to overcome if they are to continue. It is likely that the success of some horses is also due to their willingness to continue even though it is painful to do so. Research has shown that the horse can and does tolerate higher levels of lactic acid than a human athlete can endure. However, as the lactic acid accumulates, so the amount of ATP present in the muscle decreases; and when the exercise stops, the horse does not immediately cease to be fatigued: it takes time for the muscles to recover, and it takes time for the accumulation of lactic acid to be removed and normal resting levels to be restored. This is where the pay-off has to be made, because although the horse can tolerate high levels of lactic acid, it also takes a relatively long time to recover after exercise as compared to a human athlete.

7 Using a heart-rate monitor

■ Stamina versus Fatigue

During stamina events horses do not accumulate high enough levels of lactic acid to produce fatigue; they don't need to use anaerobic metabolism for this level of physical effort. Instead what happens is that in time the glycogen, which with free fatty acids is the main fuel for energy production stored in the muscles and liver, is exhausted. And without fuel only low speed work is possible.

It is useful to consider what happens in a horse's muscle when it is asked to trot for a prolonged time. At the trot only 50 per cent of the muscle fibres have to be used. However, as the fuel available in each of those fibres is exhausted, another fibre is brought into work. The high-oxidative fibres, both slow-twitch and fast-twitch, exhaust their glycogen first, and then finally the fast-twitch low-oxidative fibres exhaust their supplies. When all the glycogen has been used up the horse may no longer be able to trot, although it can probably keep going at walk or possibly a very slow trot. This is because free fatty acids in the blood (released from the fat stores) will fuel slow exercise, but the transport system will not produce sufficient of them to sustain faster work. The horse

can keep going for several days at slow speeds, though, fuelled by the fat stores.

Human marathon runners feel the onset of pain as they exhaust their glycogen and this warns them to slow down. There are two concerns about the same situation in the horse: first there is the 'welfare' argument which says that riders will inevitably cause unnecessary pain by keeping horses moving in defiance of that warning. The second problem is that some horses will, because of their temperament, cause damage to their muscles by keeping going without any check at all and without giving their rider a clue as to what is happening.

The Results of Fatigue

It is important that riders do not ignore fatigue in their desire to do well in a competition. Tired muscles lose their co-ordination, and the sudden unco-ordinated movement that results is one of the commonest causes of injury and lameness. Nor is it just the muscle that will be involved in this case: the tendons are at their physical limit when galloping, and the muscle is the only safety system left. But a tired muscle is unable to fulfil that role,

8 Walking round the saddling enclosure is not a sufficient warm-up for a horse to offer maximum performance in a speed event

and a sprained tendon may be the result. One way to help a particular rider become attuned to how a particular horse reacts when fatigue starts to develop is to use a heart-rate monitor (Fig 7). Thus when the horse is exercising at a more or less steady speed, any sudden increase in heart rate is probably indicative of the onset of fatigue. The rider can then slow down but he has learned to appreciate how the horse is moving and how it behaves at that time. During the competition proper it may not be possible to be studying a heart-rate monitor but by then the rider will know the signs given by that horse when fatigue is starting, and can then decide what to do.

Naturally we try to prolong the exercise which can be carried out before the onset of fatigue. Reducing the horse's speed will result in a higher proportion of free fatty acids being used but, of course, this may mean that the horse cannot compete. If, however, we can increase the proportion of fatty acids used without reducing the speed then this is an advantage. This so-called 'glycogen sparing effect' can be achieved by increasing fitness, in other words by training the muscles to use more fatty acids.

Feeding Before the Event

Human marathon runners use high carbohydrate diets such as pasta to build up glycogen levels in their muscles. The trouble is that every gram of glycogen stored also stores three grams of water and the result can literally be heavy legs. The naturally higher muscle-glycogen levels in the horse (50 per cent up on man) mean that it may not be possible to carry out glycogen loading in the horse, and it probably isn't necessary anyway. It is likely to take several days for depleted glycogen levels to be replaced after exercise. We don't know if a higher energy diet can influence recovery from fatigue for the better, nor is it known whether anything other than a normal high energy ration is needed for racehorses.

Warming up Before Competitions

A proper warm-up period at the start of exercise is essential if the effects of fatigue are to be minimised. This period should always consist of walking and trotting exercise only; its duration will vary from horse to horse but a minimum of five minutes will probably be needed. The idea is to increase the circulation to the muscles, opening up the blood vessels which are not in use whilst the horse is resting, in the expectation that any lactic acid formed will be more readily removed. The use of a heart-rate monitor will show that the heart rate increases from 40 beats/minute at rest to around 120 beats/minute at the trot, and when it levels out and stops increasing then the circulation is primed for exercise (Fig 9). During the warm-up period the temperature in the muscles does actually rise by about 1°C. Like all chemical catalysts, enzymes work more efficiently at higher temperatures, and so the muscle enzymes involved in the ATP/ADP cycle are brought to maximum readiness during this period. It is also thought that muscle contractions and reflex times are faster at the slightly higher temperatures. Incidentally, a 1°C rise might not seem very much to cause all these changes, but it must be appreciated that the internal temperature in all body tissues is very rigorously controlled, and it takes a reasonable amount of exercise to achieve this desirable warming.

A warm-up period is desirable for all kinds of activity. Even sprinting, where high levels of lactic acid production are an accepted feature, needs a warm-up period because otherwise sudden acceleration can cause muscle tearing. This is really a case of the horse's mind being able to insist on sudden muscle contractions without the muscles themselves being in any way ready for them.

For some reason the horse world gives little thought to warming up for speed events. At racetracks horses often only get the chance to walk from a stable to the paddock (Fig 8), and then to canter the all-too-short distance to the starting gate without any significant amount of trotting at all. You might argue that you are handicapping the activity of all the horses in the race equally, but it is not a means of ensuring maximum performance levels, nor of reducing fatigue-induced injuries.

Warming up before exercise must be distinguished from the situation when a horse gets very excited and sweats up before a competition. It is generally accepted that the horse which does sweat up is less likely to do well in the actual competition. This might be because the adrenalin-stimulated sweating does not produce any change inside the muscle mass, and when the horse starts to compete it asks the muscles for a level of work

Approximate heart rates at different speeds	
	beats/minute
Standing	40
Walking	80
Slow trotting	120
Fast trotting	140
Slow cantering	160
Fast cantering	200
Galloping	225

9 The heart rate at increasing levels of exercise

which they would have been capable of performing if they had been properly warmed up, but which starting 'from cold' soon results in fatigue.

The Cooling-off Period

The period after exercise is just as important as that beforehand. It must be realised that a horse will continue to produce heat after exercise because the lactic acid which has been produced will, in turn, have to be broken down, and this process releases more heat. The cooling-off period after exercise is not, therefore, specifically aimed at lowering the body temperature, but rather at dealing with the situation which produces that temperature. It is probably a reasonable guideline to say that cooling down should continue until no more heat is being produced, that is, until all the lactic acid has been dealt with.

It has been shown that a horse should be trotted during the cooling-down period rather than just walked or left standing. The better circulation during the trot enables more lactic acid to be removed more quickly than in either of the other two situations. It is not, however, desirable to cool down the muscle too quickly as this may result in part of the circulation closing down whilst there is still some lactic acid present. Nevertheless, hosing down with cold water (Fig 10) is now recommended to cool horses down after strenuous exercise in hot climates, and recent studies have shown that the temperature effect of cold water is greater than the cooling effect caused by the evaporation of warm water. So after a period when the organisers of major competitions were asked to provide warm water to cool the horses, we are now back to demanding cold or iced water.

Drugs and Fatigue

Drugs have been used to reduce fatigue. Amphetamines increase heart output, respiratory rate, oxygen uptake and circulation through the muscles, all very desirable ends. They have been shown to increase the amounts of glucose and free fatty acids transported to the muscles, which is also desirable. In addition to these physiological effects, in man, amphetamines remove the inhibitory influences that tell us to slow down because we are becoming fatigued. The result has been that some human athletes have driven themselves to exhaustion and death whilst under their influence. The use of drugs is naturally banned from all types of competition.

Anabolic steroids have been given to horses in an attempt to increase their muscle size, and thereby increase their power for performance. However, merely giving the drug to a mature horse probably neither increases the size of its muscles nor affects its performance *per se*. It has, however, been suggested that anabolic steroids may increase a horse's aggression and drive, and as a result it is prepared to train harder and to withstand the pain of fatigue; thus the extra work it performs results in extra muscle mass, rather than the steroids themselves being a direct cause of that increased mass. The use of anabolic steroids is banned during competition, and in a number of countries even their sale is banned.

Both human and equine athletes have been given a substance called carnitine in their diet to delay the onset of fatigue by improving the availability of free fatty acids and by acting as a buffer after sprinting exercise. However, it is still far from certain that such supplements actually result in increased carnitine in the muscles. There has also been publicity for the use of the amino acid glycine (as dimethyl glycine, DMG) to reduce lactate production and so delay fatigue. Again, scientific tests have failed to reveal any improved effect on exercise from feeding the supplement.

By giving a horse sodium bicarbonate it is claimed that the acidity resulting from lactic acid production is effectively buffered, the higher tissue pH that results encouraging the removal of lactic acid and so delaying the onset of fatigue. In human athletes the effect of sodium bicarbonate is most noticeable during middle-distance events. The use of sodium bicarbonate and other buffers are prohibited by some racing authorities.

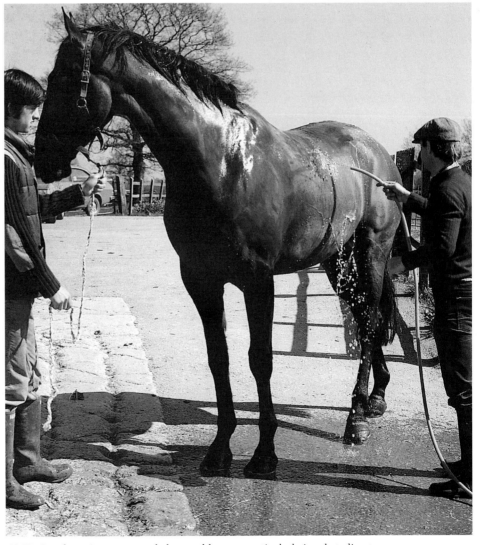

10 Hosing down is recommended to cool horses, particularly in a hot climate

■ MEASURING FITNESS ■

The Heart Rate and Fitness

The easiest measurement that can be related to fitness is the horse's heart rate. Although this can be assessed by using a stethoscope and a watch (Fig 11), or by taking the horse's pulse, neither of these methods can be carried out on the moving horse.

To measure the heart rate in this situation we have to use an electronic heart-rate monitor. This is really a simplified form of electrocardiograph, or ECG. Electrodes in contact with the horse's skin pick up minute electrical impulses in the heart (good electrical contact between the electrodes and the skin is essential to achieve this); the equipment interprets the information and sends it either to

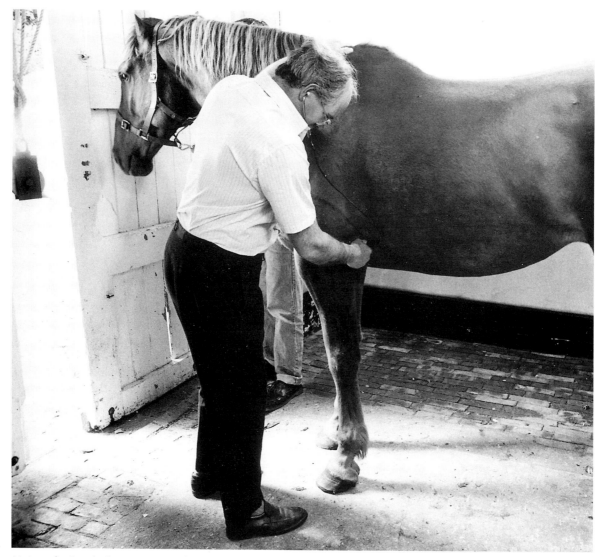

11 Auscultating the heart. Some perfectly healthy horses have abnormal heart sounds at rest

a monitor on the rider's wrist or to a recording device for later playback.

The information available from a heart monitor varies depending on the sophistication of the equipment. The most important information is the heart rate itself but other information, such as the frequency or occurrence of abnormal heart-rate rhythms, may also be available. It may be possible to produce a printout of the information or to transfer it directly to a computer for long-term storage and assessment.

When assessing a horse's heart rate it is important, as with all scientific measurements, to compare like with like. You cannot compare a heart rate from a monitor with one counted via a stethoscope in the stationary horse. More particularly you should not directly compare heart rates obtained from different monitors. They will certainly differ, but this is unimportant. Also we are more concerned with assessing different heart rates from the same horse, measured in the same way, than with comparing heart rates between different horses.

The basic expectation is that the fitter a horse becomes, the slower its heart rate will be at a particular speed. At heart rates between 120 and 200 beats per minute there is a direct correlation between the heart rate and the amount of blood being pumped around the body. Excitement will increase the heart rate even when the horse is galloping, so if a horse is startled then its heart rate will shoot up for a time just as it would in a resting horse. We must be careful not to include such episodes in any fitness assessment. A heart rate of 200 beats per minute is often held to correspond to maximum oxygen consumption. In Standardbred horses it also corresponds to a speed of around 635 metres per minute.

In addition to measuring heart rate during exercise, we also assess fitness by observing the way that rate returns to normal after exercise, because when it does so we know that the horse has repaid any oxygen debt incurred by having to obtain energy anaerobically during the exercise. In this case, the fitter the horse the more quickly its heart rate returns to its resting rate. Endurance competitors set great store by recovery heart rates in assessing whether the horse is fit to continue in the competition. Each regulatory body sets its own criteria for this, but for general purposes we usually expect a fit horse's heart rate to return to below 60 beats per minute within 30 minutes of finishing the exercise.

The Respiratory Rate and Fitness

Because it is controlled by the horse's stride pattern, the respiratory rate cannot give us any firm indication of fitness. In a way this is surprising because many trainers use the sound of a horse's breathing after exercise to indicate fitness. One subjective assessment often made is whether the horse sounds 'clean-winded' or 'thick-winded' after fast work, with the former indicating fitness. In fact being thick-winded has nothing to do with fitness and depends solely on how much mucus is present in the trachea, or windpipe. If a moderately fit horse is suddenly given an hour or two's grazing per day, or is fed its hay on the floor, then it will sound more thick-winded because mucus from the lungs will more easily run down into the trachea whilst its head is down feeding. This explains the prejudice some trainers have against turning their horses out to graze: it makes them more thick-winded and so, they think, less fit.

Despite my comments in the preceding paragraph, there is an indirect way in which the sound a horse makes whilst breathing reflects fitness. When a horse is standing quietly in the stable, it only uses a fraction of its lung volume during breathing. If that horse performs more and more work, then it will use more and more of its lung volume until it is using every last little air sac within the lungs. Every time one of these alveoli is opened up, a tiny amount of mucus is released, which eventually reaches the trachea and by causing turbulence affects the noise of breathing. Because a fit horse regularly utilises the whole of its lung, there is little mucus released when it does so. An unfit horse might release enough mucus when worked to make it sound thick-winded, but as has been explained, this is not the only cause of the noise.

It is now possible to measure a horse's tidal volume – that is, the volume of air breathed in at each breath – during exercise simply by inserting a small sensor into its rectum and measuring rectal pressure during exercise. There is a good correlation between rectal pressure and movement of the diaphragm, which in turn reflects tidal volume. This might in the future give us valuable information on how effective training methods are. A fit horse would be expected to use less volume of air and to return to normal air intake more quickly than an unfit horse over any particular piece of fast work.

The Blood and Fitness

■ Using Blood Enzyme Levels to Assess Fitness

Because blood samples are relatively easy to take it was inevitable that attempts would be made to use enzyme levels and blood cell counts to assess fitness. The muscle enzymes creatine kinase (CK) and aspartate aminotransferase (AST) can give us some information about fitness. When a horse first enters training, levels of these enzymes rise. It is assumed that the general stress of training, and the specific stress of physical exercise, is too much for the unfit muscles and some breakdown of fibres occurs, releasing the enzymes. As the horse adapts to the training, the enzyme levels return to more like their pretraining levels. When the workload is increased again, so do the enzyme levels. So CK and AST levels provide some information about whether the horse has adapted to a particular workload, but not about its ability to work at maximum potential (Fig 12). They are of

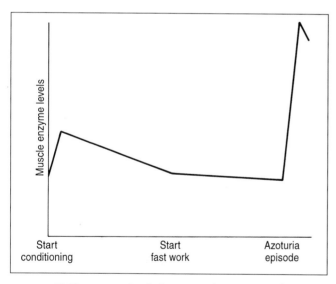

12 The enzyme levels during conditioning and early training work

most value in the early stages of training, especially for helping to determine whether the horse is sufficiently conditioned to start fast work. When a fit horse has stable muscle enzyme levels, any rise is likely to be significant and its cause needs to be investigated. Some endurance horses have high but stable muscle enzyme levels and still perform perfectly well. We do not know how or why they do this.

■ The Importance of Regular Blood Samples

It must be stressed that the value of blood samples depends entirely on having a 'normal' out-of-training level for that particular horse against which to compare any changes during training. It is not safe to compare training levels with the breed or type average because the changes with training may well be too small to register as abnormal if the horse's resting values are in the lower normal range.

■ Blood Cell Counts and Fitness

Various attempts have been made to assess fitness from blood cell measurements, in particular the routine measurements carried out to assess red blood cell (RBC) numbers and their haemoglobin concentration. To a large extent these efforts have been doomed to failure from the beginning because of the difficulty of comparing like with like. The horse's large reserve of RBCs in its spleen distorts the values after even the slightest excitement. At one time it was thought that RBC numbers (as measured by packed cell volume, or PCV) went up during training and that high levels indicated more fitness. In fact what seems to happen is that horses respond more to stimulation as training progresses and so become more excitable when they are blood sampled; thus it may be the excitement which produces the increased PCV rather than any advantageous effect of training: the raised PCV is more due to the extra RBCs pushed out into the blood from the spleen than to any overall increase in their numbers.

A detailed evaluation of the horse's blood cells can, however, be worthwhile for competition horses (see Figs 13 and 14). Samples should always be taken at the same time of day, exciting the horse as little as possible. Low RBC numbers are an indication of anaemia, which means that the horse has a reduced ability to carry oxygen to tissues via the bloodstream. Contrary to popular opinion, horses do not commonly develop anaemia due to lack of iron or of vitamin B12, and supplements containing these substances are a waste of time and money from the point of view of performance. The only substance which has ever been shown to increase the number of red blood cells is folic acid, which is present in fresh green forage and so may be deficient in stabled competition horses. If a horse has low RBC numbers but the size of each cell or its haemo-globin content are higher than normal, then it probably means that the horse is aware of the problem and is taking steps to overcome it temporarily whilst new RBCs are formed. It takes approximately thirty days to manufacture a working red blood cell, so improvements in RBC measurements occur only slowly.

The white blood cells (WBC) are concerned with the body's ability to fight infection and stress, and both situations will give rise to a raised WBC count. Thus trainers who have a horse blood-sampled immediately after a poor performance and find that the horse has a raised WBC count cannot therefore assume that the horse has an infection which was responsible for that poor performance. Stress alone can give a similar result, so a raised WBC count needs to be maintained for

24–48 hours after the competition before we can really say that an infection is probably present. As a rule of thumb, horses have 60 per cent neutrophils and 40 per cent monocytes and lymphocytes, but small alterations are not usually significant. Neutrophils are particularly involved in dealing with bacterial infections, and high numbers may confirm that a problem is bacterial in origin. The significance of changes in monocyte and lymphocyte numbers is less reliable. A horse may, for example, have an active virus infection without raised numbers. At the other end of the spectrum numbers may remain raised after the horse appears clinically normal.

It is starting to become possible to measure lactate levels in the blood quickly and easily. This is, of course, of great interest in assessing fitness because in many circumstances the accumulation

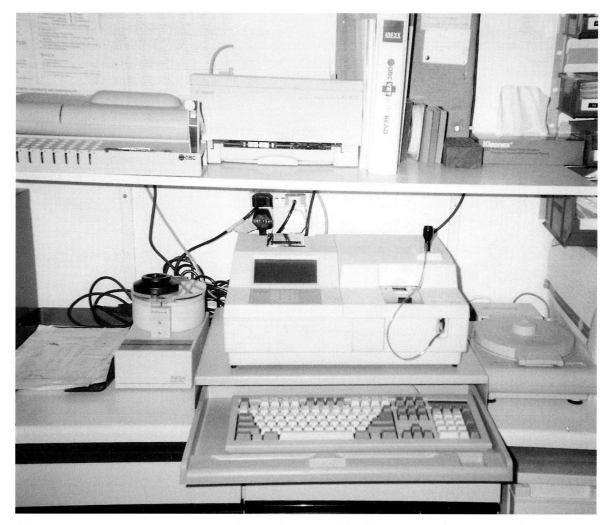

13 Many veterinary practices now possess sophisticated equipment like this Vet-Test machine to give on-the-spot results for haematology and biochemistry on blood samples

Gillham House Veterinary Group
Wells Rd, Fakenham, Norfolk
Tel: 01328 862137
Fax: 01328 855913

Species : Adult Equine   Ver: 4.4
Patient : Richardson   Date : 23-Apr-1996 05:46PM

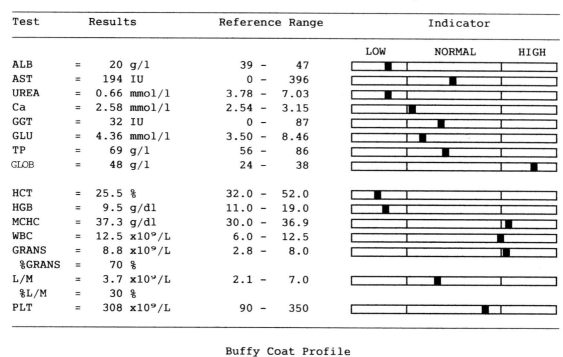

Test		Results	Reference Range	Indicator
				LOW NORMAL HIGH
ALB	=	20 g/l	39 - 47	
AST	=	194 IU	0 - 396	
UREA	=	0.66 mmol/l	3.78 - 7.03	
Ca	=	2.58 mmol/l	2.54 - 3.15	
GGT	=	32 IU	0 - 87	
GLU	=	4.36 mmol/l	3.50 - 8.46	
TP	=	69 g/l	56 - 86	
GLOB	=	48 g/l	24 - 38	
HCT	=	25.5 %	32.0 - 52.0	
HGB	=	9.5 g/dl	11.0 - 19.0	
MCHC	=	37.3 g/dl	30.0 - 36.9	
WBC	=	12.5 x10⁹/L	6.0 - 12.5	
GRANS	=	8.8 x10⁹/L	2.8 - 8.0	
%GRANS	=	70 %		
L/M	=	3.7 x10⁹/L	2.1 - 7.0	
%L/M	=	30 %		
PLT	=	308 x10⁹/L	90 - 350	

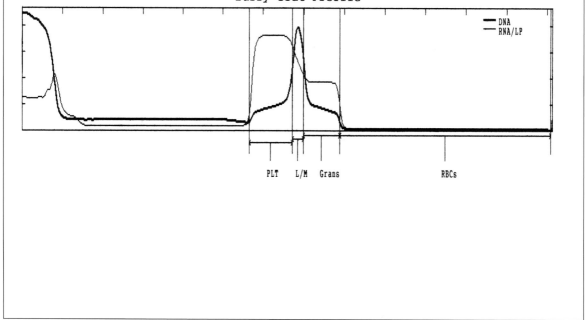

Buffy Coat Profile

PLT   L/M   Grans   RBCs

14 The printout produced details both biochemistry and haematology. Of particular note here is the high globulin level where the horse is producing antibodies against infection. The high WBC numbers and in particular the high number of granulocytes, or neutrophils, also show that the horse is fighting an infection

of lactate indicates fatigue, and fatigue indicates a lack of fitness. We can use lactate in two ways. First we can measure the onset of blood lactate accumulation (OBLA): this refers to the speed at which the horse can work before lactate starts to accumulate. In fact there is general agreement that the danger level of lactate from the fatigue point of view is 4mmol per litre. So the second, and more useful way to use lactate levels is to measure the speed of work which results in a lactate level of 4mmol/litre. It has been shown that as fitness increases so does the exercise level that can be performed before this lactate level is reached. We are in effect measuring the speed at which anaerobic energy production really takes over from aerobic energy production. An even simpler way to use blood lactate levels is just to measure them at the end of a standard exercise test. What the test comprises is immaterial, it is the comparisons which are valuable.

Fitness and Performance

Naturally we can use performance to indicate fitness. This is the method which trainers have used over the centuries. The easiest way is to work the horse concerned against a horse which you think is fit and to see how it compares – is it as fast, or faster? Is it slower? The drawback here is that the benchmark may not be accurate. The trainer usually assumes that if a horse competes successfully it must be fit, but this may not be the case. A horse of great ability could well be successful at many levels of competition without being fit and so without showing its maximum potential. And if the trainer compares a mediocre horse to a horse of such talent they may appear equal, although of course they are not.

If horses are assessed as individuals, then one way to put a figure on fitness is to work a horse over a fixed distance and to measure the time taken, the idea being that as fitness increases so the time taken for the test decreases. However, this involves working the horse at maximum intensity, and so there is an associated risk of injury during the assessment. It may be slightly safer from an injury point of view to record the speed (distance travelled divided by the time taken) at which the maximum heart rate is reached. Maximum heart rate itself does not alter with fitness. An alternative to this is to measure the speed at which a heart rate of 200 beats per minute is reached. This has been shown to correlate quite well with fitness,

although because different horses have different maximum heart rates, it results in different work intensities being compared. So a horse whose maximum heart rate is 215 beats per minute is working harder at 200 beats per minute than a horse with a maximum heart rate of 220 beats per minute. One way around this is to use the speed which results in a heart rate of 80–90 per cent of maximum heart rate.

■ The Treadmill

Research into fitness has come to rely heavily on the use of the treadmill. The horse is restrained within four walls, but the ground surface is a belt of rubber or other suitable material that moves at specified speeds; the horse then literally runs on the spot. In fact horses adapt very quickly to the treadmill, and it is possible to attach all kinds of sophisticated measuring devices to the horse and use them whilst it is galloping in the treadmill. Altering the incline at which the treadmill operates enables even higher workloads to be imposed. Treadmills are expensive, however; also their use is quite labour-intensive and they are certainly time-consuming because only one horse can be exercised at any one time. From the trainer's point of view their most important advantage is their ability to impose a particular speed of movement on a horse, or conversely to measure easily the speed at which a horse is working.

Treadmill assessment enables very precise measurements to be made, especially of speed. The step test is particularly useful because it adapts so well to both stamina and speed competitions. The horse is given a warm-up of 8 minutes at 4 metres/second, followed by 90 seconds at 6 metres/second. The horse then does one-minute steps at 8, 10,11,12 and 13 metres per second. It takes a fit horse to complete all the steps, especially if the treadmill is set on an incline. Fitness is measured either by how far along the programme the horse can proceed, or by how long it takes to complete the full programme. If stamina is the aim, the time spent at each step can be increased.

■ Peak Fitness: A Valid Objective?

The ability to measure fitness in this way has produced a rather surprising piece of information: fitness does not reach a peak after 6–8 weeks and then level out; it continues to increase as long as the workload is sufficiently demanding. Traditionally a horse was trained to competition fitness and then just kept ticking over between competitions. However, it transpires that this might result in the horse not achieving its full potential. The stress and physical exercise of competition is certainly the equivalent of a considerable amount of training time but if training work is continued even though the horse is competing successfully, it will either be able to move up to higher levels of competition or to compete more safely because it is at a higher level of fitness. Measurement of fitness during continuous training for nine months showed that at the end of the period, fitness was still increasing.

■ Measuring Lost Fitness

Familiarity with an objective measurement of fitness is useful when, as unfortunately so often happens, the horse suffers an injury of some kind. In many cases this requires rest or at least a decrease in work level, and inevitably the question is 'How much has the horse's training programme been put back by the rest?' Measurement of fitness will put an actual figure on the lost fitness and so enable the trainer to ensure that when the horse does return to competition it does so at least as fit as it was before. The evidence we have is that the length of continuous training prior to the injury is more important in this regard than any other aspect of fitness. Rest periods of 4–5 weeks without losing any fitness are possible if the previous training period was long enough.

Investigation of Poor Performance

One of the major reasons for us wanting to be able to measure fitness accurately is to help us to investigate poor performance. When a horse's performance does not match our expectations we need to know whether it is simply because the horse was not as fit as we hoped, whether it was because it did not have the ability which we hoped, or whether there was some other, perhaps pathological reason.

Professor Reuben Rose at Sydney University has made a study of investigating poor performance and has identified the following key questions:

● Has the decrease in exercise capability been sudden or gradual?

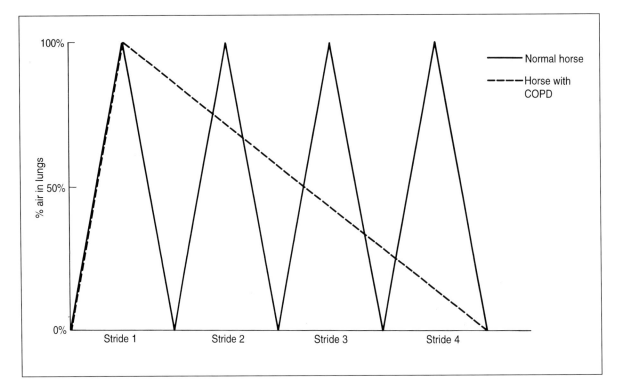

15 A horse with COPD would only take one breath every 3–4 strides. Because the horse tries to synchronise stride to breathing, the result is fewer strides and fewer breaths

- Is there any respiratory distress after exercise?
- Is there any respiratory noise during exercise, and if so at what speed does it occur?
- Is the problem continuous or intermittent?
- Does the horse train well but not reproduce its form in competition?
- Is there any sign of lameness or alteration of gait?
- Are there any signs of ill health such as weight loss, coughing etc?
- Are there any changes in the horse's appetite?
- Has the horse had any recent drug therapy?

If a horse performs poorly because of a lack of fitness, then the obvious answer is to train it harder or longer. If, on the other hand, it really is fit but is nonetheless performing badly, then it is likely that training harder or longer will make the situation worse; it will certainly exacerbate any lameness problem present. The Sydney clinic found that the majority of horses showing reduced performance had some lameness problem present.

In recent years there has been a tendency for most cases of poor performance to be blamed on a virus, whether there is any evidence for this or not. This is especially so when two or more horses trained by the same person perform badly. What people tend to forget is that most trainers use surprisingly little individual variation during training and so if they have overtrained one horse they are likely to have overtrained others as well; similarly if one horse is unfit then it is likely that others will also be unfit. In such circumstances a history of objective fitness assessment for individual horses can be invaluable in investigating the problem.

Exercise-Induced Pulmonary Haemorrhage (EIPH)

When a horse is found to have blood visible at its nostrils after exercise, it is assumed that its performance has been impaired. In fact the blood comes not from the nose itself, as was once thought, but from the lungs, and it is assumed that if blood is present then it will have reduced both the airway and the efficiency of the lung tissue. In fact most Thoroughbreds show EIPH at some time or other, and if horses are routinely examined with an endoscope after exercise, blood will often be found in the trachea, or windpipe (Fig 17) even though none was visible at the nostrils. Racing authorities in some countries have very

strict rules about such 'bleeders', and after a second occasion when blood is spotted at the nostril the horse may be banned from the track. This seems rather unfair, granted the high percentage of runners which will also have bled from the lungs but which will escape penalty simply because the blood was in fact swallowed from the pharynx rather than drained down the nose. There does not appear to be any connection between the amount of haemorrhage and the chances of it becoming visible at the nostril.

The source of the haemorrhage is a small area at the back of the lungs, where the lung lobe is relatively thin. Because of chronic inflammatory changes in the walls of the alveoli, or air sacs, the pressure changes during breathing are greater here than in any other part of the lungs, and the resulting suction ruptures the blood-vessel walls. The inflammatory changes – thought to be the result of respiratory infection – are unfortunately irreversible, so once a horse is a bleeder, whether visible or not, it will tend to remain so. New research has implicated a chemical called nitric oxide in the pattern of events which ends up with a 'nose bleed'. As we learn how to control nitric oxide levels we would hope to be able to control the frequency of haemorrhage.

Although the USA Turf authorities allow the use of frusemide to control EIPH, there is considerable controversy as to whether this is an effective treatment. Scientific papers have, over the years, claimed to prove both that it does and that it does not do so. It has been suggested that the reason why trainers want to be allowed to use frusemide to control EIPH is that the drug also speeds up the rate at which other drugs disappear from the urine: by using frusemide at the same time as a prohibited drug it may be possible to produce a 'clean' urine sample for testing even though the effect of the prohibited drug is still present.

Respiratory Infections and Reduced Performance

Respiratory infections are widespread among competition horses, and are certainly a common reason given for reduced performance. The problem is that most respiratory infections are spread in droplets of water, breathed out or coughed out by an infected horse and carried in the air for a considerable time and distance. It has been

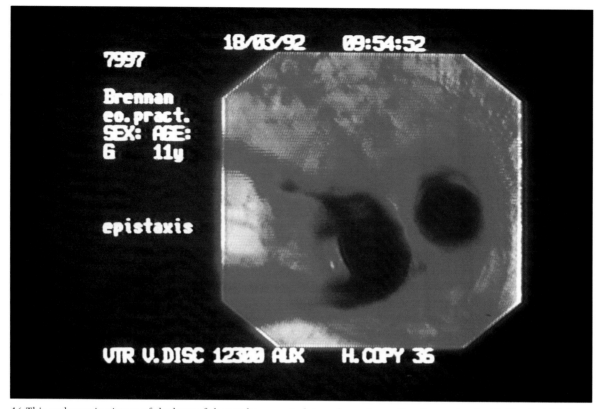

16 This endoscopic picture of the base of the trachea, or windpipe, shows the walls splattered red with blood which has come from the lungs via the two bronchi in the centre of the picture

shown, for example, that virus particles can infect another horse 200 metres downwind of the original clinical case.

During the seventies, eighties and early nineties it was always assumed that the majority of outbreaks of equine respiratory disease were due to viruses; equine herpes virus (EHV) in particular was implicated on many occasions. However, recent work shows that in fact bacteria are responsible for more than half of the infectious respiratory diseases common in competition horses, and even where viruses such as EHV are involved, they may have been triggered from their dormant state – where inactive virus is present in bone marrow or lymph nodes – by the stress of bacterial infection. The important thing that does follow from this new research is that it changes the way that we control such outbreaks in stables, because bacteria are susceptible to antibiotics whereas viruses are not. So where conventional wisdom has maintained that there is littlel point in using antibiotics in a yard affected with 'the cough', it now looks as if they do have an important role to play. Before dealing with how best to cope with such an outbreak of res-

piratory disease, it is worth considering what symptoms to look for. If two or more horses in a yard start coughing or develop a nasal discharge within 7–10 days of each other, then there may be an infection in the yard because the incubation period for most of such infections is 3–10 days. Merely having two or more horses in a yard perform badly within 7–10 days of each other, in the absence of any clinical symptoms, does not indicate the presence of a respiratory infection – there are other, more likely, causes of this reduced performance.

If an outbreak of respiratory disease is suspected, proceed as follows:

1   Take immediate steps to limit infection. Avoid contact between horses as much as possible, and avoid indirect contact via grooms, grooming kit and tack. Remember that you have a moral responsibility not to knowingly spread the disease further, so stop all movements out of the yard to competitions. All too often we see trainers quoted as saying that they think horse X will perform well because even though they have an infection in the yard, that horse has not

shown any symptoms. They are knowingly spreading disease and by subjecting their horse to the stress of competition they are increasing the likelihood of its developing clinical disease as well. In my opinion anyone admitting that they have sent a horse to a competition from a yard with clinical infection should be heavily penalised by the regulatory authorities.

2   Consult your vet and have your suspicions confirmed. In particular it is important to eliminate chronic obstructive pulmonary disease (COPD) as the sole cause of the problem. Feeding a new batch of hay containing large numbers of invisible fungal spores can result in several horses in a yard starting to cough at more or less the same time, even though no infection is present.

3   Consider symptomatic treatment: this can take two forms. We can use a mucolytic such as dembrexine to reduce the viscosity of any mucus present and therefore ease its removal. We can also use bronchodilators such as clenbuterol to open up the small airways and so increase the efficacy of breathing. Both these approaches are likely to reduce coughing and an initial increase as mucus is eliminated. Owners often ask vets for something to stop a horse coughing, and although there are drugs which will act directly on the cough centre in the brain, it is not necessarily a good idea to do this because a cough is a protective mechanism. If we stop a horse coughing before the mucus has been removed then we will be given a false sense of security that the horse has recovered.

4   Consider antibiotic therapy in view of the high chance that bacteria are present. Single injections of antibiotic, even in so-called long-acting form, are not sufficient. It is likely that blanket treatment of all horses in the yard for a minimum of 5–7 days is needed, and there is some practical evidence that 14 days' treatment is needed to eliminate infection. There is one antibiotic, a mixture of trimethoprim and sulphadiazine, which can be given orally to horses. If other antibiotics are used then each horse will have to be injected every day.

5   Disinfect the stable, starting when the antibiotic therapy is underway. Remember that because the bacteria and viruses are airborne you must disinfect the ceiling as well as the walls of the stable. Disinfecting dirty surfaces is a waste of time.

6   Feed horses at ground level, thus encouraging any mucus to drain down the trachea to the mouth rather than back down into the lungs. Turning horses out to pasture is good in this respect, as long as it does not mean mixing groups of horses together. It has the added advantage that infectious agents are killed by sunlight and drying, both of which are more likely to occur outside.

7   If a horse has been sufficiently affected to put it off its food, a six-week rest period should be observed before strenuous exercise. This allows the heart and lungs to recover fully, and will avoid future problems.

TRAINING

The conflict between the old and the new in the horse world is nowhere more sharply defined than over the question of training horses for competition. On one side are trainers who have a lifetime's experience (and in some cases a lifetime of success), whilst on the other side are the scientists who may have trained few horses but have studied the subject in great depth. In actual fact there is no real conflict because both camps are seeking the same goal, namely success in competition, and they may use very similar methods. The difference is that a scientist needs to know exactly why a particular training method works whereas many trainers are more concerned with the result than the reason why. Nevertheless, I would suggest that all trainers of competitive horses should know the scientific background to their craft even if they do not make daily use of that knowledge. Science can be very practical.

The Aim of Training

The aim of training has been said to be 'to increase a horse's fitness so that it can compete more successfully, and with less risk of injury, against horses of equal ability'. Because fatigue is a major limitation of performance, training is very much about delaying the onset of fatigue during competition. However, there is one thing that training cannot achieve and that is to improve a horse's natural ability; that is fixed at birth. As the American trainer Stanley Dancer said, 'A great horse is a great horse regardless of the training system you use'. It is probably the case that training is more important for horses of low ability than for the great horses, and the reason for this is quite simple: even using half of its ability – ie being only half fit – a great horse will be successful up to a certain point, whereas a horse of only low ability may need to utilise every scrap of its ability, and be 100 per cent fit, in order to achieve any success at all.

The Successful Trainer

Trainers do more than plan the exercise schedule for their horses, and there are therefore other reasons for their success than how they carry out those schedules. If we look at the most *successful* trainers we find that:

1 They have a relatively high turnover of horses. This is not because their training methods are so severe that they lead to injury and retirement; it is because they do not waste time trying to achieve success with a horse which has proved to have little ability. This is in direct contrast to the majority of owner/riders who spend months or years of work on just one horse trying to persuade it to achieve the impossible.
2 Strategy can be as important as ability. So a trainer might travel a horse hundreds of miles to a competition which it stands a good chance of winning rather than competing just down the road in an event above the horse's capabilities. Strategy is also important during the competition. Successful trainers employ good strategists as riders, or give very precise instructions to riders who are prepared to do as they are told.

Training's Main Limitation

There is one great limitation on training horses which does not apply to training people, and that is the limitation of pain. As mentioned earlier, human athletes refer to 'the wall', a point during both routine training and in competition when the pain of fatigue is so great that they want to stop, but know that if they want to succeed they must carry on. The horse does not understand this. It has no concept of financial incentives for success, nor can it appreciate that a long breeding career beckons if it can be successful. So the majority of horses slow down with fatigue. There are, however, some horses which produce such

17 Racehorses on Newmarket Heath

high levels of endorphins (a natural painkilling substance released into the bloodstream) that even if they injure themselves during a competition, they will carry on. These horses are generally found to be injured a minute or two after the finish and people wrongly imply that the horse made a conscious decision to carry on despite the injury. In fact the horse doesn't deserve any credit for courage or character because in these circumstances it wouldn't have felt the injury anyway.

Overtraining

It is important to realise from the start that a horse can be overtrained. This is not a concept which commercial horse trainers like to dwell upon. Many of the horses whose lack of success is put down to a virus infection are actually overtrained, but to admit this would be to admit a fault. In some horses the gap between peak fitness and overtraining is very small and it can be very difficult indeed to keep such horses performing regularly and successfully.

Overtraining is the loss of performance despite continuing, or even increasing, training efforts. The horse may start to lose weight despite a good food intake. Its coat becomes dull or dry and it loses its enthusiasm for work. Its heart rate at a particular level of work will often increase significantly, although this is not always the case: some horses have excessive activity of the vagal nerve, which slows the heart rate via the parasympathetic nervous system, and this over-rides the increased heart rate of overtraining. Another way in which overtraining shows itself is by the horse working at a slower speed than is normal for a particular heart rate.

A distinction must be made between horses which have been in training for a long time and those which have been overtrained. In the case of the former, there is evidence that the horse will continue to get fitter and fitter as training continues, although once it reaches the genetic limits of performance it will not perform any better. In the case of the latter, the horse will become *less* fit if training continues. Perhaps one of the problems is that the term 'overtraining' gives the impression that both time and severity of training may be involved, whereas it is only the severity which produces the unfortunate side-effects. It is also possible that when a horse has stopped improving with training then trainers have assumed that they are using the correct training methods but have reached maximum fitness. Our recent understanding that fitness *can* keep on improving shows that a plateauing out should be treated with great caution because it may be the first sign of overtraining before the horse really starts to deteriorate.

Many cases of overtraining involve muscle-fibre breakdown as a result of lactic acid accumulation. Blood levels of aspartate aminotransferase (AST) and creatine kinase (CK) rise as a result. The solution to overtraining is rest. Owners must never attempt to work the horse through it, and they must certainly never increase the horse's feed rations in a futile attempt to make the horse more lively. If the AST or CK levels have been raised, then the rest must continue until they are back to normal, no matter how well the horse appears to the naked eye. If in any doubt, have the horse blood-tested.

Training for What?

The key word in training is 'specificity': in other words, the training programme has to be specifically related to the target competition because the type of fitness required will vary from one discipline to another. Pure endurance training will not prepare a horse for a power event such as a five-furlong sprint. Indeed to a degree the training requirements for the two are completely incompatible, which is why a three-day event poses such a challenge to the horse trainer. Stamina events want wiry muscles with the least distance between the centre of the muscle fibres and the oxygen-supplying blood vessels; sprint events want bulky muscles that provide power anaerobically for short periods.

Specificity also means training the horse as an individual: training the horse you have, rather than the horse which you wish you had. Anyone giving three or four horses exactly the same exercise, or giving one horse the same amount of work week in and week out, is not achieving their maximum potential (Fig 17, p77). In addition to the signs of overtraining already mentioned, each horse's mental attitude, appetite and physical response to exercise must be considered daily. This requires time spent just observing the horse, and the ability to correlate what you see with the changes you have made.

What can Training Achieve?

Most training will have three aims:

1 To improve energy production but reduce fatigue.
2 To improve the horse's structure to enable it to withstand the stress of work.
3. To improve the horse's skill and co-ordination.

Fig 18 shows the relative contribution various means of obtaining energy make to different equine activities. We are much more likely to be successful at increasing a horse's ability to provide energy aerobically than we are at increasing its anaerobic metabolism.

It has now been shown that training can alter the horse's physical structure, and the shape and strength of bones such as the cannon bone and the sesamoid bones are affected by increased workloads. It has also been possible to prove

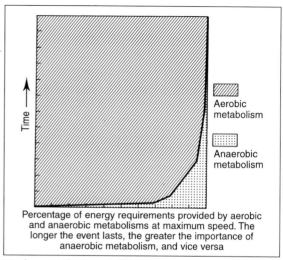

Percentage of energy requirements provided by aerobic and anaerobic metabolisms at maximum speed. The longer the event lasts, the greater the importance of anaerobic metabolism, and vice versa

18 The contribution of different energy sources to different activities: the longer the event lasts, the greater the importance of anaerobic metabolism

scientifically what tradition has said for centuries, namely that training strengthens, or hardens, the tendons. The research compared the breaking strain of samples of suspensory ligament from horses which had undergone various amounts of training, and showed that the breaking strain increased with training. We expect that this also holds true for the vitally important flexor tendons. Unfortunately we cannot yet point to specific aspects of training which produce these changes.

Nor must we forget the need to improve the horse's neuromuscular co-ordination. This is particularly the case in jumping events. With practice the nerves transmit impulses more quickly to the muscles, with important gains in reaction time. A jumper must be asked to jump a reasonable number of jumps during training, although the height and complexity of the jumps is probably not important. In other words training can take place over small jumps, with consequently reduced risk of injury.

■ Responding to Stress

It is a general principle of training that the horse should be exposed to similar stresses to those it will meet in competition. The General Adaptation Syndrome Theory says that when the body is subjected to a new stress that it has not responded to before, it will seek to undergo sufficient change to allow it to withstand that stress. Training is a stress in this respect and the response to training is a beneficial response. You can overstress the system though, and this produces damaging effects such as physical injury or overtraining.

19 Horse walkers can be used to replace some roadwork, but horses must be walked on both circles

Stress can also reduce the efficiency of the immune system and thus reduce the horse's ability to fight disease. A horse which has just had its training regime significantly increased in severity will be more likely to show clinical symptoms from a virus infection than a horse which is on a steady exercise programme. Herpes viruses can stay dormant and undetected inside the body for months, but they start multiplying when the body is stressed. That is why human beings develop cold sores (which are caused by a herpes virus) at times of stress and why horses may appear perfectly healthy before a competition but be suffering a herpes infection very shortly afterwards. The stress threshold varies, of course, from one horse to another.

The First Stages of Training

All training starts with preliminary stamina training. The horse is exercised at the trot, or possibly eventually at a slow canter, over long distances; in many cases this is achieved by hacking around the roads. The immediate result is an increase in the amount of oxygen the muscles can handle. It has been shown that although a 10–23 per cent increase in oxygen consumption can be achieved within a short period of 2–6 weeks, the aerobic capability of the muscles will continue to increase steadily for at least 9 months of such work. Unfortunately horses are rarely given such a long period of conditioning, especially in the case of the very horses who need it the most, namely young, immature Thoroughbred racehorses.

■ Hillwork

Roadwork on the flat is not the only way of conditioning. Working a horse on an incline has the same effect as weightlifting in people: the same physical effort is expended when working at a slower speed uphill than at a faster speed on the flat, and because there is a reasonable correlation between speed and the risk of injury, this is a safer way to prepare for physical effort. Even walking up a hill our limbs have to accelerate continually to overcome the continuing slope.

■ Work on the Treadmill

Treadmills provide an alternative way to condition for stamina, and many models can be used at an incline to give the advantage of hillwork. An alternative is to hang some weights over a pulley behind the horse and attach them to the girth strap; again, the horse has to accelerate in order to compensate for the extra weight.

20 Swimming does little to improve a horse's cardio-vascular efficiency, but it helps the respiratory system and maintains fitness without percussion on the legs

As already discussed, horses usually adapt very readily to working in a treadmill. They can achieve speeds greater than 30mph (50kph), producing heart rates of over 200 beats per minute, which is similar to the effect of racing. Even so, a recent study which compared the effect of the same horse being ridden by the same rider on both the track and in a treadmill showed that exercise on a horizontal treadmill proved to be significantly less demanding than exercise at the same speed on the track. Increasing the speed of the work on the treadmill gave a better equivalent to the workload on the track than did putting the treadmill at an incline.

■ Swimming

Some trainers enthusiastically send their horses swimming (Fig 20). The great drawback of this exercise is its complete lack of specificity: there are very few swimming races for horses, so we are training for an event that does not exist. Heart rates in horses swimming are relatively low, around 160–180 per minute, so swimming does little to improve cardiovascular efficiency. Nevertheless, it does achieve two things: it enables an already fit horse to remain fit without percussion on its legs if it has been injured; and it also helps the respiratory system. A swimming horse takes quick breaths in and has laboured breaths out. This is because water pressure on the abdomen requires considerable effort from the thoracic muscles to keep air in the lungs, and to control its expiration. If horses are swum regularly they must be swum in alternating directions to prevent uneven leg-muscle development.

The Introduction of Fast Work

Although there are some differences in how the second stage of training is carried out in different countries, the standard tends to be that traditionally used by Thoroughbred trainers in the UK, namely trotting and slow cantering every day with fast work twice a week. The horses are usually worked only once a day and spend the rest of the day stabled.

Again, tradition has it that fast work is necessary to 'clear the horse's wind'. The heart and circulation were not considered to need any special training. This is probably due to the fact that any trainer can hear the sounds that a horse makes during or after a gallop, but they cannot always take a pulse or use a stethoscope. There is some danger of us now going to the other extreme and getting so wound up in assessing heart function that we forget the lungs. An unfit horse's breathing will be noisier, or 'thicker', than that of a fit horse. However, that is not really a function of fitness, but the result of periods when airways are wide open during fast exercise, allowing mucus to be removed from the lungs. Presumably a clean-winded horse can perform slightly better than a thick-winded horse, but the difference will only be small. If an apparently clean-winded horse is given an hour a day at grass its wind will appear to become noisier even though the horse is no less fit; this is because during grazing mucus can drain down the trachea from the lungs, making breathing more noisy.

Working a horse at 70–85 per cent of its competitive speed stimulates vital aspects of muscle adaptation; these are: increased percentage of type II muscle fibres; increased buffering capacity; and increased concentrations of the enzymes involved in anaerobic energy metabolism. Training the heart and circulation for maximum effort requires a heart rate of around 200 beats per minute to be reached. The exercise does not necessarily need to be prolonged at this intensity. Even horses whose competitive demands in respect of speed are relatively low, for example dressage horses, need to have their heart rate raised to 200 beats per minute once or twice a week to achieve the kind of cardiovascular capabilities which will be needed to supply the long hours of work such horses are often asked to perform.

■ Heart-Rate/Speed Graphs

One of the most useful training aids is a pad of graph paper, because maximum speed graphs can then be drawn at regular intervals during the training period. The concept of these graphs is quite simple: each horse's maximum heart rate is constant throughout training, even though its maximum speed is obviously not constant. Frequent maximum speed testing would involve considerable risks of injury, so instead a graph is used. The horse is galloped over a relatively short distance (100 metres) four times at different speeds. The first time it might be galloped at approximately 550 metres per minute, then at 600 metres per minute, then 650 metres per minute and finally at 700 metres per minute. Each time

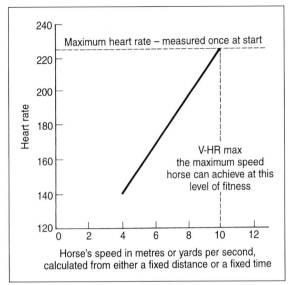

21 Graph to show the heart-rate/speed values

Interval Training

Depending on one's point of view, interval training is either a scientific alternative to the 'gallop twice a week' school of training, or a posh name for a way of training horses which has been around for a long time. The basic idea behind interval training is to enable the horse to experience more intense work over several short periods of activity than would be possible if the work was carried out in one block. So the horse is given periods of activity interspaced with rest periods, and each period of activity can vary from easy aerobic exercise to high-intensity, mostly anaerobic exercise.

The easiest way to understand the principle behind interval training is to consider what you would do if you were required to run a mile faster than at four-minute-mile speed. A small number of athletes could do so, but most people could not. However, most of us could run two hundred yards at that speed – so put nine blocks of two hundred yards together separated by intervals of rest, and we have run a mile. That is how interval training works. It increases the amount of high intensity work that can be carried out whilst avoiding fatigue (and the risks of injury associated with it). Interval training still requires the involvement of a high percentage of the possible muscle fibres and the production of lactic acid in those fibres, but the rest interval allows partial removal of that lactic acid.

■ A Flexible Workload

By varying the length of each work period, the speed of the work, the number of work intervals and also the length of the relief intervals, a very flexible workload can be built up. Obviously when a horse starts interval training the time allowed for the work interval will be greater and the number of repetitions fewer than will be set for a fit horse. It must be stressed that interval training is not intended to replace a horse's routine daily exercise. It replaces the twice-a-week fast work, with the exception of short weekly gallops to take the horse's heart rate very briefly up to 200 beats per minute if this value is not reached during the interval work. Such gallops are still necessary because interval training is concerned with aerobic and anaerobic muscle metabolism rather than simple cardiovascular fitness. All interval training is preceded by adequate warming-up exercise.

the heart rate is determined at the end of the exercise. At the start of training the horse is given one flat-out gallop to determine its maximum heart rate. The four heart-rate/speed values are plotted on a graph and a straight line drawn up to the maximum heart rate (Fig 21). This enables the maximum speed to be read off the bottom of the graph. Repeating the four heart-rate/speed workouts at intervals during the training period will hopefully produce a series of graphs where the straight line plot becomes ever less steep, and the maximum speed ever greater.

One great advantage of these graphs is that a trainer can assess the progress of an individual horse, even if he does not have another horse of known ability and fitness to gallop it against, in the way that racehorse trainers with large numbers of horses will gallop an unraced horse against one which has just raced in an attempt to assess the former's speed. The other advantage is that anyone can use the system even if he does not have another person to help him: all that is needed is a measured distance marked out and a stopwatch to time the horse as it passes the start and finish points. Although a heart-rate monitor makes it easier, jumping off the horse at a fixed point shortly after the finish and taking its heart or pulse rate is still valid as long as the same point is used every time. The heart rate at 700 metres per minute, for example, will not be the same when measured in this way as with a heart monitor, but it will have slowed down by the same amount today as it did when the horse worked at the same speed last week.

Interval training should be carried out with the horse carrying at least the same weight as it will carry in competition. If it carries more weight, then it may be possible to reduce the intensity of the work interval slightly; but if the weight is less than during the competition, then the work intensity will need to be unnecessarily increased.

■ Setting Up the Intervals

The relief interval can be set in two ways: it may be set at an arbitrary time such as three minutes and not altered when the work interval is altered; the alternative, and more scientific way is to set it at the time taken for the heart rate to return to 110 per cent of the heart rate after the initial warm-up period. When the aim is to improve anaerobic metabolism rather than aerobic capabilities, complete recovery of the heart rate to the warm-up level must be allowed, even though the result will be very long relief intervals. Of course the horse does not just stand still during the relief interval. It is walked and trotted just as it would be during the warm-up period.

The work intervals can increase in severity in three ways. We can alter the number of intervals performed, the speed at which the work is performed, and the duration of each work interval. As the workload is increased we might, for example, increase the number of intervals performed but slightly decrease the duration of each interval. When the workload is increased, the heart rate at the end of the rest interval or at the end of the last work interval will rise. As the horse adapts to the new workload that heart rate will fall again, and only when it has done so satisfactorily can a further increase in workload be contemplated.

■ Suitable Recipe

The type of recipe used will depend on the type of competition for which the horse is preparing (Fig 22). Speed is important for racehorses, so the speed of the work interval will be higher than it will be for endurance horses. It is accepted that interval training is particularly effective at increasing aerobic capacity, and so it can reduce a horse's sprinting capability. As the muscle cells increase their utilisation of oxygen, low-oxidative, fast-twitch fibres will decrease in size to allow easier passage of oxygen through the fibres. As power output is related to muscle mass, a reduction in muscle-fibre size will result in a decrease in

muscle mass and a decrease in power output. Sprinting requires a high power output to increase oxidative capability, so this formula means reduced sprinting capability: it is impossible to achieve maximum power and maximum stamina at the same time, no matter what type of training is used.

That does not mean that interval training cannot be used to prepare horses for either sprint races or other activities such as showjumping which make sudden energy demands. The recipe used in such circumstances is one of short work intervals carried out at fast speeds. As already mentioned, the relief intervals must be long enough to allow complete recovery between each work interval. The aim is to bring the majority of muscle fibres into work, but not for any great length of time or their stamina will be affected. Short,

Interval Training Recipe Suggested for Three-Day Eventer

Day 1 is a rest day. Days 4 and 7 are interval training days, unless the horse competes on day 7. Hacking, flatwork or jumping is carried out on the other days.

Week	Day 4	Day 7
1	3 x 3 min	3 x 3 min
2	3 x 4 min (500m/sec)	3 x 4 min
3	3 x 4 min	3 x 4 or competition
4	3x 5 min	3 x 5 min
5	3 x 5 min	competition
6	3 x 5 min	3 x 5 min
7	3x 5 min (550m/sec)	competition
8	3 x 6 min	3 x 6 min (570m/sec)
9	4 x 6 min	competition
10	3 x 7 min (550m/sec)	competition
11	3 x 7 min	
12	First 3-day event	

22 Interval training example recipe

sharp intervals will improve neuromuscular co-ordination and nerve-firing frequency, both of which are important for rapid acceleration.

■ The Advantages of Interval Training

Interval training claims to get horses fitter than traditional training methods, although it may take a long time to do so. Because the horse's aerobic capacity is increased, its performance in the latter part of the competition will be particularly improved. Interval training is not a soft option for the horse in the early stages, and some studies have shown an increased incidence of injuries then. However, if the horse survives the first few weeks of interval training without injury, it is much less likely to suffer future musculoskeletal injury. Adequate foundation work beforehand is essential. Interval training is time- and labour-intensive, so it is more expensive to carry out. It also requires good record-keeping.

The traditional training methods developed in the racehorse training centres of England are based entirely on the racecourse as the arbiter of fitness. According to this method, everyone trains their horses in the same way, and in theory they are all equally fit, so the winner is the horse with the most innate ability rather than the fittest. However, the lack of individual variation, whilst understandable on economic grounds, means that not *all* the horses will reach maximum fitness even if *some* of them do. Training horses as individuals will always have the potential to achieve greater fitness than training them in groups, and interval training in its pure form has to be an individual assessment.

Maintaining Fitness

Keeping a horse fit does not require an intensive routine, and once it is competing regularly the frequency of fast work can be reduced. In particular it should be appreciated that strenuous activity during competition will deplete the horse's glycogen stores, and it will take several days after the competition for these to be replenished. One of the reasons why the standard of showjumping in a three-day event is lower than in a specialist showjumping competition is that the horses have used up a high proportion of their glycogen energy stores going across country the previous day and have not had sufficient time to replace them. The muscles therefore lack power.

The art of training is to bring the horse to peak fitness at exactly the time of the competition. The ability to do this cannot be taught because it requires an infinite flexibility to respond to the horse's progress or lack of progress. Those mere mortals who do not have this natural gift will benefit from keeping detailed records of every horse's work schedule, so that they can look back after either success or failure and see the heart rates, speeds, intervals and feeding that contributed to that result.

FIRST AID

The First-Aid Kit

If horses which are just standing in a stable can injure themselves, then competition horses will certainly do so. A comprehensive first-aid kit is therefore essential, and it must go everywhere with the horse. Even if the horse is competing at a venue with a vet in attendance, a first-aid kit is still essential in case the vet is already dealing with one emergency when he is needed. In any case, first aid is all about the first action that needs to be taken, not about what one does to try to prevent a vet being needed.

■ Wound Dressings

The choice of wound dressing in a first-aid kit will depend on a number of factors, but there are two attributes which are important: it must be non-adherent, so that even if the wound bleeds and clots, it will not stick to the wound and disturb that clot when it is removed; and it should provide ideal conditions for healing. This means that the wound should be kept slightly damp, but that any discharge should be removed from contact with the wound itself.

Many owners do not realise the advances which have been made in wound dressings in recent years. Applying a square of gauze impregnated with an antibiotic and bandaging it in place might have been state-of-the-art treatment at one time, but all it does is to provide a non-stick dressing and not much else. The first-aid kit will need a range of dressings for different situations:

- Dressings which take the form of a piece of thin 'felt' made of calcium sodium alginate; this is very effective at providing a scaffold for clotting when a wound won't stop bleeding.
- Dressings which provide a very flexible polythene membrane that forms a second skin over the wound, keeping any moisture in, but keeping dirt out. These are not suitable for discharging wounds, but because they stick to the skin themselves they may not need any other bulky bandaging.
- Dressings consisting of a plastic membrane with a layer of special gel applied to it; this promotes the natural cleaning-up mechanisms at a contaminated wound site.
- Dressings manufactured from special polythene membranes where any discharge passes through the membrane and is then taken up in an absorbent pad on the other side. The most sophisticated of these uses a hydrophilic polyurethane foam that can absorb ten times its volume of fluid. These dressings are particularly effective at limiting the development of proud flesh as a wound heals, an especially undesirable aspect of equine wound healing: the granulation tissue which fills the gap in a wound just keeps on forming until it rises proud above the skin level. This prevents the skin healing across, leading to a chronic open wound. Naturally this delays the horse's return to training, so any step which will prevent or limit the formation of such proud flesh is worth taking.

■ Padding and Bandages

The first-aid kit should contain two or three **unopened rolls of gamgee**. I specify 'unopened', because gamgee is a vital padding for all kinds of purposes and so is constantly being used, and only too often the result can be two remnants of a roll left in the first-aid kit. Gamgee is vital for the application of a Robert Jones bandage.

On the subject of bandaging, the kit should not contain any white open-weave (WOW) bandages; these are dangerous because they do not adapt to the contours of the horse, and so have to be put on very tightly if they are to stay in position. **Crêpe bandages** are much better. They are reasonably cheap and cheerful, and they stretch to adapt to the body contours. Unfortunately that very elasticity also means they have the propensity to be applied too tightly, and owners bandaging their horse's legs after a competition have quite frequently caused tendon damage as a result. Bandages are being developed that automatically provide a specified degree of tension whether they are applied tightly or not, and these could be very useful for bandaging a horse's legs.

Perhaps the most useful type of bandage is the **cohesive bandage**, which sticks to itself, but not to anything else. It also has a degree of elasticity. The difference between a crêpe bandage and a cohesive bandage is that when a crêpe bandage is applied, the elasticity of each layer acts independently, sliding over the other layers above and below until an average tension results. When a cohesive bandage is applied, the second layer fixes the tension of the first layer by sticking to it, and that tension will never change. A leg can swell underneath a crêpe bandage because the bandage will stretch, but it cannot swell at all under a cohesive bandage because that cannot stretch once it has been applied. As a general rule, swelling of an injured area such as a sprained tendon is an undesirable side effect of inflammation. Indeed, much time and effort has to be put into reducing swelling after it has arisen. A distinction is therefore made between the danger of applying a bandage so tightly that the pressure causes damage to the underlying tissues, which is a bad thing, and applying a bandage at a neutral tension that will not allow passive leakage of tissue fluid out into the tissues to cause swelling, which is a good thing. If swelling is anticipated then the leg should be bandaged right down to the hoof, so that a swollen area does not develop between the bandage and the foot. Cohesive bandages also have the advantage that they won't unroll when dropped, or if the horse tries to eat them as it stands in its box. They are reasonably expensive, but not everyone realises that if they are removed carefully, and the folds and creases pulled straight, they can be re-applied several times.

In order to cut dressings and so on, the first-aid kit must also contain a sharp pair of blunt-ended scissors.

■ Thermometer

The kit should contain a stubby-bulbed, clinical thermometer. Some owners routinely take their horse's temperature once or twice a day because this can provide the earliest indication of the start of viral infections. When competing in hot condi-

tions, it can also be valuable to take the horse's temperature after the end of strenuous exercise, and again after ten minutes of gentle strolling; if it has not started to go down, then there are problems, and emergency cooling measures should be instituted. These would include soaking the horse with water which as it evaporates cools the body, and possibly the use of fans to speed up that evaporation.

■ Poultices

There should be some kind of poultice in the first-aid kit, whether Animalintex or kaolin. And more important, there must be a means of applying cold to injured tendons and ligaments. No serious competitor should rely on using ice for this purpose if that leaves them at the mercy of the bar tent, who might be either unwilling or, if sales of gin and tonics have been good, unable to help. A number of the proprietary applications available need to be cooled in the fridge or freezer, and this takes time. It is not enough, therefore, simply to have them in the first-aid kit: they need to have been activated by cooling beforehand, and then to be kept cool.

	Kaolin	Animalintex	Ice
Can provide warmth to increase local circulation	Yes	Yes	No
Can provide cold to decrease local circulation	Yes	No	Yes
Long-lasting effect	Yes	No	Ice melts but packs stay cold longer
Convenient to use	No. Heavy. Stored in metal container	Requires source of hot water. Light. Readily available	Needs to be kept in insulated container. Readily available
Draws pus and fluid out of wound	Not proven	Not proven	No

23 Comparative table of commonly used poultices

■ Topical Antiseptics and Antibiotics

Of course, not all wounds need to be bandaged, or are in a position which can be bandaged. Often it will suffice to apply some antiseptic or antibiotic to such a wound, but the question is, in what form? Oily ointments are not suitable: the act of applying them disturbs the wound, and although they prevent further infection, they also form a barrier against the oxygen of the air, which the wound needs. Besides, if subsequent veterinary examination shows that the wound could or should be stitched, then all that oily ointment will have to be removed if the wound is going to heal quickly.

Wound powders can be useful, especially those that combine an antibiotic with a fly repellent. The point that almost everyone forgets, though, is that these powders are designed to be applied as a light dusting several times a day, not as an avalanche once a day. One of the advantages of antibiotic aerosols is that even though they, too, are often overdosed, this does not inhibit healing (although in the past when they contained gentian violet, it could do so). Antibiotics go out of date, so first-aid kits should be checked from time to time to make sure that expiry dates have not been exceeded, and that containers are not empty.

■ Liquid Antiseptic

Away from home it can be difficult to find a 'clean' water supply – from the infection point of view – with which to wash any contaminated wounds. The first-aid kit should therefore contain a bottle of antiseptic which can be added to the cleanest water that is available. There should be some guidance as to the dilution of this antiseptic; just upending it into a bucket of water is not good enough because if the solution is too strong it may damage some tissues, and if too weak it will fail to kill infection. Chlorhexidine is a good antiseptic for this purpose.

Dealing with Potential Lameness

Armed with a first-aid kit, there are certain common situations which befall horses during training and competition. The first of these is the discovery of heat around a joint or tendon area. As long as the horse is not lame, cold should be applied for a total of twelve hours, and then left off in order to assess whether the heat returns. If it does not do so, then the horse can remain in normal work. If the heat returns, or if it is accompanied by a slight swelling, then the horse should be reduced to half work, with cold applications between exercise periods. If the swelling remains after three days then veterinary advice should be sought. When ice is used for cooling localised areas it should be remembered that water expands to form ice – so when it melts, even if all the water is retained in the dressing, inevitably the dressing will become loose. Thus, bandaging a cannon region with ice cubes, for example, will result in a loose, slipping bandage when the ice has melted; and remember that although bandaging may keep the cold in, it also prevents the normal body heat from escaping and so speeds up the melting of the ice. Owners are often amazed how rapidly cold packs defrost, and by the high temperatures they can reach if left in place.

Actual cooling of an inflamed area is clearly a better ploy than a perceived cooling, and in this respect I do not consider that most of the chemical coolants sold to be applied to horses' legs are as effective at lowering internal tissue temperatures as are methods based on freezing either water or a gel pack. For example, freezing a polystyrene foam cup of water provides a large block of ice than can be taken to an event and if necessary held in place directly over the injured area. However, if it were held directly against the skin for a significant time it would literally freeze the skin to the ice because of the intensity of the cooling effect. Cooling washes or compounds spread on the skin may feel cold to us, but they never in fact provide *that* amount of cooling, even of the skin.

I would suggest that if a competition horse goes lame, even slightly, then veterinary advice should always be sought. The horse's competitive future may be at risk and until a precise diagnosis is known, we cannot tell whether even a couple of days' delay may be significant. This is not necessarily the advice I would give the owner of a horse just used for hacking, but when success depends on a horse completing a course one hundredth of a second faster than all the other competitors, very minute residual changes can be significant.

Prohibited Substances and Testing Procedures

At this point I should point out that it is the owner's responsibility to ensure that a horse does not end up competing whilst receiving prohibited substances. It is no defence to say that 'I didn't realise what the vet gave my horse'. I would suggest that if any drug is being given within eight days of a competition, then the owner should ask the vet to write down what has been given and how much. Even with such precautions some drugs will still be detectable for much longer periods. Naturally one should inform the vet that the horse is likely to be competing before he gives any treatment, rather than when it is too late to alter things afterwards. Some regulatory bodies now no longer penalise the presence of antibiotics, although procaine (which is often part of the penicillin molecule) is still banned because it has other properties.

When treating lameness, the nearer the competition, the more we have to rely on physical treatment methods. This can be extremely time-consuming, but it is better than giving painkiller and hoping the horse will not be dope tested. Owners should be familiar with what should happen when a horse is dope tested. If the procedures are breached, it might not be appropriate to draw attention to that breach at the time, but it should be carefully recorded as soon as possible because this could invalidate any results, positive or negative, and avoid any disciplinary action.

■ Taking Samples

I would suggest that the owner stays with the horse throughout any official sampling, ignoring even the calls of nature. In most cases the regulatory authorities will want to obtain a urine sample, because many drugs are present for a far longer time in urine than in blood. For this very reason many owners may prefer a blood sample to be taken, and may use a long journey home as their excuse for not wanting to wait for the horse to pass urine. The rules usually state how long they must wait unsuccessfully for a urine sample before a blood sample may be taken.

Any samples taken should be divided into two and sealed with tamper-proof seals on the spot, in the presence of the horse's owner. It is increasingly important that the samples are stored correctly and transported to the analytical laboratory promptly. This is because some drugs continue to undergo chemical change after the sample has been taken. When analysts were only looking for the drug itself, this did not matter, but now that sophisticated equipment can detect and measure these breakdown products, it is more important. A high level of a breakdown product might be the result of a high

level of drug which has broken down over 12 hours, or the result of a much lower level of the drug which has broken down over 48–72 hours of poor storage. Ideally, samples taken for dope testing would be watched by the owner until they were either stored in the laboratory or were in the hands of the courier who would take them directly there. It is certainly no longer acceptable for samples to be taken at a competition on a Saturday and left in the vet's car until he can post them on Monday.

■ Sample Analysis

If the first analysis of a sample reveals the presence of a prohibited substance, the owner should be given the opportunity to be present at the confirmatory analysis, accompanied by a technical adviser. Recent experiences in the human athletic world have emphasised the importance of ensuring that owners take up this option, and that they employ the best analyst they can to be their observer. Small errors in technique can produce small but vital errors in results, and once the confirmatory analysis has proved positive, there is very little chance of avoiding disqualification. It is a principle of dope testing that the authorities do not have to prove who administered the drug, they only have to prove that it was present. Saying that a horse was never out of an owner's sight makes matters worse rather than better, because if the presence of a prohibited substance has been confirmed, it can therefore only have been given by the owner.

■ Veterinary Treatment during Competition

Animal welfare concerns have pushed for treatment of horses during a competition to be allowed, on the grounds that otherwise horses will be left without treatment in an attempt to complete the competition. In theory this is the situation already at FEI competitions. Vets who have treated injured horses should report the details to the Grand Jury, and the Jury then decides if it will disqualify the horse or not. In practice, however, such horses are usually disqualified no matter how fit they are to continue competing. I would suggest that before any treatment is given, owners ask for an official dope test to be taken; this would then allow them to argue that the horse should not be disqualified at that stage because it would prove that the first-aid treatment had not masked any other drug, and had only restored the horse to its previous state.

The Treatment of Colic at Competitions

Colic is another situation which can arise during a competition. When this happens, some owners try to avoid the use of drugs to relieve the pain by walking the horse around in hand instead. I do not support this because the exercise uses up muscle energy reserves and a horse which has just been walking around for two hours will not give its best performance even if it is allowed to compete. Moreover care must be taken in the use of any proprietary colic drinks: just because they can be bought without a veterinary prescription does not mean that they do not contain any prohibited substances which can be absorbed into the bloodstream. There is also the very real risk of some of the fluid going down the wrong way, into the trachea, and causing problems there which will affect the horse's ability to perform to its maximum level. There are some circumstances when a mild saline purgative, given by stomach tube, would relieve colic. If it does not do so, then the problem is probably so serious that it would significantly affect performance anyway.

The Treatment of Wounds

■ Small Wounds

The first-aid treatment of small wounds in competition horses can expose conflicting priorities. On the one hand there is the need to ensure that there is absolutely no future impairment of movement by the formation of adhesions, nor the formation of proud flesh (granulation tissue) that will delay the return to full work. On the other hand, stitching small wounds may properly require the use of local anaesthetics that are prohibited substances for competition purposes.

The first essential is to stop the bleeding, and whether this is from a pin prick or from a cut artery, the treatment is the same. Firm pressure must be applied, using a folded handkerchief or a clean stable rubber if by some mischance the first-aid kit is not to hand. If a very tight bandage is applied to a leg wound, it must either be released for ten minutes in the hour to allow the circulation to equalise, or the whole of the leg on the hoof side of the wound must be bandaged as

well; otherwise that part of the leg will become swollen and oedematous because the pumping action of the arteries will push more blood past the dressing than the passively draining blood vessels can remove. As a general rule I would recommend that wounds longer than one inch are stitched. Increasingly, however, surgical staples are used rather than actual stitches because these are quicker to apply and don't penetrate so deeply. The result is that they hurt less than stitches when they are put in, and local anaesthesia may not need to be used anyway, just a twitch.

■ Serious Wounds and Major Injuries

Movement is the enemy of both serious wounds and major injuries to tendons and bones. None of these can be dealt with on the training ground or competition course, so the horse will need to be transported to a veterinary clinic for treatment. That period of transportation is of crucial significance. It can, for example, convert a simple fracture of a pastern that does not break the skin and is perfectly repairable, into a multi-fragmented compound fracture through the skin that is not repairable and ends up in euthanasia. That is why the first-aid kit must contain the wherewithal to apply a Robert Jones bandage, because this will stop the situation getting any worse.

A Robert Jones bandage basically consists of at least four layers of gamgee wrapped around the leg from the hoof to the elbow, with the whole being compressed as tightly as possible with cohesive bandages. These need to be applied at least every two layers of gamgee, and they cannot be applied too tightly. The result is a padded tube that will bend very little (Fig 25). It can be further improved by including a broom handle or similar rigid object or splint down the front or the back of the leg, or to either side of it. An alternative to a Robert Jones bandage for the lower leg is to use a commercial Monkey splint (Fig 26); this keeps the front of the hoof, the pastern and the cannon stable in a straight line, and it is rapidly and easily applied.

It is always better to fear the worst and immobilise the leg unnecessarily than to risk further unrestricted movement making a situation worse. No diagnosis is required to justify applying a Robert Jones bandage. If the horse doesn't want to take weight on the leg, that in itself justifies the precaution.

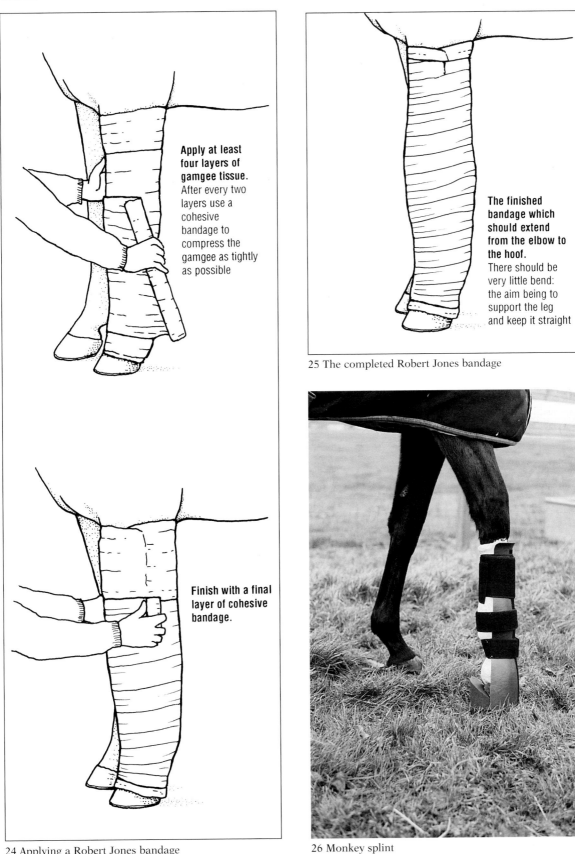

Apply at least four layers of gamgee tissue.
After every two layers use a cohesive bandage to compress the gamgee as tightly as possible

The finished bandage which should extend from the elbow to the hoof.
There should be very little bend: the aim being to support the leg and keep it straight

25 The completed Robert Jones bandage

Finish with a final layer of cohesive bandage.

24 Applying a Robert Jones bandage

26 Monkey splint

Euthanasia at Public Events

The public nature of competitions introduces an extra factor into the consideration of what is treatable and what is not, and that is the animal welfare lobby. Pressure for horses to be 'put out of their misery' means that some horses are put down rather than having their injuries evaluated and treated. In steeplechasing, for example, a horse might fall and be badly winded, but if it does not get to its feet in 10–15 minutes it is likely to be shot and removed from the course, even though in 30–40 minutes it might have walked away unaided. The higher the profile of the competition, the less apparently is the understanding of the so-called 'welfare' lobby, and the less chance the horse will have of reaching a veterinary clinic for treatment.

Of course, there are some conditions that justify immediate euthanasia on the grounds that they involve excessive pain which cannot be relieved, from a condition which cannot be cured. These include a fracture of a long bone above the knee or hock; this cannot at present be mended. Even fractures below this where the skin is broken and the fracture therefore contaminated will stand such a small chance of healing because of infection that euthanasia is usually justified. Also complete rupture of the flexor tendons, recognised by the fetlock on that leg sinking down towards the ground. And finally spinal damage that results in paralysis, although there will be grey areas when the horse can walk but does not have proper control over its limbs. Some of these cases may well recover.

If a horse is insured it is important to consider the insurance company's interests. Obviously it will not usually be possible to discuss the case with them at the time, but they will not include some of the factors specific to the competition in their assessment as to whether immediate euthanasia was justified or not. For example, a racecourse management may require a horse with a broken cannon to be removed from the course within twenty minutes to allow the next race to proceed. If it is not possible to make the diagnosis, immobilise the leg, load the horse into a horse ambulance and remove it from the course within that time, there will be great pressure to put the horse down and drag it out of the way. However, the insurance company looking at the post-mortem report might conclude that the horse could have been saved and that the decision to opt for euthanasia was not made on strictly veterinary grounds.

Heat Stroke, Sweating and Dehydration

During strenuous exercise the horse produces a considerable amount of heat. Even at rest 75 per cent of the energy released in the muscles is in the form of heat energy, and during sprinting the amount of heat produced can be forty to fifty times that produced at rest. The result is that if the horse is working hard enough to raise its heart rate to 150 beats/minute, every three minutes of exercise will raise its body temperature by 1°C (1.8°F). Obviously something has to be done about this or the horse's temperature would reach the point (111.2°F or 44°C) where the muscles literally start to cook.

The horse can lose heat by convection. This means that the heat generated in the muscles is transferred to the skin by the blood and then lost to the cooler air passing over the horse's body; the greater the difference between the skin temperature and the air temperature, the more heat is lost. Also the greater the amount of air movement over the body, the more heat is lost, so horses recovering after a competition can be cooled by fans to compensate for the fact that there is no wind in hot, humid conditions.

The horse can also lose heat by evaporation of sweat, and I cannot stress too highly that every drop of sweat which drips off the horse's body without evaporating is a lost opportunity to cool it. Evaporation is much reduced in hot, humid conditions. Horses also lose heat through breathing: they heat up the air in their lungs before breathing it out, and this is one of the reasons that they breathe more quickly after exercise or in hot and humid conditions.

Any horse which is hot (ie with a body temperature above 104°F or 40°C) and competing in a hot environment (ie above 80°F or 26.5°C) will be less likely to suffer heat stress and will recover more quickly if it is cooled quickly during or after the competition. Such a horse will be less likely to become dehydrated and will almost certainly perform better.

The requirements for cooling a horse are some large buckets of water and ice, large sponges and elbow grease. Before even removing the tack, one person should start to apply cold water liberally over the body, especially the hindquarters. Take the horse's temperature at this time. Cool it for thirty seconds, then walk it around for thirty

27 Do not be afraid to let a hot horse stop and drink cold water. It will not have any adverse effect

28 When competitions are held in hot, humid conditions, fans may be needed to evaporate the water used
to cool the horses down

29 After a competition electrolytes may need to be given to replace those lost in sweat. Care must be taken to mix these in the correct concentration

seconds before cooling it again. The alternating cooling and walking is important because the walking increases skin blood-flow and the movement of it helps evaporation. Ideally, of course, all of this should take place in the shade. It should be possible to reduce the horse's rectal temperature by around 0.56°F or 1°C every ten minutes. It is safe to allow the horse to drink up to half a bucket of cold water. Cooling should continue in this way until you are sure of the following:

● The rectal temperature is less than 102°F or 38–39°C.
● The skin feels cool to the touch over the quarters after a walking period.
● The respiratory rate is less than thirty breaths per minute.
● The horse begins to shiver.

It is perhaps worth mentioning at this point that riders need to be cooled as well as horses, because they, too, have been undertaking exercise in hot conditions.

There are some things which you should not do:

● **Do not** place ice directly into the horse's rectum; this makes it impossible to measure its temperature accurately.
● **Do not** hold small bags of ice over its head and neck because localised cooling will reduce local blood flow.
● **Do not** place wet towels on the neck and quarters. Although they will start off wet and cold, they will soon warm up and in fact insulate the horse against further heat loss.
● **Do not** apply excessive grease prior to cross-country events. It acts as an insulator and prevents sweat evaporation.
● **Do not** let the horse stand still for prolonged periods.

There is no evidence to suggest that cold-water cooling causes other problems such as 'tying-up'. Cold water has the added effect of reducing the amount of sweat produced and thus, too, the risk of dehydration.

■ The Evaporation of Sweat: its Vital Role

The horse loses heat by conduction, radiation and convection, like any other hot object. Most importantly, it loses heat by the evaporation of sweat, and it is important that the owners of competition horses understand this process. The most essential point to grasp is that the production of sweat achieves nothing, it is only in evaporating that it has a cooling effect. So every drop of sweat that falls to the ground is wasted, and every drop of sweat which is removed from the horse by someone using a sweat scraper is also wasted. On the other hand, every litre of sweat that is allowed to evaporate will remove the heat produced by burning 180 litres of oxygen. It is also important to realise that heat continues to be produced long after the horse has pulled up from the strenuous exercise, because its body has to pay the price of the short cuts used to produce enough energy for the exercise; so sweating must be allowed to continue after exercise.

The air temperature, wind velocity and relative humidity will all affect the way a horse loses heat. In a hot dry atmosphere, evaporation of sweat is most effective. In a very humid climate, however, up to two-thirds of the sweat produced will just run off the horse before it can evaporate. Owners of competition horses must therefore give some consideration to the climate when deciding whether to compete, particularly as the organisers of competitions, even at the highest levels, have sometimes shown themselves quite unwilling to consider the horse's welfare in this respect. We have known for some time how to judge whether the climate will present unacceptable problems to the horse, but often the organisers refuse to take this into consideration, being more concerned with gate money, sponsors and costs.

The air temperature should be adjusted in view of the effects of humidity, and an 'effective temperature' assessed: in its simplest form this is the sum of the air temperature in degrees Fahrenheit and the relative humidity as a percentage. When the effective temperature is below 130, there are no problems; when it is between 130 and 150, especially if the relative humidity makes up more than half of the total, then caution is needed because the efficiency of cooling will be reduced. When the effective temperature is above 180, however, then cooling will be almost entirely ineffectual and horses should not compete in such conditions;

indeed they should only exercise for brief periods.

For major competitions it is reasonable to expect the facilities to be available for more sophisticated measurements to be made: this contrasts the ordinary dry-bulb (db) thermometer reading with the wet-bulb (wb) temperature to represent humidity and the temperature of a black-globe (bg) which represents radiation. The wet-bulb globe temperature (WBGT) is calculated from the formula:

$$WBGT°F = (0.7 \times wb) + (0.2 \times bg) = (0.1 \times db)$$

In human sports activities the following have been suggested:

WBGT Precautions
80–85°F Caution. Frequent water breaks needed
85–88°F Limited activity for trained people
88°F+ No activity allowed

It is hoped to be able to develop precise equine WBGT values.

■ Coping with Dehydration

Although sweating is a vital part of the important process of temperature control, its formation represents a cost to the horse. First there is the water loss, which on an endurance ride, for example, might be 7.5 litres of water every hour of the ride. Sweat contains electrolytes, or salts, such as sodium, potassium and calcium; it also contains large amounts of protein – indeed it is the protein content which causes sweat to lather. The loss of water and electrolytes can result in the horse becoming dehydrated.

Water makes up around 60 per cent of the horse's bodyweight, and water lost via sweating has to be made good. Most of that loss will be from fluid outside the cells themselves, especially from the fluid that bathes the tissues. In the normal horse, when a large pinch of skin is pulled up over a shoulder or the neck, it recoils immediately when released. In a dehydrated horse, the loss of fluid from the tissues decreases their elasticity and the fold of skin subsides only very slowly. It has been shown that by the time this change becomes noticeable, the horse has lost 3–5 per cent of its bodyweight in water. When we consider that in man a loss of 2–4 per cent has been proved to have an adverse effect on physical performance, then any competition horse that is dehydrated enough to give a positive pinch test should not be expected to compete further.

The main way that we prevent dehydration is by making sure that the horse drinks enough water. Horses are naturally periprandial drinkers, which means that they drink around feeding time. So water should be available before, during and after feeds. It is also sensible to encourage horses to drink during a competition that lasts any length of time, whenever there is a rest period. Even when they do this, endurance horses still finish slightly dehydrated, but at least it is then a relatively easy matter for that water deficit to be replaced during the recovery period. When a horse does not normally drink during competition, every effort should be made to teach it to do so. Incidentally there is no evidence that drinking cold water causes colic. Indeed, horses which have taken part in strenuous exercise may find the cooling effect of cold water on their core temperature very valuable.

■ The Role of Electrolytes

With prolonged exercise, it is not enough to give water to deal with the problem of dehydration: electrolytes also need to be given to replace the 7.5–10.5g of sodium chloride and the 1.5–3.5g of potassium chloride lost in each litre of sweat. During an 80km (50-mile) endurance ride, Thoroughbreds can lose 350g (¾lb) of salt. During shorter periods of moderate exercise, lasting up to two hours, there will not be any obvious result of the electrolyte loss. The diet is unlikely to be able to replace that which has been lost, though,

and that is why electrolyte supplements are so important.

It is vital to realise that the horse is not able to store any electrolytes against a future need, and that any excess electrolytes are just excreted via the kidneys. Therefore there is absolutely no point in giving electrolyte supplements before the competition, except to aquaint the horse with the taste of the supplemented water. There is a variety of electrolyte supplements on the market now. These should contain four times as much sodium as potassium, although users should appreciate that for moderate sweating, only the sodium will be needed and ordinary salt will do this at the rate of 17g of sodium chloride for every tablespoonful added to a litre of water. When commercial supplements are used, they may contain glucose, dextrose or citrate to increase the absorption of the supplement. These are not an energy source for the horse.

■ The 'Thumps'

Horses taking part in endurance events in hot conditions, and in some other circumstances, may develop a condition know as the 'thumps'. In this, the diaphragm contracts in rhythm with the heart, rather than with the breathing, and the diaphragmatic movement may be sufficiently violent to produce a thumping noise. This may not arise until during the cooling-off period. Giving the horse electrolytes whilst competing will prevent the 'thumps' occurring. Clinical cases respond well to calcium solutions given intravenously.

FEEDING

OVERLEAF:
Successful competition horses such as Master Craftsman
will benefit from periods turned out to graze a good pasture

CONTENTS

THE DIGESTIVE SYSTEM

The evolution of the horse's digestive system has been only a partial success. It has produced a solution to the problem of how to digest the cellulose which makes up so much of plant material, but the anatomical considerations leave much to be desired. The result is that digestive upsets, some of which are fatal, are relatively common in the horse. It is important to understand the general anatomy of the digestive system before you can really understand how the horse uses its food.

How the Horse Eats

■ The Teeth

The digestive system starts at the mouth. The horse has what are known as prehensile lips, meaning that they are very mobile and can grasp hold of objects. In the horse's case the aim is to grasp hold of the grass or other roughage and put it into the mouth, ready to be cut off by the two opposing sets of cutting incisor teeth. Immediately we have a difference between the horse and the cow, which also lives on grass but which opens its mouth and wraps its tongue around a clump of grass tearing it off. In the horse, the cut grass is then chewed quite thoroughly by the molar teeth, which lie in the cheek region. This chewing is vital for several reasons: first, it crushes the plant material to expose the inner parts of the leaves and stems, breaking through the protective outer layer; second, it cuts the fibrous material up into smaller pieces; and finally, it stimulates the production of saliva, which contains the first digestive enzymes. Indeed the horse cannot produce saliva unless it does chew something: it never salivates in anticipation of a good meal.

If the conformation of a horse's jaw is such that it is badly over- or under-shot (Fig 1), then because its top and bottom incisor teeth cannot meet, it will find it all but impossible to bite off grass. The molar teeth, however, are still able to grind food, so once it is in the mouth the horse's digestive

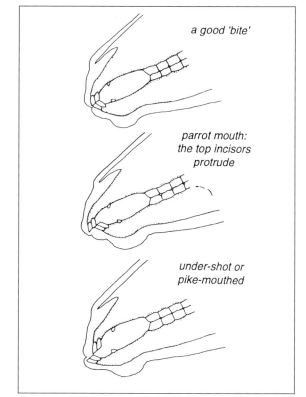

1 The conformation of the horse's jaw has an effect on the way the horse eats

system works normally; but it may be necessary to provide ready-cut forage in order to overcome the problem. Moreover great care is needed to ensure that the fibre we do provide is readily digestible and not too long, so as to obviate impaction problems further along the digestive system because of long, coarse, undigested fibre. Thankfully a wholly over- or under-shot jaw is rare, and more commonly the upper and lower incisors meet but are not exactly aligned. In this circumstance the horse can graze perfectly normally. Over the years though, uneven wear develops on the teeth (Fig 2), the practical significance of this being that it makes it impossible even to guess at the horse's age by looking at the amount of wear on the lower incisors; it will look a completely different age to a horse with normal teeth.

At some time in the life of most horses, sharp points develop on one or more molar teeth, usually on the outside edge of the upper molars or the inside edge of the lower molars. It is perhaps wrong to say that the points 'develop' because it is really the rest of the grinding surface of the tooth which wears away, leaving just a part of the tooth sticking out generally in a sharp, jagged point. Because of the discomfort these cause to the tongue and cheeks, the horse does not chew as enthusiastically as it should and so the food passing into the stomach is less ground down than it

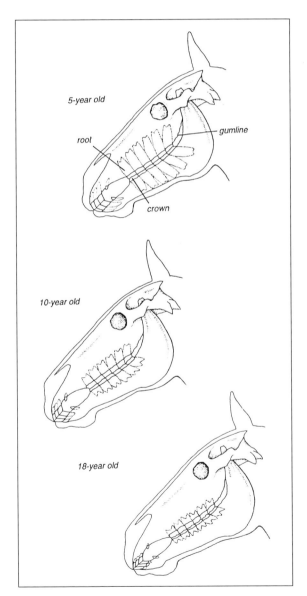

2 A horse's teeth grow continually, to compensate for what is worn away through eating. As the horse gets older the roots diminish, and the grinding surface of the teeth wears smooth

should be. In these circumstances impaction colic can be the result further along the line. The horse may also resent the bit and bridle pressing the sensitive skin of its mouth against any sharp points, and try to prevent this happening by rearing, head shaking and refusing to respond to the aids. Regular tooth rasping is therefore essential, both for nutritional and competitive reasons, and all horses should have their teeth checked every 6-12 months. In some cases the way a horse moves its jaw positively encourages the development of sharp points on its teeth, and its performance will undoubtedly benefit if it has its mouth checked professionally every 2–3 months.

When that mouthful of food has been chewed sufficiently, the tongue packages it into one lump and pushes it right to the back of the mouth ready

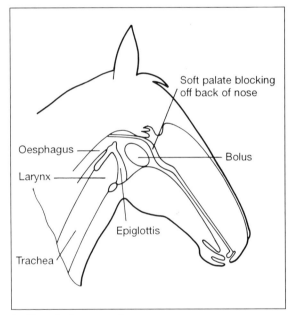

3 How the horse swallows

for swallowing. This involves some very precise co-ordination between different structures. The horse's larynx, which is the opening to its trachea, or windpipe, is pulled out of its position in a hole in the soft palate, which is the position it occupies during breathing, and is covered over by the epiglottis to prevent any food going down the wrong tube. The food is then pushed backwards down the remaining open tube, which is called the oesophagus. Once the lump, or bolus, of food has gone into the oesophagus, the larynx can return to its position in the soft palate, and the horse can start breathing again (Fig 3).

Swallowing is a conscious act, but the further down the oesophagus the food passes, the less conscious sensation and control there is. At the end of the oesophagus the food passes through a narrow opening into the stomach. It is that narrow opening which prevents the horse from being able to empty its stomach by vomiting. If a horse does regurgitate food, whether through its mouth or down its nostrils, it is a sign that it is very ill indeed. The exception to this is a foal with food material coming down its nostrils because it has a cleft palate, but even this is very serious because it is difficult to correct a hole in the palate surgically in the horse.

The Stomach

The horse does not have a particularly big stomach because it is only designed to deal with the more or less constant small quantities of grass produced by grazing. These small quantities are significant for the performance horse because it means that when we ask the horse to use large amounts of energy during work, it may not be able to process enough food through the stomach to provide that energy. The very description 'concentrate feed' recognises the fact that man has always had to use unnatural feedstuffs, such as oats, which provide a higher concentration of energy by volume than the horse's natural roughage diet. And in our search for ever higher levels of performance we are having to use ever more concentrated energy sources.

The Intestines

The horse's small intestine does not really have any special features, and functions very like our own intestines, digesting carbohydrates and simple proteins. Also, like ours, it cannot digest complex cellulose protein molecules. Where the small intestine changes to the large colon, however, there is a marked difference from the human digestive system: here, human beings have a small, blind-ending sac called the appendix which, as everyone knows, performs no real function and our digestive system works quite happily without it. The horse also has a blind-ending sac at this point, but it is very large in comparison and is called the caecum. Although in theory the horse should be able to digest its food without the caecum, as we do without the appendix, because it is more prominent it has to function properly;

thus the regular muscular contractions which pass along the intestine, moving food material along the system, must also involve the caecum. The junction of the small intestine, or ileum, with first the caecum and then the large colon results in a narrower section of the continuous tube which makes up the horse's digestive system, or to be more precise it provides an area which cannot easily be stretched to allow bulky material to pass on. As a result, impactions of fibrous material can occur here.

The Large Colon

The large colon of the horse acts as a fermentation chamber. The food material entering it is like a thick soup in consistency, and here it meets millions of commensal bacteria which break down much of the remaining solid material even further to very simple proteins and free fatty acids (the simplest carbohydrate unit). The bacteria specialise in dealing with cellulose, but many different species and subspecies of bacteria are present, each one looking out for its own specific foodstuff. The percentage of each bacterial species present depends on the food which the horse has been eating. Those bacteria which find abundant food material in the diet increase in numbers accordingly, whilst those that no longer find much food to work on decrease in numbers. As the food passes through the large colon, much of the water it contains is re-absorbed until only the characteristic balls of faecal material remain. If the horse's diet changes, and more fibrous material is present than can be broken down by the bacterial mix present, then eventually as the water is absorbed the undigested bulky fibrous matter may become impacted. This is why it is so very important that any equine diet changes are made very gradually, to allow the balance of bacteria present to adapt to the new situation.

In order to allow all this fermentation to take place, the horse's large colon is very long. However, it has evolved into a compact layout which enables it to fit into the abdomen, looking like two letter 'U's on top of each other, joined at one end. Unfortunately this layout means that there are the two large 180° bends, and one very sharp 180° bend. Fibrous matter passing along the colon can become impacted at any one of these bends, especially if it has not been properly digested. To make matters worse, the diameter of the colon almost halves at the very sharp bend, which is called the pelvic flexure, and this makes impaction even more likely (Fig 4).

■ Do Probiotics Have a Role to Play?

From time to time we hear a great deal about pro- biotics for horses. These are bacterial mixtures which an owner mixes with the horse's food to sup- plement the existing bacteria in the colon. All kinds of claims are made for probiotics, and it is worth remembering that they can do no more than the natural bacteria. They have no magic effects, and the best thing they can achieve is to ensure normal fibre digestion. Of course, in animals which are very stressed, or which have received antibiotics by mouth for a long period, or whose diet has been changed accidentally or on purpose, this is a very desirable achievement. Nevertheless, there are a number of points concerning probiotics that owners should consider if they are not to be misled by often ignorant salespeople.

1 Ensure that the bacteria are equine strains, not just any old Lactobaccilus grown in a lab for some other purpose and now being sold to horse owners. If the probiotic is not of equine origin, its effects will be limited.

2 Ensure that the product has a proper sell-by date and is well within that date. Bacteria are sensitive, living organisms and have to be at their best to multiply in the digestive system.

3 Make sure that the product will supply a known number of live bacteria on adminis- tration. We do not know how many of any particular species constitutes the ideal, but the product should have a reliable bacterial content which does not change.

4 Different foods require different bacterial mixes, and the probiotic manufacturer should indicate the purpose for which the product is sold.

Foals gradually pick up their own intestinal bacte- rial population from exposure to the live bacteria passed out in faeces by other horses. The ultimate probiotic is to transfer large colon contents from a recently dead horse to another horse via a stom- ach tube. Failing that, a 'soup' can be made from fresh faeces, strained and given in the same way. A crude form of probiotic, but no worse than some of the commercial products, is to add a carton of ordinary live unpasteurised yoghurt to the horse's feed every day. This will not provide equine selected strains of the Lactobaccilus bacteria, but the bacteria will be in large numbers and healthy.

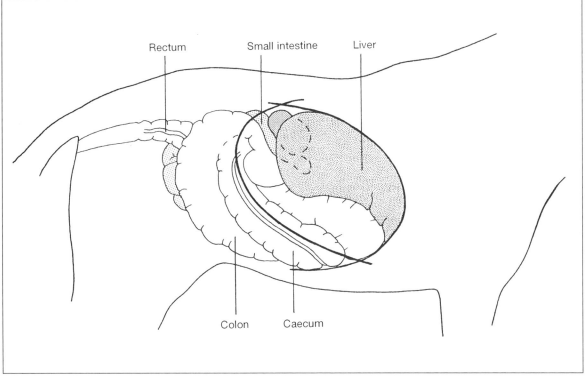

Rectum Small intestine Liver

Colon Caecum

4 Anatomy of the colon

The Grazing Horse

It is worth looking in a little more detail at what happens when a horse is grazing. The horse prefers to graze short rather than long grass, and it bites it off with its incisor teeth. When horses are kept in a reasonably confined space such as a paddock they tend to eat some areas literally down to the ground, and to dung in other areas which naturally they will not willingly graze. The former areas are referred to as 'lawn', and the latter as 'rough'. The rough becomes further contaminated with weeds which take advantage of the lack of grazing to grow more profusely. Horses may therefore have two acres of paddock, but in effect only one acre of pasture which they will eat.

When hay is fed the stalks are taken in whole, so large strands of fibre are present. These are not cut into shorter pieces during chewing by the molar teeth. They are, however, crushed to allow contact between the digestive enzymes and the food material. Supplementary feeds need to be ground down by the teeth because the smaller the end particle, the more surface area it has, and the better it will be digested. Where a horse is being asked for maximum performance, regular dental care is essential both to remove sharp points which develop on the teeth and to ensure efficient food digestion. Incidentally it is not necessarily a good thing for a horse to finish its food quickly: slower feeding improves digestibility and reduces boredom, and with this in view it may be advantageous to mix some chaff or other fibre into concentrate feeds to slow down their consumption.

One practical point to mention is that because the horse cannot produce saliva unless it is chewing, a competition may result in the mouth being very dry. The horse can do nothing about it, but the practice of sponging its mouth out with fresh water during the break between the roads-and-tracks section and the cross-country section of a horse trials is obviously advantageous (Fig 5).

Storing Energy

The horse very rarely obtains its energy from food at the same time as it needs that energy, so it has to be stored, and one way that the horse does this is by using a chemical compound called

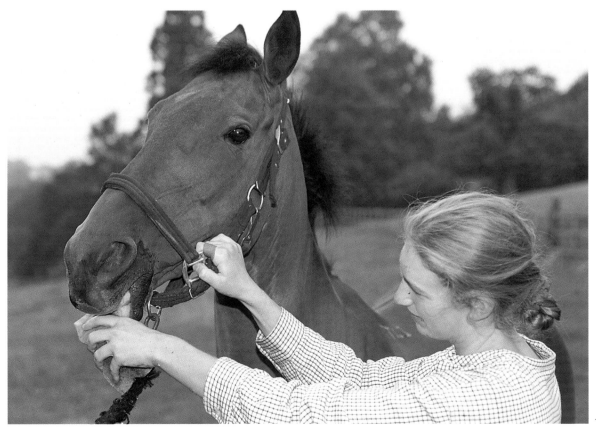

5   Sponging a horse's mouth

glycogen. This is made up of thousands of glucose molecules which are formed into a single, branched, glycogen molecule: when energy is needed, glucose molecules can be broken off it. The horse also stores glycogen in its liver and in its muscles. The liver glycogen is used to supply the glucose for general body use, for example for nerves and blood cells; there is a constant release of glucose into the bloodstream from the liver to meet these requirements, and there has to be a complicated system of hormonal control to ensure that even at times of peak demand from the body, the blood glucose levels stay constant. The muscle glycogen supplies glucose and energy for use in the muscle itself during contraction.

The other way the horse stores energy is as fat. Fat is made up of triglyceride molecules, each of which contains one molecule of glycerol and three molecules of fatty acids. Triglycerides can be present all over the body, as well as in the larger deposits of fat itself. The major fat deposits are underneath the horse's skin, around the major organs such as the heart, and in the abdominal cavity. Fat is a vital energy source because there is more than thirty times the amount of energy in the horse's fat deposits than in all the glycogen stores. Even a competition horse in lean condition will have enough fat to supply the energy to keep it exercising at a moderate speed for several days. A fat horse, however, has disadvantages to set against the advantage of its stored energy, first because it has to use energy to move the extra weight of the fat around; and second, because the fat also acts as a layer of insulation. This prevents heat loss from the horse, and can seriously affect metabolism generally, especially after strenuous exercise.

Proteins: Building Blocks, not Energy Sources

Although the horse needs to have a means of storing energy because strenuous exercise results in a sudden great demand for that energy, there is no means of storing protein. Proteins are the building blocks that make up muscle and much of the ligaments, tendons, hooves and so on. These are built up slowly and there are no normal situations when large amounts of protein are required. Of course the performance horse has a greater requirement for protein than a horse resting in a stable, because wear and tear on the muscles means that some have to be replaced, but that demand is met out of the daily food intake. If large amounts of protein are fed, the horse does have the ability to break down some of it and release energy, which can be stored, but this is a rather inefficient process and is not to be encouraged. It is surprising the number of people who talk glibly about feeding plenty of protein to performance horses, without realising what a waste this is.

Maintaining Mineral Levels

The way the blood levels of glucose are maintained has already been mentioned. There are similar systems for maintaining the blood levels of minerals, such as calcium and magnesium, and of electrolytes such as sodium and potassium. The maintenance of the blood calcium level is particularly interesting because the horse's skeleton acts as the reservoir of calcium. Thus if blood calcium levels go down, more calcium is released from bone breakdown. And if extra calcium is fed, then once the bones have been restored to their normal density, the rest is just discarded. After very strenuous exercise horses may develop a form of hiccup, where the diaphragm moves violently. This condition, known colloquially as the 'thumps', is due to low calcium levels in the blood which the system mentioned above just cannot rectify quickly enough. It can be fatal if the calcium level drops low enough, but equally can be treated quite simply by administering a calcium solution directly into the horse's bloodstream.

Bodyweight and Feeding

Ultimately the aim of feeding is to achieve a stable bodyweight, and that stable bodyweight can be looked upon as the pointer on a set of scales. If exercise is increased without increasing nutrition, the pointer will show that the weight has gone down. If feeding is increased without increasing exercise, the pointer will show that the weight has gone up. It has been suggested that the one change that will have the greatest effect on a trainer's success with performance horses is to change from feeding by sight to feeding by weight.

When we feed by sight, we look at the horse and say 'that horse looks more or less the same as it looked when it was successful in the past, so

I must be feeding it right'. However, few owners or trainers have eyes that are accurate enough, and memories that are good enough, to make that kind of quantitative judgment about one horse, let alone a whole yard of horses. When people feed by sight they look at the food in a scoop and decide that it looks like half a scoop, or they look at a quantity of food and decide that it looks like 1.3kg (3lb) of food. Again, it is unlikely that they will be consistently right (or even just consistently wrong by the same margin).

When we feed by weight we say 'that horse is 2.2kg (5lb) heavier than it was when it was successful before, so it needs less food or more exercise'. It also means that if a planned ration is 1.1kg (2.5lb) of corn, it really will be 1.1kg rather than 0.9kg (2lb) or 1.3kg (3lb). Most horses have an effective competing weight which usually has to be discovered by trial and error: there is no magic way to find this weight out. The starting point is a horse which performs well and where you can see the last rib, but not really count the other ribs. Trainers have to be prepared to experiment by increasing and decreasing the horse's weight even when competing successfully. After all, a horse may satisfy its owner's wildest dreams by coming third in a competition, but it might have been capable of coming first. As even the leanest horse has more than enough supplies of fat for competition, trainers need not be afraid that they will be criticised if their horses do not carry enough 'condition'. It should be obvious that a horse which is overweight due to fat is handicapped just as much as one carrying an overweight rider. In showing classes, obesity is seen by outsiders as one of the major welfare issues of the competition horse, especially when it affects a young horse whose skeleton is still immature.

Obviously a weighbridge provides the most accurate way to determine a horse's weight, but it is not really practical for regular use in most cases. In any case, it has been shown that it is possible to estimate a horse's weight very accu-

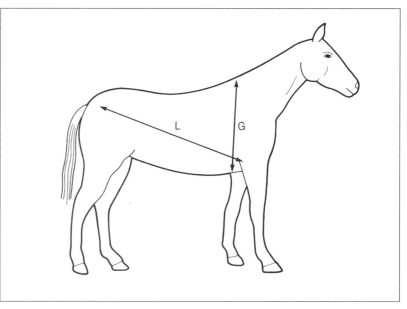

6 Estimating a horse's weight by measuring its girth (G) in inches behind the shoulder, and its length (L), and using the formula given in the text

rately using only a tape measure. There are weighbands available that read off a weight instead of a girth measurement, but these are not very accurate because they do not differentiate between a deep-chested horse and a fat horse, and fat weighs heavier than lung tissue full of air. The accurate way to estimate a horse's weight is to measure its girth (G) in inches behind the shoulder (Fig 6), and also to measure the length (L) from the point of the shoulder to the tuber ischii (the bony prominence just to the side of the tail). The formula used is

$$\text{WEIGHT IN LB} = \frac{G^2 \times L}{300}$$

In greyhound racing, dogs are weighed at the track, and are not allowed to race if that weight varies significantly from their standard racing weight. Only in a few countries, such as Japan, has a similar system been tried for horse racing. Interestingly a horse's ideal racing weight does not vary very much between its two-year-old and three-year-old careers. If a horse loses more than a couple of pounds' weight during a competition then something has gone wrong. It is not desirable just to increase its feed until stored fat makes up the weight loss, because muscle will also have been broken down and lost. Time and exercise are also needed – in other words, further training to enable the horse to withstand the stress of such a competition more successfully in the future.

ENERGY

Competitions are all about movement, and movement requires energy. If one understands fully how that energy is produced, one can appreciate the limitation on its production in various situations and so the limitations on performance.

Where Does Energy Come From?

The basic source of energy is a chemical molecule known as adenosine triphosphate (ATP). Within that molecule, energy is stored in the bonds which hold the three phosphate particles making up the triphosphate. If any one of these phosphate particles is broken off, energy is released. This can only take place in the presence of an enzyme or catalyst (defined as a substance which is vital to a chemical reaction but which is unchanged at the end of that reaction). The chemical formula is:

$$ATP + H_2O \text{ --- enzyme----> } ADP \text{ (adenosine diphosphate)} + P + energy$$

Only about 25 per cent of that energy will be mechanical energy that can produce movement; the rest will be lost as heat. Because it is a rather inefficient system, relatively large amounts of ATP have to be broken down during movement; one stride of a man, for example, is said to require the energy from more than a billion billion molecules of ATP.

Faced with such huge requirements, and the fact that any one muscle cell only contains enough ATP molecules to fuel two or three contractions, it is obvious that muscles cannot power significant movement without a continual supply of further ATP. In fact there is no huge store of ATP. What happens is that the ADP is recycled. So:

$$ADP + P + energy \text{ --- enzyme----> } ATP + H_2O$$

The regeneration of ATP has to keep pace with its breakdown if the horse is to keep on moving.

As movement is using the energy released by ATP breakdown, another source of energy has to be found for the ATP regeneration. This is the energy provided by food. Glucose, free fatty acids, proteins and a substance called phosphocreatine can all produce the energy needed to rebuild ATP molecules. As long as oxygen is present, carbohydrates can be broken right down to carbon dioxide and water, releasing considerable amounts of energy. This is where we get the concept of burning oxygen to produce energy. The respiratory and circulatory systems have to supply one litre of oxygen for every 20 kilojoules of energy released from the breakdown of carbohydrate or fat.

Energy and Diet

The various fuels that are provided from a horse's diet ultimately provide the energy for the reconversion of ADP to ATP. Glycogen in the muscles does this by releasing glucose molecules to be used there and then. Further supplies can be obtained from the glycogen in the liver, but only after a delay while the glucose is transported to the muscles. There are very few triglycerides in the muscle cells because fat is stored elsewhere, so the fatty acids from the triglycerides must also be transported to the muscles; moreover they have to be combined with a protein called albumen in order to be moved.

If we evaluate glucose and fatty acids as relative sources of energy, we find that 1 molecule of glucose will reform 39 molecules of ATP. However, 1 molecule of free fatty acid will reform 139 molecules of ATP. From a practical point of view, though, perhaps we ought to be concerned with the weight of these fuels rather than with single molecules. 1g of triglyceride provides twice as much energy as 1g of glycogen. When we consider the water which is tied up in the glycogen as well (3g of water for every 1g of glycogen), it is obvious that fat (as triglyceride) is a more efficient way of storing energy than starch (as glycogen).

When a horse is working it uses a blend of fuels rather than just one at a time. At rest, muscles get

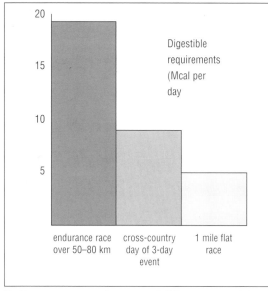

7 Extra energy requirements of different competitions

most of their energy from free fatty acids, but as they start to work they start to use glucose more as a fuel. By the time the horse is doing fast work, almost all of the energy is being obtained from glucose. The proportion of free fatty acids used at any particular speed will depend on the horse's fitness, because one of the effects of fitness is to increase the availability of the enzymes needed to break down free fatty acids. In other words, we will need to provide slightly different food for a fit horse to obtain a given amount of energy than we will for an unfit horse to carry out the same amount of work.

In order to calculate how much food will be needed to fuel a given amount of work, we usually consider digestible energy, which is the energy the horse actually receives, rather than the theoretical amount of energy, the amount the fuel would produce in a laboratory. Thus a stabled 400kg (880lb) horse needs 50MJ of digestible energy to remain balanced, and a stabled 600kg (1,320lb) horse needs 79MJ of energy. In other words, the bigger the horse, the more energy proportionally that is needed. When we come to assess energy requirements for strenuous exercise, they can be as high as 210MJ in the UK or 160MJ in the USA, where training methods usually involve a shorter time in work. It is not always appreciated that the energy requirements for endurance competitions can be even higher than for racing (Fig 7).

7a When horses of more or less equal ability compete against each other the feeding programme of each may be significant in determining which horse wins

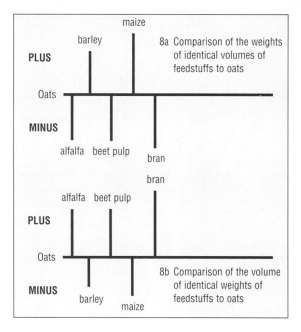

8a Comparison of the weights of identical volumes of feedstuffs to oats

8b Comparison of the volume of identical weights of feedstuffs to oats

As we need to provide more and more energy, we reach the limiting factor of the size of the horse's stomach. A horse can only consume 2.5–3 per cent of its bodyweight as dry matter. So a 400kg (880lb) horse can only eat 12kg (26lb) of dry food per day, and this might well not be enough. It is in this situation that feeding fat, usually in the form of vegetable oil, can be useful.

■ 'Heating' Foods

When choosing a feedstuff to provide their horse's energy requirements, a surprising number of horse owners look only at the feed's quoted protein levels. There should be no connection between the two, because proteins are literally the energy source of last resort. What we should be seeking, and finding, is a Megajoule value per 1kg (2.2 lb). Owners often claim that certain feedstuffs are 'heating', or make their horse 'hot', by which they mean that the horse is so lively and full of energy that they have difficulty in controlling it. This is a very ignorant concept. I use the word ignorant because it shows a complete lack of understanding of how any food acts as a fuel for energy production. If we just consider the cereals, which are the feedstuffs most often accused of being 'heating', they *all* produce glucose, glycogen and a small amount of free fatty acids. It is not the case that any particular cereal produces anything that specifically makes the horse active, or which provides a different type of energy. What does happen is that feedstuffs differ in the amount of digestible energy they contain in a given weight of the food. They also differ in the weight of a given volume of food. The feedingstuffs which so many people accuse of having a heating effect are simply those that contain more digestible energy per unit weight, or which weigh the heaviest per unit volume (Figs 8a and 8b).

■ Oats as a Feedstuff

There is no special nutritional reason why oats are fed to the horses; they are no more its natural food than any other cereal. Oats are actually the cereal with the lowest digestible energy concentration, and also the lowest weight per volume. This does, however, make them a 'safe' cereal to use because a relatively large change in the weight or volume of oats fed will make a relatively small difference in the amount of digestible energy provided. Crimping (rolling) oats can improve their energy availability by 7–10 per cent. Even so, there are practical problems with feeding oats: their quality seems to be particularly variable, and the energy yield will vary from source to source and from season to season; therefore 1kg (2.2 lb) of oats might provide only 10Mj of energy, but it might provide as much as 12.6Mj. This makes accurate ration planning difficult.

■ Corn as a Feedstuff

Corn, or maize, supplies more digestible energy than oats, and so the weight of corn fed has to be adjusted down from that of oats fed. Tests on both polo ponies and endurance horses have confirmed that once this adjustment has been made, horses perform just as well on corn as on oats. Barley is midway between corn and oats as a digestible energy source, although it may be less palatable than either of the other two. Barley needs to be crimped (rolled) before it is used for horses. It is often processed in other ways as well, such as steam flaking or micronising. These processes may improve palatability but they do not change a 'hot' food to a 'cool' food: when you feed the same amount of digestible energy, you get the same performance. Milo, rye and wheat can all be used for feeding horses as long as they are cracked, rolled or steam-rolled, although rye is not very palatable and should never constitute more than a third of any grain mixture. The decision to incorporate one of these grains is usually an economic one to utilise a local price advantage.

Other Energy Sources

Of course sugar, as in sugar lumps, would be a good though impractical energy source, and the byproducts of its production are widely used. Molasses are often added to coarse mixes to reduce dust and improve palatability. Molasses provide 10Mj per 1kg (2.2lb), but are probably too expensive to use specifically as an energy source. Some horses prefer food without molasses, and this may be responsible for palatability problems with certain horses on some commercial mixes. Sugar-beet pulp provides 11Mj of energy per 1kg (2.2lb) of dry matter, which is almost as high as oats. The problem is that such products must never be fed dry because they swell up immediately on contact with water and can cause obstruction of the oesophagus, or choke. Although it has been claimed that sugar-beet products will swell up to their maximum volume in only 3 hours and are then safe to be fed to horses, it is usual to allow 24 hours of soaking to elapse before feeding them.

Roughage

All the energy sources I have dealt with so far are artificial, and are not part of the horse's natural diet. Grasses and hay form the natural energy source, but unfortunately the horse just cannot consume enough of them to provide all its needs for work. Legumes such as alfalfa and clover have a higher digestible energy content than grasses such as fescue, timothy and ryegrass. When a horse is grazing, the energy it obtains will depend on the stage of maturity of the main grasses at that time. When a horse is being fed hay, on the other hand, although the digestible energy content is lower, it will have been fixed at the stage at which the hay was cut. Young plants have a greater digestible energy content than old plants, although of course the volume of available grass is lower than with older plants later in the growing season. The chart (Fig 9) shows the stage of growth at which alfalfa grazing and hay are most efficient energy sources.

Hay will still be able to provide all the energy a resting horse needs as long as it is well made. Good grass can, however, be turned into poor quality hay. The longer the hay takes to dry, the more vitamin content is lost and the more leaf that is lost due to weathering. Legume hay has

Per cent dry matter and per cent digestible energy for alfalfa grazing and hay		
Alfalfa	Percent dry	Digestible energy
Grazed before flowering	21%	0.52 Mcal/kg
Grazed in full flower	25%	0.57 Mcal/kg
Hay made in early flowering	90%	2.18 Mcal/kg
Hay made in mid flowering	89%	2.04 Mcal/kg
Hay made in full flower	89%	1.92 Mcal/kg
Dried meal	92%	2.26 Mcal/kg

9 The energy values of alfalfa at different stages of growth

more leaves and is more difficult to dry than grass hay. Products such as HorseHage and other bagged grasses that rely on a cold fermentation in a sealed polythene bag to preserve the grass, have a higher digestible energy content than hay but without the variability through the season that occurs with grass. The product should state its average nutritional content on the label, because this will vary from source to source.

Fat as an Energy Source

Fat is a valuable energy source because it contains about 2.25 times as much energy per unit volume as carbohydrates. The whole process of converting that digestible energy to movement energy is also very efficient. It has been shown that in ponies the conversion of digestible energy from corn oil to net movement energy is 85 per cent efficient. The efficiency for a hay/grain energy source is only 60 per cent.

Including fat in the diet enables us to provide more energy without having to cut down the amount of roughage fed any further. As a general rule we should provide at least 1kg (2.2lb) of roughage per 100kg (220lb) bodyweight in order to maintain healthy digestive tract function, and this limits the amount of concentrate feed we can expect the horse to eat. Feeding 10 per cent of a concentrate mix as corn oil will actually increase the digestible energy content by about 15 per cent. It has also been suggested that when fat is fed long term, it encourages the muscles to use free fatty acids as their fuel for exercise rather than glycogen, and this is a stamina advantage.

PROTEINS

Proteins are often referred to as the building blocks of the body. It is certainly true that much of the mass of the body is mainly protein, because as any lover of a good steak knows, muscle is almost entirely protein. Tendons and ligaments rely on fibres of a protein called collagen for their strength, and there is even protein in bones. However, the building-block analogy can be overdone, because there are many vital proteins which are not structural. The haemoglobin in the blood is a protein, and the whole concept of immunity against disease is based on proteins called antibodies. Even the fluid component of blood is held inside the blood vessels, rather than escaping into the surrounding tissues, by the hydrostatic pressure of its protein content. So if a horse loses a great deal of protein due to disease, it will start to develop oedema as fluid escapes into the tissues.

The Role of Amino Acids

Proteins are in turn made up of building blocks that are called amino acids. Although there are many different proteins in the body, they are all constructed from different arrangements of only about twenty amino acids. Some of these are called essential amino acids because they have to be imported into the body in the diet, the other non-essential amino acids can be manufactured by the horse itself. Lysine and methionine are two of the essential amino acids, and they are sometimes also included in feed supplements in an attempt to prevent any problems occurring. Methionine is known to be a vital component of the bonds that hold the keratin molecules (which is a protein) firmly together in healthy horn. Lack of methionine can lead to poor quality horn, and feeding extra methionine can improve horn quality. As so often happens though, the amounts of methionine included in feed supplements are often too low to really make a difference – they are there so that they can be written about in the advertising blurb rather than as a therapeutic measure.

The Role of Proteins Through Life

The body structure is not built up once and for all as the horse grows. Even mature horses are continuously breaking down existing protein structures and replacing them with new. It is a dynamic situation. So even old horses need protein in their diet to supply their anabolic needs, and young growing animals need particularly high levels. The term 'anabolic' will probably be familiar because of the use of so-called anabolic steroid hormones to stimulate the body to make abnormal amounts of new muscle. These drugs have been abused, and used to provide instant muscle rather than building up muscle in response to lengthy training, and have featured in many doping cases involving both equine and human athletes.

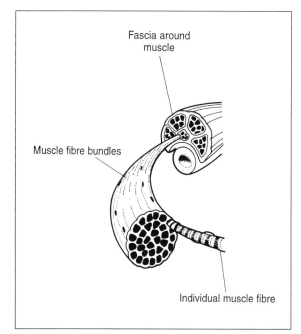

10 Cross-section of a muscle showing the muscle fibres

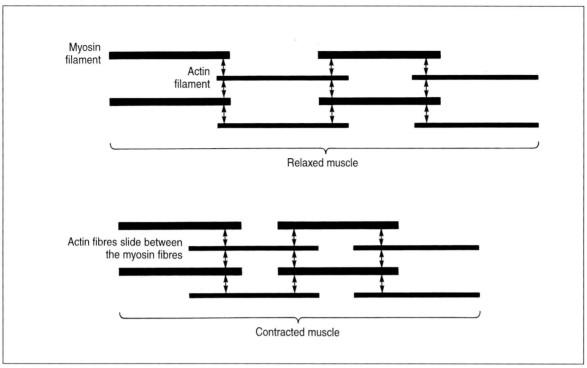

Myosin filament

Actin filament

Relaxed muscle

Actin fibres slide between the myosin fibres

Contracted muscle

11 What happens when a muscle contracts

The Structure of Muscles

It is important to understand a little about the structure of the muscles. When training increases the size of a horse's muscles, it does so by increasing the diameter of the muscle cells rather than by increasing their numbers (Fig 10). When a young horse's muscles increase in length as it grows, the number of muscle cells again remains the same, but each one is longer. The protein content of muscles is made up of two proteins, actin and myosin. Filaments of these inter-digitate with each other, and the muscle contracts by pulling them more closely in, and relaxes by letting them slide apart from each other (Fig 11). Very strenuous exercise invariably results in some muscle tearing and damage and even the initial fibrous repair of this requires protein. As time passes this fibrous tissue will be broken down again and replaced by actual muscle tissue.

Can the Horse Have Too Much Protein?

It is possible to have too much of a good thing, and to feed too much protein. This is very wasteful, both because proteins tend to be expensive

components of a diet, and because protein cannot be stored at all for later use. So any excess is just broken down in the body, and the nitrogen – which is the key part of all amino acids and proteins – is excreted via the kidneys. During this process some energy will be released, but when an equation is drawn up that includes the cost of feed protein, the amount of energy that is obtained when it is broken down, and the amount of energy which is required to break down and eliminate the nitrogen from the body, the balance is only just in profit, if at all. In some circumstances the horse will break down its own muscle tissue to produce energy, relying on its food to replace that protein quickly. If it is unable to do so, it will rapidly lose weight.

Owners often attribute all kinds of effects to too much protein in the diet, mainly because of the basic flaw of equating protein levels with a feed's energy content. So if a horse is lively and difficult to control whilst out riding, they will consider changing to a feed with a lower protein level, which in fact will have no effect unless (as is so often the case) it has a lower energy level, too. Some owners also have the idea that high protein levels cause skin problems, especially sweet itch or other allergic-type reactions. Again, lowering the protein level will have no effect on such problems. Excess protein in the diet has no visible effect at all on an adult horse, although in young animals high protein diets have been associated with leg deformities. But even this is probably not due to the protein but to the high levels of minerals such as calcium and phosphorus which many protein sources also contain.

At one time human shot putters and the like used to consume enormous quantities of meat, and this led to the idea that horses in strenuous work needed high protein diets. It is, after all, easy to suggest that whilst building up its muscles during training there will be an extra protein requirement, and it would be understandable if there was also a protein requirement to replace muscle tissues broken down or damaged during that exercise.

In fact a horse performing strenuous exercise will automatically be fed more protein because it is fed more food. If a horse is receiving a diet with 7.7 per cent protein, which as shown in the chart (Fig 12) has been suggested to be sufficient for an adult horse, then increasing its daily feed consumption from 8.5kg (18lb) at rest to 15.5kg (35lb) in work will automatically increase the protein supplied from 655g (23oz) to 1,194g (42oz). Of course, there may be a protein loss as a result of exercise because of the protein content in sweat, and there will be some protein required to build up muscle in the early stages of training, especially in young horses; but a diet containing 7.7–8 per cent protein is sufficient. Indeed, diets with protein levels as low as 5.5 per cent may be sufficient if the protein is of sufficient quality, ie contains good levels of the essential amino acids.

Most feeds already contain protein levels in excess of the working horse's requirements. Good hay will contain 7 per cent protein, corn will provide 9.6 per cent protein and oats and barley 11–14 per cent. So protein supplements are not necessary. One of the problems associated with protein, though, is that quality and digestibility appear to be linked. The highly digestible leaf part of grass, for example, has a higher protein quality than the far less digestible grass stems. If a diet is being balanced to compensate for using a feed with poor quality protein, the amounts will have to be further increased to offset the poor digestibility of that protein.

Hay is an important source of protein for all horses that are stabled, although the protein levels will vary enormously. As with energy levels, there is a distinction between legume and grass hays. Legume hay often provides too much protein for mature animals, with the result that they end up urinating more as they excrete the nitrogen remaining after the protein has been broken down. Young growing horses and mares with foals can make full use of the protein though. Because the protein levels of grass hay can be as low as 2 per cent, concentrate diets may contain specific protein-rich feedstuffs. The accompanying chart (Fig 13) shows their protein levels and the relative quality of that protein (as measured by the percentage of the essential amino acid lysine that they contain).

Protein requirements of different types of horse as a percentage of their total diet	
Type of horse	Protein requirement
Mare in late pregnancy	10.0%
Lactating mare	12.5%
6-month-old weaned foal	16%
Yearling	14.5%
Two-year-old	12.0%
Adult horse, not in work	7.7%
Adult horse in work	7.7%

12 The protein requirements of different types of horse as a percentage of their diet

The protein quality of some common feedstuffs		
Feed	Percentage protein	Percentage of protein as lysine
Alfalfa hay	14%	5.6%
Alfalfa meal	18%	5.0%
Brewers grains	27%	3.3%
Fish meal	72%	7.9%
Linseed meal	33%	3.6%
Dried skimmed milk	33%	7.8%
Soybean meal	48%	6.7%

13 The protein and lysine levels of some common feedstuffs

FEED SUPPLEMENTS

The Role of Minerals

Minerals such as calcium, iron, zinc and selenium may only make up 4 per cent of the horse's weight, but they are vital for many aspects of its life. Most of these minerals are obtained from plant material, which in turn means that the horse's supply will depend upon the mineral content of the soil in which those plants grow. It is important to realise that a horse can become deficient in a mineral whilst living in a 'safe' area simply because so much of its diet consists of hay, for example, which might have been grown in a mineral-deficient area.

The mineral levels in soil change, too. For example, acid rain will lower the pH of soils, and this results in copper being washed out of the soil. Aluminium, on the other hand, is much more available to animals in such conditions. Also, the levels of one mineral in the diet can affect the availability of many other nutrients. The amount of calcium in the diet, for example, affects phosphorus, magnesium, zinc and copper availability, but those very calcium levels will in turn have been influenced by iron levels, and in a reverse way by phosphorus and magnesium levels. It is not only minerals that are involved, either. Calcium absorption by the horse's gut is affected by some dietary proteins, amino acids, carbohydrates, oxalates, phytates and vitamin D.

The horse's body does its best to maintain constant levels of minerals where they are needed, no matter what levels are present in the feed. As a result, blood levels of some minerals remain surprisingly constant in what might be considered difficult conditions. For example, blood calcium levels will not initially be affected by high or low calcium diets because calcium can be stored or mobilised from the bones. However, a high phosphorus diet will cause a drop in blood calcium. Interestingly, feeding a horse high levels of copper or zinc produces little increase in their blood levels, but feeding a diet deficient in zinc or magnesium causes a very marked drop in blood

levels. The horse can cope with too much better than it can too little.

So it can be very difficult to assess mineral levels accurately in horses. Blood levels, as with calcium, may not reflect the true situation, and in any case the samples may be easily contaminated. The rubber stoppers on some blood tubes, for example, can cause high zinc levels just from contact with the blood. At one time it was suggested that hair analysis could reveal a horse's mineral status. We now know that this is not so. Coloured hair, for example, will contain three or four times the amount of calcium or magnesium than will white hair from the same horse.

Calcium and Phosphorus

When a horse's body is literally burnt away to ash, more than 70 per cent of that ash will be calcium and phosphorus. These two minerals are so closely linked with each other in the body that they will be considered in tandem. Bone contains more than 99 per cent of the body's calcium and 80 per cent of its phosphorus. The bone crystals have a calcium:phosphorus ratio of about 2:1. However, the two minerals have many other vital functions: calcium is involved in blood clotting, the transmission of nerve impulses, the contraction of muscles and the secretion of many hormones, each of which function is absolutely crucial. Phosphorus is present in many structural proteins in the body, and is involved with many enzyme systems as phosphate, for example adenosine triphosphate.

Young horses obviously need calcium and phosphorus for bone formation. Mares need these minerals during the last quarter of pregnancy for their growing foal, and then after foaling for milk production. However, too much calcium and phosphorus in food must be avoided because high calcium intakes will slow down the normal turnover of bone that occurs in the skeleton, and high phosphorus intakes will reduce the absorption of calcium.

The calcium and phosphorus of roughage seems to be particularly well absorbed by the horse. Indeed, hay will provide more calcium than cereals, especially legume hay. Cereals generally are poor providers of calcium but reasonably good providers of phosphorus. Specific calcium and phosphorus supplements are often fed, and their values are show in Fig 14.

Signs of calcium deficiency may not be due to a simple lack of calcium in the diet. Substances such as phytates in wheat bran and oxalate in some grasses bind calcium to themselves and prevent its absorption in the small intestine; by the time the calcium is released again in the large intestine, it is too late for it to be absorbed. Because the signs of calcium deficiency so commonly affect the horse's skeleton, the young racehorse is particularly susceptible to problems. The walls of the major long bones in the legs may become thin and fragile. Particularly worrying is the fact that more than half the skeleton's mineral may be used up in maintaining calcium levels in the body before obvious disease is noticed; the horse even continues to grow at almost a normal rate. Ultimately, however, the weakness is manifested by the skeleton becoming accident-prone, which means time lost from training.

A horse which is deficient in phosphorus, on the other hand, fails to grow properly, possibly because it only has a poor appetite. Such horses may well be lame as well. Diagnosis of calcium or phosphorus deficiency can be difficult. 30 per cent of the body's calcium has to have been lost before x-rays will show any changes in the bones, although phosphorus may be detected from circulating blood levels.

The Role of Magnesium

Magnesium has some links with calcium and potassium. It is also very involved in the chemical reactions that take place during energy production. Although magnesium deficiency does not occur naturally in the horse, there is a condition called transit tetany which is in part associated with the need of some horses to receive extra magnesium. The condition shows itself by sweating, muscle twitching, ataxia and even death, and is brought on by stress such as long journeys. Treatment consists of intravenous infusions of both calcium and magnesium, but prevention can sometimes be achieved in susceptible horses by feeding extra magnesium. The normal magnesium requirements are about 0.1 per cent of the diet, ie about 5–6g/day for an average 450kg (1,000lb) horse. Hay (especially legume hay) and most good protein sources give good levels of magnesium. Cereals are again a poor feed source.

Vital Salts for Life

At school we learn that salt is sodium chloride. As far as the horse is concerned, although **sodium** and **chloride** exist and function as separate ions within the body, their functions are very closely related. Sodium on its own is vital for maintaining the stability of the cell wall membranes, and in the transmission of impulses along the nerves. Sodium and chloride are a vital part of the control of fluid movement from the bloodstream to the extra-cellular fluid to the intra-cellular fluid. Sodium levels in urine and faeces can give a crude

Calcium and phosporus levels in horse feeds				
Supplement	Percentage calcium	Percentage phosphorus	% Calcium absorbed	% Phosphorus absorbed
Bonemeal	30%	13.3%	71%	46%
Monosodium phosphate	0%	23.3%	-	47%
Limestone	33%	0%	67%	-
Maize	0.13%	60%	-	38%
Wheat bran	0.4%	1.13%	-	34%
Timothy hay	1.3%	0.2%	70%	42%
Alfalfa	-	0.27%	77%	38%

14 The calcium and phosphorus values of certain supplements

indication of body levels, but a creatine clearance test is more reliable. This looks at the level of sodium and other electrolytes in blood and compares them to the levels in urine, having compensated for any individual variation by correcting them with reference to what has happened to the inactive substance creatine.

Horses know when they really need salt. Routine requirements will always be met if the horse has access to a salt lick, or even to loose salt. Iodised mineral salt is perfectly suitable for horses. Left to their own devices, horses will eat about 10–75g (0.3–2.5oz) salt per day, although the amount eaten by each individual horse might vary from 15g (0.5oz) to over 200g (7oz). Although the horse seems able to control sodium levels in its body so accurately by altering its intake, excesses can occur if the horse has free access to salt but only limited access to water. The symptoms of such salt poisoning include colic, diarrhoea and hind-leg weakness. Horses which compete in hot conditions but are not allowed to re-hydrate are at risk.

Potassium is very often linked with sodium. However, most of the body's potassium is inside cells, where it has a role in muscle contraction and in the passage of foodstuffs into the cell. The horse needs about 0.5 per cent of its diet to be potassium. Because forage contains around 1.5 per cent potassium, the grazing horse has no problems. The competition horse that is on a high cereal diet may have problems, however, because cereals may contain less than 0.4 per cent potassium. Endurance events in particular may cause problems. Loss of appetite is one symptom of potassium deficiency which might be particularly serious in a horse expected to recover after the competition.

Horses in really hard work will require 125g (4.4oz) of sodium, 75g (2.6oz) potassium and 17g (0.6oz) chloride daily. If they are being given diuretics to help control lung haemorrhage, they will need more than this because the extra urine they produce will remove more of the electrolytes. The electrolytes can be given in feed or water. As potassium tends to be only necessary on a very low roughage diet, salt is an acceptable electrolyte supplement, and certainly cheaper than many commercial supplements that are salt-based anyway. A 30g (1oz) salt supplement is worth considering for all horses in strenuous work. This has to be introduced gradually, though, or the horse may not eat or drink as much as normal.

Electrolytes cannot be stored in the body, so it has to be a case of replacement rather than prevention. There is, however, a suggestion that giving a horse a high-fibre meal with electrolytes prior to strenuous exercise does produce a short-term electrolyte reservoir in the gut rather than in the body tissues.

Iron and Anaemia

Many people know that iron is a vital part of haemoglobin, the complex molecule which has the ability to carry oxygen around the body and to swap it for carbon dioxide when the tissues have a low oxygen but high carbon dioxide level. Fewer people realise that iron is also a vital part of a substance called myoglobin in muscle, and of some enzymes involved in respiration.

If an animal is deficient in iron it becomes anaemic. That may mean that it has fewer red blood cells, smaller red blood cells, less haemoglobin per red blood cell, or even all three. Anaemic horses are weak and tire easily because the lack of haemoglobin means that tissues cannot get enough oxygen. In the horse, the mucous membranes around the eyes, lips and so on may not appear pale in anaemia because the large store of red blood cells normally held in the horse's spleen can be pushed out into the general circulation if the horse does become anaemic. So it is not possible just to look at those membranes and say that a horse is anaemic. Such a diagnosis can only come from having a blood sample tested for the number of red blood cells present and their haemoglobin content. Even then it is important that the sample is taken from a quiet, resting horse, because just the excitement of eating can cause the horse's spleen to contract and squeeze more red blood cells into the circulation, thus giving an artificially high result.

The body takes good care of its iron. Little of it escapes into the urine or faeces. An adult horse only needs about 40 parts per million (ppm) in its diet, and this is easily obtained from good quality feeds. Iron deficiency due to a lack of intake is very rare in horses. Apart from other sources, horses invariably take in some soil when grazing and this has a high iron content. Chronic worm problems can result in sufficient blood loss to result in anaemia, and some infections (such as equine infectious anaemia) can also result in anaemia.

Giving iron supplements to horses which do not have a clinical iron deficiency is of no value. There is no correlation between the amount of iron fed and the amount of haemoglobin or red blood cells manufactured. Indeed it is possible that giving too much iron may interfere with phosphorus intake. If iron supplements are needed, then ferrous iron salts are more effective than ferric salts. Contrary to some manufacturer advertisements, chelated iron is not absorbed any more readily than iron in feedstuffs or simple iron salts. The basic message, though, is that iron tonics or haematinics are usually a waste of time and money. The horse does not need them.

Mineral Deficiencies

■ Copper

Copper has a role in the process by which iron is incorporated into haemoglobin, and in ensuring the proper development of red blood cells. This role in the horse's blood is often not appreciated. Copper is also a vital part of certain enzymes, including those involved in the production of collagen and elastin, which are an essential part of tendons. Copper deficiency can occur in two ways: the horse may simply not get enough copper in its food, or the food may contain too high a level of molybdenum, which prevents the absorption of the copper which is present. High zinc intake can also affect copper levels. This has been shown to occur in foals, with the result that they develop osteochondrosis in their joints. The important point about this disease is that although the damage occurs during the first year of life, the lameness does not appear until the horse is put into hard work for the first time, for example prior to competition.

Adult horses need around 3.5ppm of copper in their diet, although young horses may require three times that amount. There is much dispute at the present time about what the normal copper levels should be in the horse's blood. Deficiencies have occurred on both molybdenum-high and copper-low soils. The coats of affected animals go grey, and they become anaemic.

■ Zinc

Straightforward zinc deficiency has not been reported in the horse, although the mineral is an essential part of many enzymes. Too much zinc, on the other hand, can be toxic because it interferes with copper metabolism and causes the symptoms of copper deficiency. The horse's zinc requirements vary from 40–100ppm, depending on whether high levels of calcium, copper and phytin (found in cereals and soybeans) are present to reduce its absorption. Good quality roughage will certainly supply enough zinc, as will trace-mineralised salt.

■ Cobalt

Cobalt is an important part of the vitamin B_{12} molecule, of which more later. It is interesting that although the horse therefore needs cobalt, neither deficiency nor toxicity has ever been reported. Indeed horses appear to be able to graze safely cobalt-deficient pastures that would cause clinical disease in cattle and sheep; dietary levels of 0.1ppm are thought to be adequate.

■ Iodine

Iodine is mainly incorporated in the thyroid hormone thyroxine. Problems can occur both as a result of deficiency of iodine in the soil or plants, and as a result of substances called goitrogens that affect the thyroid glands and are found in members of the cabbage family as well as in linseed, soybeans and peanuts. Iodine deficiency results in an enlargement of the thyroid gland (goitre) but decreased thyroxine production. Breeding mares that are affected have irregular oestrus periods and prolonged pregnancies. Their foals may be stillborn or weak.

It is more usual to test a horse for evidence of thyroid function by measuring thyroxine[4] levels in the blood than to measure iodine levels *per se*. The horse needs 0.1ppm of iodine in its feed. If there is any doubt, then the use of iodised salt will prevent a deficiency occurring. Feeding kelp can result in too much iodine, and then goitre.

■ Selenium

Selenium is an anti-oxidant, or rather it is a component of an enzyme that is a tissue anti-oxidant. It shares its anti-oxidant role with the sulphur-containing amino acids and with vitamin E; when any one of these is in short supply, the others can often replace it. Selenium-deficient soils are relatively common in the USA, and both forage and cereals grown on these soils are low in selenium. Horses living in these areas need to be fed food grown elsewhere.

Selenium deficiency affects the muscles, causing a condition known as white muscle disease. It is particularly serious in foals, which become weak, have difficulty in walking, and tremble. The affected muscles themselves become swollen and hard. Death may occur if the heart muscles are affected. The name 'white muscle disease' stems from the fact that *post mortem* the muscles are white rather than red. Treatment consists of selenium injections.

Horses need 0.1ppm of selenium in their diet. It may be worthwhile giving pregnant or suckling mares 1mg per day of selenium to help the foal. Soybean meal, linseed meal and alfalfa are good selenium sources. Horses that suffer from exertion rhabdomyelosis, or azoturia, may benefit from selenium supplements, although no precise link has been shown with the condition.

Selenium toxicity can also occur, usually as a result of giving too much selenium supplementation, although there are selenium-rich soils that cause problems. In the chronic disease the horse develops laminitis, it may lose the hair from its mane and tail, and the hooves may slough right off. More acutely the disease is called blind staggers or alkali disease, and horses do become blind and ataxic, or even paralysed.

What Are Vitamins?

Vitamins are organic compounds that are required in very small amounts for the horse's metabolism. In the horse, unlike man, many vitamins can be synthesised in the body, and so these are not an essential part of the diet. Ascorbic acid, or vitamin C, is produced in such quantities in the horse's liver that even deficient feeds can be compensated for. The bacteria in the horse's caecum and colon also produce vitamins, especially the B group, in large quantities. The tendency for each vitamin to be identified by both a single letter and by a full name can be confusing, and lead people to think that there are more vitamins than there actually are. Vitamins are divided into two groups: those that are soluble in fat, and those that are water soluble. The fat-soluble vitamins are A, D, E and K; the water-soluble vitamins are B and C.

■ Vitamin A

Vitamin A has a number of roles in the body: it is concerned with sight, with skin cells, with bone development and with reproduction; the underlying factor is that it is involved in the development and specialisation of new cells. So when there is a vitamin A deficiency the new cells that are formed are very basic, and have reduced resistance to infection. This is especially so for the surface epithelial cells that line all the tubes of the body, such as the respiratory system, the urinary system and the reproductive system.

Vitamin A deficiency results in a slowing of bone growth. At the same time there is also a reduction in the amount of bone that is reabsorbed – a process which normally goes on all the time and which in the adult horse has to match the rate of new bone growth, but which in a youngster does not do so, with the result that their bones increase in size. Deficiency can occur when diets are low in carotene from green foods. Young horses show symptoms reasonably quickly, failing to grow as fast as normal because of the effects on bone. Adult horses take a long time before symptoms appear: vision is affected, especially at night; mares fail to conceive and stallions lose their sexual urge. If too much vitamin A is fed, it is stored in the liver. This can be toxic and result in weak bones that fracture easily. Vitamin A levels in the blood can be measured quite accurately.

Vitamin A is not present in the diet as the vitamin itself but as a substance called provitamin A that can be converted by the horse into the vitamin. Carotene, for example, is converted into vitamin A in the liver, the body fat (an example of why the classification of vitamins as either fat- or water-soluble has practical implications) and the gut wall. There is a great deal of carotene in green feeds, but it is not very stable; much of it is lost in hay-making, around 90 per cent just by making the hay, and up to three-quarters of that remaining by even six months of storage. The practice of feeding over-wintered hays therefore ensures that it has little or no carotene. Legume hay has more carotene than grass hay, and as a general rule the greener the hay looks, the higher its carotene content. Out of the cereals only corn contains any carotene, and then only low levels.

Mature horses need about 25 international units (IU) of vitamin A per kilogram of bodyweight. This means that a 500kg (1,100lb) horse needs 12,500 IU of vitamin A, which in turn will require a daily intake of 30–40mg of carotene. If a horse has not had access to grazing for several months, extra vitamin A should be fed. Because vitamin A is rather unstable, commercial supplements may not actually realise the levels on their labels, especially if they originate from fish oils.

Horse owners usually fail to appreciate how delicate vitamins are. They leave bottles of vitamin supplements lying around in the sun, or just lying around for months on end, and expect them still to have their stated vitamin contents. Such supplements must be bought fresh (and check that they have not been stored for a long period by the merchant) and used fresh; they are definitely not a thing to buy in bulk for long-term use.

■ The B Group of Vitamins

Vitamin B$_1$ is thiamine; it is concerned with energy metabolism, especially the safe aerobic production of energy. Lack of thiamine results in the accumulation of lactic acid in tissues such as muscles, which is very undesirable. Deficient horses go off their food and lose weight, and they lack muscle strength. Both bracken and horsetail (Fig 15) contain a thiaminase enzyme which destroys thiamine, so grazing pastures containing these plants (or hay containing them) can be dangerous. The horse normally needs around 15–20mg of thiamine per day, but horses in strenuous work will need more than this. Thiamine is plentiful in most horse feeds, especially cereals. It may be lost during the production of poor quality hay, though. Brewers' yeast is a good source of thiamine for supplementing horses in strong work.

Vitamin B$_2$ is riboflavin. It is mostly concerned with the eyes, although it can affect how well feeds are utilised in the horse's body. Horses require around 2–2.5mg per kilogram of feed, which can be plentifully obtained from good hay. Yeast is a good source of riboflavin, but cereals are not.

Vitamin B$_{12}$ actually refers to a group of substances. In the horse it is vital for the utilisation of propionic acid, produced by the bacteria of the large colon. Propionic acid is a valuable energy source. Horses never become deficient in vitamin B$_{12}$ because they can always manufacture their needs in the large colon, or rather bacteria will manufacture it for them. Under normal conditions, therefore, horses do not need any vitamin B$_{12}$ in their diet – yet to read the labels on some feed supplements and tonics, you would think that it was the most vital of vitamins in the

15 Horsetail is dangerous to horses because it contains a thiaminase enzyme which destroys thiamine

diet! This is due to the fact that in human beings it *is* important, and can cause deficiency diseases which are not, however, found in the horse.

■ Vitamin C

Vitamin C is ascorbic acid, and it is important for the manufacture of collagen. Horses manufacture all the ascorbic acid they need, mainly in the liver; indeed, even if they are fed diets artificially free of the vitamin they will still excrete excess in their urine. Horses suffering from respiratory virus problems and those suffering from loss of performance may have low blood levels of vitamin C because the vitamin may be involved in the immune response to viruses and may also affect natural cortisol production. 20g (0.7oz) per day of ascorbic acid given in the feed will raise the blood levels. Vitamin C is not included in manufactured feeds due to its instability.

■ Vitamin D

Vitamin D helps to control the blood calcium levels by balancing the amount of calcium which is absorbed from the gut, the amount which is released by destroying bone, and the amount which is excreted in the urine. Vitamin D_2 is ergocalciferol, and is found in plants that have been sun-dried, such as hay; one kilogram of hay may contain up to 3,000 IU of vitamin D_2. Vitamin D_3 is cholecalciferol, and is made in the horse's skin when it is exposed to sunlight. Either source of vitamin D is effective.

Vitamin D deficiency causes rickets in young animals because the new bone is weak and easily deformed, but classic rickets does not appear to occur naturally in the horse. It is possible to have too much vitamin D: in the long term this leads to calcium being deposited in the walls of blood vessels, the lungs and so on – there are some plants, including yellow oat grass and day-blooming jasmine, that increase vitamin D activity sufficiently to cause such toxicity. Horses need 3,300 IU of vitamin D per day for a 500kg (1,100lb) horse; supplies manufactured by the skin and obtained from hay are usually sufficient to meet this. There is no value in supplementing vitamin D to compensate for calcium and phosphorus problems, and care must be taken with any supplement not to exceed the total daily requirement. Fish oils are good sources of vitamin D_3, and yeast is a good source of vitamin D_2. Cereals have little vitamin D.

■ Vitamin E

Vitamin E is an anti-oxidant; it stabilises the cell walls by preventing their destruction by oxidation. It has been associated with reproductive and muscular problems, but it is not a simple relationship because other anti-oxidants such as selenium are also involved. Some horses that are susceptible to azoturia appear to benefit from vitamin E, and it has been claimed to improve performance in endurance horses, but there is no real evidence of this. Recommended levels in the feed have been increased because of a suggestion that it is involved in the immune system's response to viruses. Cereals and green forage (including hay) are excellent sources of vitamin E, although processing of feeds tends to destroy it. Alfalfa is a good source, a point worth remembering because its mineral content makes it useful in the prevention of azoturia as well. It is even possible to manufacture vitamin E artificially.

■ Vitamin K

Vitamin K is involved in blood clotting. It is found in green forage, such as hay. It has been used in an attempt to stop exercise-induced pulmonary haemorrhage (EIPH), but toxicity can occur.

■ Folic Acid

Folic acid affects the manufacture of red blood cells. The vitamin is normally found in grazing, especially legumes, so deficiency is most likely in stabled horses. Deficient horses have a low red blood cell count and so are anaemic. Feeding folic acid to them is the only situation where it has been proved that a supplement can increase the rate of red blood cell formation. Good quality legume hay will provide some folic acid for stabled horses, although much of it is lost during drying. A supplement is preferable. Absorption of folic acid is poor, so high levels need to be fed, ideally 200–500mg per day, which is much higher than the levels usually included in feed supplements.

■ Biotin

Biotin is sometimes included in supplements to improve horn quality. The scientific evidence that this actually occurs is limited, one of the difficulties being that the horn formed one day will not reach the weight-bearing part of the hoof wall for another six months or so, during which time many other influences will have come and gone.

FEEDING FOR PERFORMANCE

The quality of the food which we purchase for a competition horse has the potential to affect its performance as well as its general well-being. It will certainly affect us financially. Everybody wants value for money in both financial and nutritional terms, but it is certainly not just a case of buying the most expensive feedstuffs that are available and hoping that they *are* the best.

Assessing General Food Quality

Assessing the quality of concentrate feeds just by appearance is fraught with difficulty. Small variations can make a significant difference to the horse's overall nutritional intake. It is sometimes said that cleanliness is next to godliness, and certainly a clean, bright-looking sample often indicates that at least the foodstuff has been stored well and so will not have lost excessive amounts of its vitamin and other contents. Cereal grains should be plump and starchy. Flaked cereals should therefore consist of large flakes rather than small or fragmented ones. This also applies to bran. It is all too easy to make a coarse mix look and feel attractive by the addition of more molasses, whereas we are buying it for the nutritional value of the other contents.

Analysing the Nutritional Value of Feeds

The nutritional analysis of feedstuffs can be carried out in a variety of ways. We are interested in an assessment of its value as an energy source, and the digestible energy (DE) may be expressed in megacalories (Mcal) or in megajoules (Mj). The analysis should also include a fat level; as discussed earlier, fat is a very concentrated and valuable source of easily accessible energy.

There are a number of ways in which the protein levels of feeds can be expressed. The percentage fibre gives an indication of protein level, but the most useful criterion is the percentage of digestible crude protein. In some cases an attempt is made to measure the quality of the protein by giving a percentage content of lysine, an amino acid which is important to the horse, especially youngstock.

In some cases the levels of individual minerals in a foodstuff are given; in others only an indication of the amount of ash that would be obtained by burning the feed is given. Such ash consists mainly of the mineral content, and calcium and phosphorus usually make up 70 per cent of it. The vitamin levels given for manufactured feedstuffs usually represent minimum levels obtained by adding a vitamin supplement during manufacture, rather than a precise value obtained by analysing the foodstuff.

Concentrate Feeds

There are three types of concentrate feed: horse cubes, coarse mix and individual feedstuffs mixed by the owner. Cubes are often less wasteful than other feeds because a horse generally considers that a single cube dropped on the floor is worth picking up and eating but a single grain of barley is not. Cubes generally take up less storage space. They also take up less space in the horse's abdomen, so it may look less fat. Cubes avoid the problem of a horse sorting through its food, eating only what it fancies and leaving the rest; this can be particularly worrying when a horse is in really strenuous work and is having difficulty in eating enough food anyway to fulfil its energy requirements. On the other hand, because cubes can be eaten quickly they may leave the horse with more time in which to feel bored. There is also an often expressed fear that the feed manufacturer might use poor quality or unnatural ingredients in horse cubes, where the contents cannot be identified by eye.

The First Commandment of Feeding

The secret of good feeding is to weigh everything. There are a few lucky, experienced individuals who can weigh by eye, but they are rare indeed. It is a salutary experience to estimate 2.2kg (5lb) of oats into a bucket and then to weigh it and see how accurate that estimate was. The feed room needs a good, accurate spring balance, and buckets which either all weigh the same or have their individual empty weight painted on them. Also, we must not forget to weigh the horse that the food is being fed to; as a weighbridge is rarely available, a weigh-tape will be quite adequate for this purpose.

Inexperienced horse keepers often fail to realise that different samples of the same foodstuff – for example, samples from different farms or merchants – will occupy different volumes for the same weight; so a level scoop of oats from one source will not weigh exactly the same as the same scoopful of oats from another source. What is potentially even more dangerous is the idea that a scoopful of one foodstuff weighs the same as a scoopful of another foodstuff and so can be interchanged. Rations must be worked out by weight and measured out by weight every day. A serious competition yard should never acknowledge the existence of a 'scoopful' as a measure.

Devising a Ration

When devising a horse's ration it is safe to feed concentrates to provide the energy for work, and hay to provide the overall maintenance. The energy levels of the commoner feedstuffs are shown in Fig 16. The average horse requires 5 Mj of energy for every hour's walking exercise, 10 Mj

Nutrient value of some common feed components

Feed	Digestible Energy Mcal/Kg	Crude Protein
Oats	3.2	13%
Barley	3.6	13%
Maize	3.8	10%
Beet pulp	2.8	9%
Molasses	3.4	7%
Bran	3.3	17%
Dried alfalfa	2.3	18%

16 The energy levels to be found in common feedstuffs

of energy for every thirty minutes of trotting exercise and 8.33 Mj of energy for every ten minutes of galloping, and the number of combinations which can provide such of these is legion (see Fig 17). Of course these are only a guide, rather than commandments written in stone. Basically we add up all the exercise undertaken in a day, find the total number of megajoules of energy needed, and then devise a suitable and available mixture to fulfil those requirements.

Supplying the energy needs of a working horse

Exercise	Energy requirement	Diet 1	Diet 2	Diet 3
1 hour walking	5 Mj	0.4 kg sugar beet	0.3kg maize	0.15kg maize + 0.2kg sugar beet
30 minutes trotting	10 Mj	0.75kg oats	0.5kg sugar beet + 0.25kg maize	0.52kg oats + 0.27kg bran
10 minutes galloping	8.33 Mj	0.5kg maize	0.6kg oats	0.2kg oats + 0.25kg sugar beet + 0.24kg bran

17 The different mixtures described will provide the same amount of energy for a given amount of exercise (1kg=2.2lb)

One aspect of feeding which is commonly overlooked is the timing of feeds in relation to exercise. The energy-providing feedstuffs are digested quite rapidly, resulting in a raised blood glucose level and a requirement for insulin production. Competition horses need to be fed in such a way that their blood glucose levels stay as constant during exercise as possible. Research has shown that concentrate feeds need to be given at least five hours before exercise to achieve this, so a horse which is going to perform in the morning needs its feed very early in the day. I do not envisage this particular piece of information being very popular with those who actually have to get up early to do the feeding!

When devising rations for a horse we must remember that although we can change the diet quickly, the horse will take time to adapt to any changes; the intestinal bacteria in particular will only adapt slowly, over 4–7 days, to a new diet. There is a great potential for triggering off colic in horses whenever we change their diet, so any dietary changes must be gradual, spread over several days. Furthermore, not only does the horse's digestive system expect the same amount of the same foodstuffs every day, it also expects them at the same time every day. Some competition yards are so disorganised that they cannot provide this bedrock of regularity in feeding; the result is at best inefficient feeding, and at worst lost performance and even colic. Feeding should take precedence over everything else when it comes to day-to-day management decisions.

Forage: The Foundation Stone of Feeding

The basis of all horse feeding must be a bulk feed such as hay or grass: unless the horse's digestive system has enough bulk passing through on a regular basis there will be problems such as colic. Furthermore, as the horse can only eat a certain amount of food in any one day, we must be careful not to increase the amount of concentrate food past the point where the horse's hay consumption has to be reduced below a minimum level. Horses consume 1–2 per cent of their bodyweight daily.

Harvesting a hay crop even two or three weeks early or late can reduce the digestible energy of the resulting forage by as much as a third. We traditionally expect meadow hay with its variety of plant species to be superior nutritionally to

seeded hay containing one species. However, against this we must set the fact that each species of plant will reach its maximum nutritional value at a slightly different stage of maturity, and so will reach that maturity on a different day from the others. So although alfalfa hay may potentially have a high digestible energy content, the time of its harvest is still critical compared with mixed hay.

Horses used for showjumping or dressage and working for two or three hours per day can maintain their bodyweight as long as they receive 8kg (17lb 10oz) of hay and 3kg (6lb 10oz) of oats per day. Racing training usually involves more intense work but over a shorter time; racehorses therefore need around 7–10kg (16–22lb) of hay and 8–10kg (18–22lb) of grain daily (see Fig 18).

Average daily diets fed at four American racetracks					
Type	Hay	Oats	Corn	Coarse mix	Bran
Standardbred	8.8 kg	4.4 kg	0.5 kg	1.8 kg	0.2 kg
Standardbred	8.3 kg	4.5 kg	0.5 kg	1.6 kg	0.2 kg
Thoroughbred	6.6 kg	6.2 kg		1.0 kg	0.5 kg
Thoroughbred	7.3 kg	5.8 kg		1.3 kg	0.5 kg

18 Comparative weights of hay and concentrates fed to racehorses and to Standardbred horses

Assessing Hay Quality

When assessing hay quality, first look at the outside of a number of bales for signs of discolouration due to moulds (Fig 19). This may show as an area of yellowing, perhaps with a white border. Then break open a bale to make sure that it is uniform right through, again without any colour changes towards the centre. At the same time, watch how much dust is thrown up into the air as a result of doing this. Lay out the dried grass stems and assess their quality. The aim is for leaf rather than stem or flowerhead; the stems should bend in your hands rather than break, and the colour should be well preserved. A range of grass species is usually better than just one, not least because this usually indicates that the hay came from a well established pasture rather than from a seeded (and possibly heavily artificially

19 Poor quality hay: the discolouration is due to mould

21a A microscopic view of the dust from good hay

20 Ragwort, highly dangerous to horses because it is poisonous even when dried

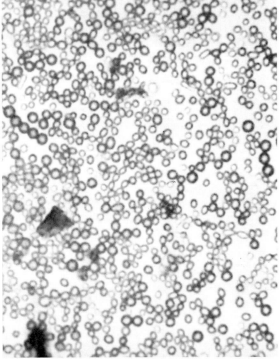

21b Slit-sample analysis of the dust from mouldy hay. Fungal spores obliterate almost everything else

fertilised) ley. There should be very few weeds such as thistles, docks, ragwort (Fig 20) or bracken; the last two can be poisonous even when dried. Finally it is a general rule that the heavier a bale is for its size, the better value it represents. This may be because of the amount of hay which has been compressed into the bale, or because the grass has not been over-dried and lost too much of its water content as a result. Loss of water also means loss of water-soluble vitamins.

The more hay one is buying in one transaction, the more desirable it is to have it assessed in a laboratory for its actual nutritional quality; this will ensure that any feeding calculations are based on fact rather than on hope. It is also possible to have a slit-sample analysis made of the dust that inevitably accompanies hay, in order to assess the number of fungal spores present (Fig 21b); there have been many instances where expensive hay of high nutritional value has also contained a high number of fungal spores, and so posed a definite health risk to any horse consuming it.

Assessing Pasture Quality

It is worth remembering that the water meadows and open grazing which we generally think of as being ideal grazing are not at all natural, but the result of quite intensive grazing by horses, sheep and cattle over the past centuries. However, we can benefit by looking at their advantageous features and investigate how to establish and encourage these in the rather poor quality paddocks that so many horses have to graze nowadays.

First is the density of the plants, or the number of stalks or leaves per square foot. This not only provides the potential for a relatively high yield of grass, but also a cushioning effect when the horse moves around the paddock. The close-knit root system helps in this, holding the soil together but in small amounts, rather than in the solid lumps that can otherwise develop in compacted clay soils. It takes decades, even centuries for such a root system to develop – but when new paddocks are laid down, so many owners make the mistake of grazing them too early with the result that the relatively widely disseminated young plants have their growth checked unfavourably by grazing and don't spread as well as they would otherwise do. In some paddocks the bare ground can still be seen between the grass plants even years after seeding

because of this impatience. Let the grazing establish itself properly before grazing it, especially on light sandy soils, because when the well spaced out plants are grazed right down the horse will tend to take in some of the soil as well and this can lead to sand colic, where the caecum becomes filled with sand. The other point to note is the diversity of the plant species growing in the good, well established pasture. This means that the grazing horse will take in herbs – a posh name for wild flowers and weeds – as well as grass. A variety of herb species is useful because they flower at different times through the year, and similarly reach peak nutritional value at different times. Therefore a pasture might contain significant quantities of a herb which reaches its peak nutritional value in April, rather than when the grasses reach their peak, and obviously this evens out the overall nutritional value of the grazing throughout the year.

Most herbs are broad-leaved, rather than narrow-leaved as are grasses. However, most of the undesirable weeds, such as nettles, are also broad-leaved, with the result that if the grazing is treated with weedkiller which is safe for grass but not for broad-leaved species, then the advantageous herbs will also be killed. So if you want to keep the herbs then you cannot use weedkillers. Where it has been necessary to use weedkillers, the general rule is that horses must be kept off the pasture for at least three weeks, or until there has been substantial rain, in order to reduce the risks of chemical poisoning.

The way to help herbs establish themselves and spread in a field is to mimic the effect of the continuous grazing that the old grasslands received. Thus frequent topping allows the sun to reach the often low-growing herbs, and encourages the grasses to spread outwards rather than upwards. Unfortunately neither weedkillers nor topping removes the dangers inherent in ragwort, which is just as poisonous when it is wilting or dried as it is when it is growing.

Certain herbs have been used medicinally over the centuries for both horses and people, and in a few cases these medicinal claims have been proved scientifically. However, I would make two points about using herbs to treat a horse's ailments: first, do not delay seeking veterinary advice just because someone recommends a herbal remedy. Treat with the remedy alongside any treatment your vet prescribes, but don't compromise the success of a treatment by start-

22 Endurance horses are trained to drink at every opportunity around the course to combat dehydration

ing it too late. Second, remember that in the past the herbs themselves were used, and not in concentrated form as in the products which are available today. Overdosage of any chemical can be dangerous, whether it comes from a veterinary drug or a plant. There is nothing inherently safe about using herbs – after all, there are a great many poisonous plants – so take care. The best 'herbal remedy' is a field of grass with as wide a variety of other plants as possible.

The Horse Must Drink

I have mentioned elsewhere the fallacy that horses in hard work require a high protein diet. It has been suggested that excess protein can increase heat production and decrease performance rather than the other way round. High protein levels will certainly increase the horse's water requirement because the extra nitrogen has to be got rid of via urine production. Besides the effects this water consumption may have on the horse's weight, we must be aware that failure to allow the horse sufficient opportunity to drink may result in a dehydrating effect, and in a toxic effect if the urine cannot be passed. Horses are naturally peri-prandial drinkers, a grand term meaning that they drink around their meal times. They have to be trained to drink at regular intervals during a long-distance ride or during the few hours before a competition (Fig 22).

Feeding while Travelling

Competition horses sometimes have to travel for quite long periods to and from events, and all too often little thought is given to the physical effects of travelling on their bodies, and particularly in relation to nutrition. During travelling the muscles are constantly in action, bracing the horse against the movement of the vehicle; but the lack of proper exercise means that the blood circulation removing the lactic acid produced is relatively low. A day spent travelling is therefore best followed by a period of trotting similar to the cooling-down period after strenuous exercise; this assists in removing the lactic acid and so helps to ensure the muscles are at their best for the competition that follows. There might be something to be said for a warming-up period to prepare the muscles for travelling as well. Hay should be available throughout the journey because it provides a source of energy for the muscle activity mentioned earlier, and also helps to maintain intestinal movement.

Horses are accustomed to drinking as they eat. It is obviously not possible to have a supply of water available whilst travelling, but the horse should be 'trained' to drink during the regular stops that should take place. About half a bucketful of water is sufficient on each occasion.

For international competitions a decision often has to be made whether to take large quantities of food from home, or whether to purchase supplies in the foreign country. The order of preference would be as follows:

1 Take your own concentrate and your own hay.
2 Find a foreign merchant who supplies concentrate which is similar in respect of nutritional values and ingredients used, and take your own hay.
3 Take your own concentrate and vacuum-packed grass or substitute fibre source to which the horse is acclimatised long before travelling.
4 Change over to foreign concentrate and roughage gradually during the acclimatisation period.

23 Competing at the top level in the world of eventing often involves lengthy journeys; care must be taken to ensure that the horse is properly fed, watered and cared for to reduce the effects of fatigue and stress

WHEN THINGS GO WRONG

Colic

When we eat something which disagrees with us, we get stomach ache, and the same applies to horses. However, because of the anatomy and function of the horse's digestive system, it also gets stomach ache from many other causes. Over the centuries a single word, colic, has come to be used in the horse to describe abdominal pain (or stomach ache) due to any cause. So colic is not an entity in itself, it is a symptom of pain – but one which may manifest itself in a number of ways.

■ The Symptoms of Colic

The classic way in which a horse shows that it has colic is by rolling on the ground, sometimes in an uncontrollable way. If the pain is less severe it may just keep looking round at its belly, or kick at its belly with its hind feet. It may also paw the ground, presumably as an indication that it is thinking of lying down and rolling. The abdominal pain may cause it to start sweating, either all over its body or just in patches. Not surprisingly it may be very disturbed by the whole experience, gazing all around or becoming aggressive; and indeed we should not expect a horse with colic to behave rationally. It may, for example, throw itself to the ground with no regard either for itself or for any human being around (Fig 24, p135).

■ The Dread of Colic

Although horses with colic may die, colic itself never kills a horse: the pain is never fatal. When death does occur, it is due to shock and related circulatory problems, the tissues of the affected lengths of bowel, and the bacteria in that section of the bowel, releasing substances called endotoxins into the bloodstream, and the endotoxins in turn triggering off the shock symptoms. At the same time, tissue fluid is withdrawn from the circulation and accumulates at the site of the problem. The result of all this is that horses with colic may have a raised heart rate; the normally pale-pink mucous membranes around the eyes may become bright red and congested; the temperature may be raised (although pain plays a part in causing this as well); and the respiratory rate may be increased.

■ How to Assess the Severity of Colic

In recent years a number of surveys have been carried out to find which symptoms are most valuable at telling us whether a horse with colic is really seriously ill and likely to die. The severity of the pain is not a reliable indicator of this at all. The most reliable indicator is something called the capillary refill time, which assesses the strength of the circulation and its ability to keep open small blood vessels. The capillary refill time is measured by pressing firmly onto the pink mucous membrane of the horse's gum with a finger or thumb. When the finger is released, the underlying gum is white: the capillary refill time is the time taken for that area to become pink again. Normally it is 1–2 seconds; if it is more than 4 seconds the severity of the endotoxic shock is such that death may occur.

Another indicator which owners can monitor is the horse's heart rate. This is not as reliable as the capillary refill time at forecasting the eventual outcome of colic, but it can help to indicate changes for good or ill along the way. The horse's normal heart rate is 40–50/minute. A heart rate consistently above 65/minute is a cause for some concern; and the nearer it gets to 100/minute, the more concerned we become. The problem with the heart rate is that it is as much affected by pain as anything else, and horses vary in how they respond to pain; so some will have a heart rate of 70–80/minute with a relatively mild colic. Nevertheless, a heart rate below 65–70/minute is always a good sign, and marked changes of heart rate (both up and down) during the progress of the condition are also usually significant.

A blood sample provides useful information

about the severity of the shock present during colic. By measuring the 'packed cell volume' (PCV) we can tell whether the horse has become effectively dehydrated, whether its blood is too thick to be pushed through the tiny capillaries without putting a great strain on the heart. A raised PCV is a bad sign, but at least it is a condition we can do something about, by administering fluids via an intravenous drip.

■ Different Types of Colic

There are a number of situations which can give rise to abdominal pain. Most of them stem from the 'design' of the horse's alimentary tract, which is a compromise between the simple system in man and the complicated system in cattle. The horse probably suffers more serious abdominal problems than almost any other animal.

The least serious type of colic is probably **spasmodic** colic. The horse has obvious pain for a period of perhaps 20–40 minutes, then appears normal again; but unfortunately the pain returns about the same period later. This type of colic is due to a disturbance in the nerve supply that controls bowel movement, resulting in a situation where the bowels are over-active but the movements are unco-ordinated. Something as insignificant as a low-flying aircraft frightening the horse can trigger off spasmodic colic.

Acute pain of longer duration is usually due to **physical damage or change**. Worm damage, for example, can result in recurrent episodes of colic over weeks or months. This might be because whilst migrating through blood vessels the *Strongylus vulgaris* worm has damaged the blood vessel's wall. A decrease in the blood-vessel diameter results in a decrease in the blood supply to the bowel, and if a section of bowel is short of oxygen it will be painful.

Impactions are blockages of the bowel. The blockage may possibly be due to worms, as happens with roundworms in youngsters and with tapeworms blocking the ileo-caecal junction in older horses. Most commonly, impactions are due to dry fibrous material blocking the tube and preventing further movement of faeces. Impactions may follow the ingestion of something very fibrous, for example the horse eating its straw bed; they may occur because the food wasn't chewed properly due to dental problems; or because of a dietary change. The latter is very much a specific horse problem: the bacteria in

the colon adapt to a particular blend of grass/hay/short food, and any change in the diet may result in the fibrous part of the diet not being digested. This alone may be enough to cause a blockage, but things are made worse when the colon bends back on itself through 180°, at the same time suddenly decreasing in diameter. It is probably true that poor stable management is the commonest cause of impactions.

Although some impactions cause acute pain, in the majority the pain seems to be more like a continuous low grade pain. As a result horses with impactions may just lie flat out on the ground, not rolling, but not standing up either. Perhaps surprisingly, this type of pain can be unresponsive to painkillers. We should not expect to make an initial diagnosis of an impaction solely on the basis that the horse has stopped passing faeces. Horses will continue to pass the faeces which are already behind the blockage, and this often acts as a red herring – the further forward the blockage, the greater the volume which might be passed before we notice that the horse is no longer defecating.

When the impaction has moved on, the signs of colic can stop very quickly. The length of time which will elapse before the horse passes faeces will depend on how much of the faeces behind the stoppage were actually evacuated. When normal bowel movement returns, the horse's appetite often returns with a vengeance.

Perhaps the most acute colic is that seen with problems of **displacement**. This is the type of colic sometimes referred to as a **'twist'** or as a **'twisted gut'**. In fact it is very rare for a section of the bowel just to twist around its longitudinal axis, rather like making a sausage; more commonly a section of bowel moves through a gap between two other structures, and pressure on the bowel wall reduces or stops the circulation to it. The result of the displacement is a length of bowel which is suffering a poor blood supply and trapped bowel contents, and unless something is done pretty quickly the bowel wall will die. Endotoxins are released from it, and in time from the trapped bowel contents.

■ First Aid for Colic

Once an owner recognises that his horse has abdominal pain, he or she will have to make a quick decision whether to summon veterinary help or not. I would suggest that the vet is called in the following circumstances:

- The pain is sufficiently great to cause the horse to roll repeatedly.
- Mild pain returns within a couple of hours after apparently ceasing.
- The horse either can't be persuaded to stand, or lies down again as soon as any stimulation stops.
- Even mild pain continues for more than an hour.
- The level of pain seems to be increasing.

Conversely it is not usually necessary to call the vet if:

- The only sign of pain is that the horse keeps looking at its flank.
- The horse occasionally stamps its foot or kicks at the abdominal wall.

When a horse's attention is distracted it will often stop showing the symptoms of colic, in the same way that we sometimes forget that we have toothache when we are busy but find that the pain returns with a vengeance when we lie in bed at night. As a result of this effect a tradition has developed of walking in hand horses which have colic. It is important to recognise that walking does nothing to affect the cause of the colic or to treat it: it merely produces a cosmetic effect where we no longer see the symptoms which make us feel concerned. As such there is a degree of danger in keeping horses with colic continuously on the move because it means that we no longer have any indication of the severity of the pain, or of how the pain is progressing. There have even been occasions when the horse has been kept walking for so long that its energy reserves have been compromised.

One of the reasons given for walking horses with colic is that by discouraging rolling it prevents a twisted gut developing. The evidence which we have indicates that such displacement colics are the *cause* of rolling rather than the result of it. In other words, a horse may have a displacement but will not start rolling until the affected section of bowel becomes severely compromised – it does not develop the displacement in addition to some other cause of colic that made it roll in the first place.

In some circumstances it may be desirable to stop a horse rolling because it is causing so much self-inflicted damage. If walking will achieve this whilst veterinary help is on its way, then that is fine; but you must always be aware of the danger of the horse causing more damage to itself if it rolls whilst out walking than it would if it rolled on a thick bed in its stable.

If a horse with mild colic will accept it, then feeding a warm bran mash may be helpful because it provides bulk in the gastrointestinal tract which encourages proper bowel movements. Do not attempt to give any proprietary colic drinks or other medicines forcibly by mouth as there is a very real danger of the liquid going into the trachea and lungs if the horse has a spasm of pain whilst you are drenching it with such a substance.

■ The Treatment of Colic

Treatment of colic aims to relieve pain, remove the cause and save life. In recent years there have been considerable advances in the development of painkillers. As more and more powerful drugs become available, though, it has become possible to mask the severity of the horse's condition too much. If this occurs, the realisation that the horse needs surgery to correct a displacement, for example, may not come until too late, when the bowel concerned is too toxic to recover. The drug flunixen in particular has been implicated in many of these cases where deterioration in the horse's condition was masked by the pain relief. It has been suggested that phenylbutazone is a more suitable painkiller for acute colic cases because it has less effect on the superficial signs such as heart rate. Once a precise diagnosis has been made, and a decision reached either to proceed to surgery or not, then it doesn't matter how powerful the painkiller is that is used. Although the choice of painkiller will obviously be made by the vet, owners pressing for complete relief of symptoms have been responsible for a vet choosing inappropriately powerful drugs. The more inexperienced the vet and the more demanding the owner, the greater this temptation is.

The shut-down of circulation to the bowel is probably the cause of most colic deaths. By infusing quite large volumes – 5–10 litres (1–2 gals) – of fluid into the horse's circulation we can both 'thin' the blood so that it passes through the small capillaries more easily, and increase its volume so that blood vessels have to stay open in order to accommodate all the fluid inside the body. Fluid therapy doesn't solve the cause of the colic, but it often provides a means of keeping the horse alive whilst either the horse itself or the vet deals with

24 Horses with colic can roll quite violently

that root cause. Because the fluid doesn't stay in the bloodstream for very long, fluid therapy may have to be continued for quite some time, keeping the horse stable until the crisis is over.

■ Colic Surgery

Physical displacements of the bowel, or twists, are dreaded by horse owners because in the past they have resulted in the death of so many horses. It is important to realise, though, that not every very painful colic is due to a twisted gut. When a definite diagnosis is made, a decision has to be made as to whether surgical correction of the displacement should be attempted. This is not last-ditch treatment – if it is to be carried out, then it should be started as early as possible, because the better the horse's condition at the time of surgery, the better its chances of recovery. Owners must be aware that if they delay giving their consent for surgery, they are increasing the risk if it is undertaken later on.

The success rate for colic surgery depends on many factors, but more than any other type of surgery it is affected by the surgical team which operates and carries out after-care. The overall

success rate of different clinics can vary tremendously. It would be wrong not to attempt surgery just because the clinic's success rate was only 25 per cent, because delays before surgery was attempted might be the cause of the low success rate. On the other hand, a success rate of 70 per cent must not be thought of as an open offer that provides a safe fall-back option no matter how long a decision is delayed. When surgery is carried out, one of the problems faced by the surgeon is whether the affected piece of bowel is viable or not. If it isn't, then it must be removed, and the two open ends of healthy bowel joined together. Unfortunately the appearance of the bowel is not a very accurate guide as to whether it can recover or not. Recently, however, it has become possible to measure the oxygen concentration in the tissues of affected bowel; if they are low, then no matter how well the bowel looks at the time, its chances of surviving are poor.

The complication most dreaded by surgeons is paralytic ileus. This is not a true paralysis of the bowel, but it refers to a condition where all movement along the bowel stops. If this happens, shock develops relatively quickly. The higher success rate of some clinics than others for colic surgery depends on details such as spotting paralytic ileus as soon as it occurs, and taking prompt action. It may be possible to restart bowel movement with a drug called cisapride, but failing that there is no alternative but to open up the horse's abdomen again and massage the bowels until peristalsis, or rhythmic movement, restarts.

The fact that at the time of writing, several years after its value was discovered, the drug cisapride still has not been put on the market for horses is one of the greatest scandals of the pharmaceutical industry. Extensive research has shown that its use can markedly improve survival rates for horses undergoing colic surgery, and that means that it reduces the horse's suffering. The company which owns the patent on the drug has decided that it isn't interested in marketing it, and won't allow anybody else to do so either. It is hard to justify such a decision on moral grounds, and it is to be hoped that eventually the decision will be reversed.

■ How to Prevent Colic

It is obviously better to prevent colic than to need to treat it, and a number of preventive measures should be in use all the time, not just when there is a horse which has a history of colic problems in the yard. First of all it is important that horses are fed **sufficient roughage**; there must be a sufficient volume of contents passing along the bowel, and only roughage can provide this. Restricting hay intake in an attempt to encourage the consumption of more concentrate feeds can therefore be dangerous. Second, **the food which is fed should be of good quality.** If the horse is fed hay of poor digestibility, for example, the chances of an impaction occurring are much increased. Third, **the horse should be fed at regular intervals**, and the value of a strict feeding routine cannot be overstated. The horse and its internal bacteria will have everything primed and ready for a meal, and if this arrives too soon or too late the complicated bowel movements, and secretion of digestive enzymes and so on, will not take place. The regularity of feeding good ingredients is one of the most important factors governing the incidence of colic in stable yards.

Regular dental checks help to ensure that food is chopped small enough before it is swallowed. Competition horses should have their teeth checked every six months, and from a performance point of view sometimes sooner. **Worming**

is the other major preventive measure for colic. The frequency of worming will depend on the product used, but the important thing is to avoid significant worm build-up on the pasture. Tapeworms, which have been associated with impactions, are not killed by routine worming and require a double dose of pyrantel to remove them.

It has been suggested that letting horses drink during exercise or soon after will cause colic. This is not true, and horses need to keep taking in fluid during stamina events – indeed, they should be trained to do so. Nor is drinking at feeding time likely to cause colic. Horses in the wild naturally drink before, during and after feeding, and the truth is that artificially withholding water and then allowing access to it by the bucketful is *more* likely to cause problems.

Equine insurance companies tend to tread carefully once a horse has had colic. Actually one attack of colic probably doesn't mean that the horse is any more likely to have a second attack. However, two bouts of colic within 12–18 months would indicate that there might be some predisposing factor present. Unfortunately when we buy a horse we are unlikely to receive an entirely honest answer to any enquiries about its past colic history, and so we may buy in a problem.

Weight Changes

Owners never seem to be satisfied with their horse's weight. They want to put weight on or take it off in order to achieve the ideal they have in their mind of what the horse should look like. Taking weight off a horse is relatively easy, as long as we remember to avoid the temptation to go for a sudden drastic weight loss; this can be dangerous because the sudden mobilisation of the fat reserves releases large quantities of triglycerides into the blood (which can literally become milky in appearance as a result) – the horse's metabolism can't cope with the overload and just stops. The safe way to reduce a horse's weight is to restrict it to a hay-only diet, and to continue to exercise it. The hay will provide all its maintenance requirements, and so the work involved in exercise will have to be fuelled from its fat reserves. Slowly increase the work until the desired weight is achieved. The basic guideline is that it should be possible to see where the horse's ribs end, but not to count the individual ribs. If a horse starts to lose weight whilst receiving a constant amount of food and exercise, veterinary help should be sought immediately.

Putting weight on a horse safely can also be quite a problem, because we want the weight to represent muscle rather than fat. First of all, do not be tempted to use anabolic steroids: it is doubtful if any mass gained as a result of their use really represents proper muscle, and after the horse's first, blindingly successful competition, the weight will just fall off again. Second, do not try and just fatten up the horse like a fat bullock: providing high-energy foods but low-energy exercise will result in a layer of fat under the skin, but no extra muscle. Feeding should always follow exercise, so increase the exercise (to build up the muscles) before increasing the feed.

Male sex hormone acts like a very efficient anabolic steroid, which is not really surprising because its molecules are very similar to those of such steroids. That is one of the reasons why, even in competitions for entire stallions, the use of artificially administered testosterone is banned. It is now possible to distinguish between male hormone levels that are natural and those that are artificial, the work into this problem having received an impetus from a notorious racing case where a horse was banned on the grounds that the hormone levels in its body had been artificially administered. The horse's owner was rich enough to sponsor work into the topic, in an attempt to clear his name. Synthetic female progesterone also has an anabolic effect. This can be significant because the drug can be used to manipulate a mare's oestrus cycle in order to prevent oestrus coinciding with competitions.

The Danger of Overfeeding

It is perhaps significant that two of the commonest diseases associated with incorrect feeding, azoturia and laminitis, are actually the result of overfeeding rather than the opposite. **Azoturia** is muscle damage that results from high muscle glycogen levels being broken down to lactic acid. Every day that a horse receives more high-energy food than it can burn at exercise means more glycogen stored away for possible problems later. So never feed concentrates to a horse which will not be exercised that day. Good hay will be quite sufficient food, allowing concentrates to be re-introduced after the horse starts work again.

Some horses seem to be particularly prone to attacks of azoturia. This may be because of an inherent instability of the walls of their muscle cells, but it may also be because of faulty stable management. Because of lack of attention or of ignorance, some owners repeatedly allow circumstances to occur that increase the risk of azoturia developing. Any owner of a horse which develops a second attack of azoturia should look in the first instance to their stable management for the cause, rather than to the horse.

Subclinical azoturia poses a particular problem for competition horses, who are often receiving relatively large quantities of concentrate feeds. An affected horse performs badly, but the owner does not suspect azoturia because the horse has been in regular work and is not thought to be receiving excessive quantities of high energy feeds. Typical symptoms would be that the horse sweats more readily with exercise than expected, or breathes faster after exercise. Blood sampling (Fig 25) confirms a diagnosis of azoturia by revealing high levels of the muscle enzymes creatine kinase (CK) and amino aspartate transferase (AST), even though the horse has not 'tied-up', had difficulty urinating, or manifested any of the other symptoms of typical azoturia. This is a situation where a knowledge of the horse's past CK and AST levels is invaluable in distinguishing a truly raised level from a level which is just slightly higher than average, or normal for that horse.

The electrolytes sodium, calcium and chloride are vital for returning the stability of the muscle cell wall in such cases, and there is something to be said for taking steps to ensure extra levels of these electrolytes even when there are no problems. Feeding alfalfa hay or dried alfalfa products can be helpful because of the high calcium levels they contain. Most competition horses will also benefit from receiving 25–50g (1–2oz) of ordinary salt per day. If subclinical azoturia develops, the levels of these supplements may need increasing until an electrolyte clearance test shows that normal stability has been reached that will allow the muscle cells to function normally.

Laminitis may be the response to over-enthusiastic attempts to increase a horse's weight by feeding. Large amounts of high-energy food lead to the release of gut toxins which affect circulation in the feet. Ponies especially can develop laminitis at grass, reminding us of the large amounts of soluble carbohydrates that grass can contain at certain times of the year.

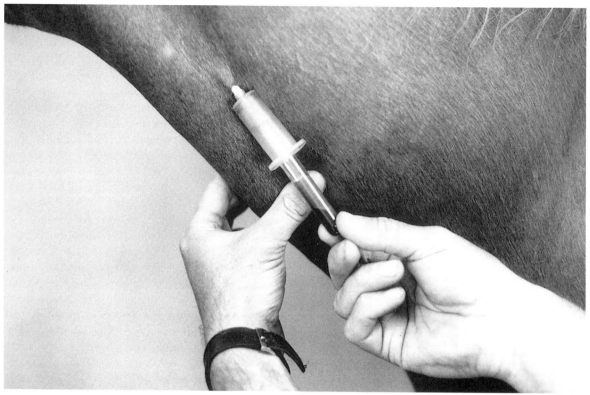

25 Taking a blood sample

It would be reassuring to think that laminitis due to overfeeding a high carbohydrate concentrate ration would not occur in competition horses because their handlers were relatively experienced. Unfortunately this is not the case, especially in the showing world where the judges want the horses to be fat, and so very often such a diet is considered to be essential. People seem to be completely blinkered when it comes to obesity; small animal vets consider obesity to be one of the commonest problems they have to deal with, and it is certainly an entrenched attitude in the showing world. Of course judges would deny this, but nonetheless they are unable to explain why a show horse has to be so much heavier and fatter than a successful racehorse, show jumper, eventer or endurance horse of the same height.

It is important that any horse on a high carbohydrate/fat diet is assessed daily for signs of laminitis, even if this only consists of observing how it moves at a brisk trot. One early symptom is that the horse tends to put the heel of its foot down first, rather than the toe or the flat of the foot. It can also be helpful to know how to assess the pulse on the pastern: this can be felt on either side of the pastern, a quarter or a third of the way down, just in front of the deep flexor tendon that

covers the back of the pastern, and in horses with laminitis it is very markedly exaggerated. Never rely on assessing the temperature of the feet to tell you whether the horse has a laminitis problem or not.

If laminitis due to overfeeding is suspected, it is important to empty the digestive tract so that the situation does not continue to deteriorate: depending on the severity of the problem, bran mashes or liquid paraffin by stomach tube will be necessary. The heavier the horse, the more likely it is that the damaged laminae suspending that weight will tear, and so support for the bony column is essential. Applying a rubber lily pad to support the frog can make the horse much more comfortable, and in an emergency situation strap one or two rolls of bandage, abut 2.5cm (1in) in diameter, over the frog; by pressing the frog upwards we prevent the pedal bone sinking downwards.

Mares which are successful in competition are often 'rewarded' by being retired to stud, but a combination of the lack of exercise and abundant rich grass – the result of our human desire to make their retirement pleasurable – can increase the risk of post-foaling laminitis. The main cause of laminitis at this time is toxin released from the contents of the mare's uterus, but failing to maintain foot care during retirement – allowing the development of a long toe/short heel conformation – is also a contributing factor, and one which can so easily be avoided.

Recurrent attacks of laminitis are a problem in ponies, possibly because food moves along the intestines more slowly in ponies as compared with larger horses, and this allows more of the soluble carbohydrate to be absorbed. In some parts of the world, though, climatic conditions produce frequent extremes of lush grass followed by parched ground, and even horses develop laminitis in such a situation. Many animals that suffer repeated attacks of laminitis do so because the laminae in their feet did not recover fully from the previous episode. As such, the increased workload to which the 'recovered' animal is subjected is as much to blame for the new attack as is the increased energy intake they are expected to consume to fuel that work.

Of course, laminitis tends to occur in relatively fat animals and there is a temptation to reduce drastically the level of carbohydrate fed to the animal in an attempt to reduce the bodyweight quickly. Terms such as 'starvation pen' are commonly mentioned by owners of susceptible animals, but this can be a dangerous way to attack the problem because if there is insufficient energy in the diet then the horse will attempt an emergency mobilisation of its fat reserves. This results in a condition called hyperlipaemia, where there are high fat levels in the blood, and because laminitis can be a result of hyperlipaemia anyway, the whole starvation process ends up being counter-productive. The aim should be a *gradual* loss of bodyweight rather than a sudden loss, so in the early stages some concentrates may be fed and certainly hay should be available.

The horse's digestive system is designed on the assumption that it will have frequent small amounts of food passing through for digestion. Our system of using concentrate foods for stabled competition horses which have great physical demands made on them results in a number of peaks of carbohydrate absorption. Regularly spaced feeds and more, smaller feeds rather than one or two large feeds will all help to reduce nutritional problems.

26 Horse on a nebulizer

Choke

Occasionally food becomes stuck in the horse's oesophagus, unable to continue down to the stomach. This can happen when a large piece of solid food such as carrot becomes lodged there, or it can happen because the tube has become constricted for some reason. Most cases of choke, as this is called, occur because the horse has eaten something which swells up on contact with water. The food mixes with saliva in the mouth, and before it is through the oesophagus it has become too big to pass further. Dried sugar-beet products are a common cause of choke. There is nothing wrong with them nutritionally – indeed, they are very useful feeds – but they must be thoroughly soaked before feeding to allow them to swell up. Although tests have shown that as long as it is mixed with enough water the sugar-beet pulp will swell to its maximum size in 3 hours, it is usually best to play safe and soak it for 12–24 hours. After all, it doesn't cost anything to leave it that extra time just in case it hasn't absorbed all the water. The rule of thumb is that at the end of the soaking period there should still be surplus water present which has not been absorbed; if there is not, add some more water and leave it another 3 hours.

When the oesophagus does become blocked, frothy saliva accumulates up its length and starts to appear at the mouth and nostrils, and the horse is obviously distressed. It can't and won't eat or drink. It may be possible to see a swelling on the left side of its neck where the obstruction is lodged. Perhaps the greatest danger is that the accumulating saliva will drain down the trachea into the lungs instead, triggering off pneumonia.

If possible, of course, the vet will want to clear the obstruction. However, great care must be taken not to damage the oesophageal wall in any way, because this might lead to scar tissue forming, thus narrowing the tube further in the long term. Modern relaxant and anti-inflammatory drugs will usually relax and open the oesophagus sufficiently for the food to pass on. Once it does so, then of course the problem is over almost immediately, and the horse will eat and drink again.

The Danger of Poor Quality Hay

Hay is such a vital part of the stabled horse's diet that it is hard to think that sometimes it can have serious health implications. Similarly, millions of horses are stabled on straw of one kind or another, and it is odd to think that just standing on straw, and not even eating it, can cause health problems.

In both of these circumstances the trouble is chronic obstructive pulmonary disease (COPD). Both hay and straw are prone to infestation with fungi. These release fungal spores into the air as small, dust-like particles, and because they are small they can be sucked right down into the alveoli of the horse's lungs. As such they should be no more of an irritant than any other dust particle but unfortunately, because they are organic matter, they can trigger off an allergic, or hypersensitive reaction in the lung. The result is the release of histamine-type chemicals that cause contraction of the muscles in the walls of the small tubes, or bronchioles, in the lungs. This bronchi constriction makes it more difficult for air to be sucked in or pushed out of the air sacs, or alveoli. Breathing in is always a muscular effort, and so air is drawn past the constriction. However, breathing out is mainly due to reflex elasticity of the lungs, and this is not able to empty the alveoli against the constriction. Muscular emptying of the lungs therefore has to be brought into play, resulting in a two-stroke expiration, otherwise known as 'broken wind'.

The commonest symptom of COPD is a cough, and affected horses may also have a mucus discharge from their nostrils; both of these symptoms may be worse around feeding time, when the adrenalin flows. In established cases the two-stage expiration can be seen easily, and the horse may develop a heave line along its flank where the muscles have increased in size as a result of the effort of pushing the air out of the lungs. The resting respiratory rate in the stable can be a useful clue that something is wrong. Rates above twenty breaths a minute are danger signs even if no double breathing is obvious. Importantly for the competition horse, athletic performance is reduced in COPD because not enough oxygen is picked up in the lungs to supply all of its needs for strenuous exercise.

There is no cure for COPD. Once a horse has become hypersensitive, it will always remain so. It may, however, be possible to eliminate the clinical symptoms. There is a drug called clenbuterol which relaxes the muscles in the bronchiolar wall and so leads to broncho-dilation; the horse can then breathe normally. It is also possible to use a drug called sodium cromoglycate by nebulizers (Fig 26); this stabilises the wall around the cells which contain the histamine, and reduces the amount released. This helps to stop the clinical problem arising, but does little to relieve it if it has already become established.

The most important aspect of treatment is to prevent the horse from coming into contact with the fungal spores. If this can be achieved, 99 per cent of horses will recover and be able to lead normal athletic lives. If it is not achieved, no amount of drug-taking will remove the symptoms. As straw is very readily colonised by the fungi, an alternative bedding must be used, such as wood shavings, paper, hemp or sand; these materials must be kept clean and dry to prevent them becoming colonised, too. Deep-litter bedding must never be used.

The stable must not have any openings that allow air to circulate from adjacent stables where straw or hay might be in use; it should also be well away from any muck heaps, and hay or straw stacks. In fact the ideal stable for a horse with COPD is a field, and all but the highest level of competition horse can be kept at grass for at least most of the day. This ensures that they are free from fungal spores. Some owners maintain that they can't provide a fungal-free environment, or that they can't keep their horse at grass. If they can't be bothered to put in that little extra effort, then they must accept that their horse will not get better. There are a few horses, though, whose COPD is pasture-related, and these horses have to be stabled. Oil-seed rape is often blamed for this condition, but a direct cause and effect has not yet been proven.

When providing clean air for a horse with COPD we are not concerned with dust, only fungi. Most visible dust particles are far too big to penetrate down into the lungs anyway, but the important thing is that the horse is allergic to fungal spores, not to dust. One point to watch is that when horses are travelling to and from competitions they must not travel in a horsebox with straw or hay. Care is also needed if they are stabled at the competition. The airways can constrict within minutes of contact with spores, so the competition performance would be affected even in that short time. Hay is a dangerous source of spores because the horse literally buries its nose into the hay and so cannot help but breathe in any spores. It is perfectly possible to buy hay that is not colonised by fungi. Neither the appearance nor the nutritional value of the hay will give any guidance on this, but a machine called a slit sampler can extract dust particles and put them onto a microscope slide for counting and evaluation. Soaking hay in water has only a limited effect at removing spores, even if it is running water, because most of the effect is due to the spores sticking to the wet hay; if the hay dries out, which it does quite rapidly in some climates, then it is just as dangerous.

As an alternative to hay, vacuum-packed grass products or silage are available. These are usually fungal free when first opened, but within 1–2 days of opening they become grossly colonised by fungi from the atmosphere. It is possible to replace some or all of a horse's roughage with special high-fibre horse nuts, but these require very careful management if they are to be used successfully.

When buying a horse, it is most important to appreciate that a horse can have COPD but be completely free of symptoms. No veterinary examination will be able to detect the problem in such circumstances. Only when the horse is bedded on straw will symptoms gradually (or occasionally all too quickly) start to appear. Always insist on seeing the horse stabled normally on straw, or alternatively insist on receiving a written warranty that the horse is not allergic to fungal spores; the latter course of action at least helps if symptoms develop shortly after purchase. It is also wise to stable a new purchase for a week or two in order to check on this possibility. Never buy a horse with a slight cough, no matter how convincing the vendor as to why it is coughing.

Overwintering

Owners are prepared to put a large amount of effort into feeding for performance, and working out what to feed for the amount of work being done, but then tend to forget their horses for the rest of the year. However, when the last competition is over, don't just turn them out into a field: no matter how 'natural' grass might be as a food, such a marked change in diet can cause digestive problems. Depending to some extent on whether the grass is growing rapidly and has a high moisture content, or is relatively fibrous, the change can produce either diarrhoea or impaction: whilst on a basically concentrate ration, the bacteria in the horse's caecum and colon will include a few of those species able to digest the fibrous component of grass and a sudden change will mean they are insufficient to cope with digesting this fibre effectively. The change in routine from being stabled all the time to being turned out must therefore be achieved gradually, ideally over 7–10 days, in order to give the appropriate bacteria time to increase in numbers.

It is only the length of time spent grazing which should be changed gradually: the amount of concentrate feed should also be phased out over a few days, and not just stopped completely on the morning of the last competition. Similarly the exercise the horse undertakes should be reduced, because this helps it to 'wind down' physically and mentally from the 'high' of competition.

The winter feeding of both the horse in full work and that which is resting needs particular attention. It will use a greater percentage of its carbohydrate/fat intake to produce heat to maintain its body temperature, and so these components will be correspondingly less available for maintaining bodyweight or for exercise. We can simplify the nutritional problem by reducing the amount of heat lost by radiation. Rugs are the usual way to achieve this, of course, although it is important to remember that a soaking wet rug cools rather than maintains the body temperature. It is also worth noting that it is better to put an extra rug on a stabled horse than it is to close the top stable door or window. Even in very cold weather ventilation is of equal importance to temperature control, especially on straw bedding.

Owners also tend to forget that bad weather will affect horses psychologically just as it does us, and they will be less enthusiastic for their work. However, it would be wrong to keep on increasing the amount of oats fed in an attempt to make a horse more lively. Careful attention to its weight will reveal whether it is having to use up its body fat to keep itself warm: if its weight is constant, then feeding extra food is almost certainly not the answer. Keep a 'weather' eye on resting horses as well: allowing them to lose weight significantly as a result of bad weather is never viable because you will have to replace that muscle and body fat at some stage in the future before they can compete again.

Vegetable oil and sugar-beet pulp are two of the best nutritional components to use to combat cold weather. As explained earlier, fats are more energy dense than carbohydrates, so a relatively small increase in the amount of fat fed will have a significant effect. The danger is that it is also easy to overcompensate and then to end up feeding more energy than the horse requires. Sugar-beet pulp is bulkier, and it is easier to avoid overcompensating when measuring it out. It is also probably true that the longer the feed takes to act during cold weather, the better it is. More heat is lost by the resting horse than by one just chewing and feeding.

27 Correct management of performance horses during the winter months is just as important as their care during the competition season

LAMENESS

OVERLEAF:
Horses landing at speed from a jump; the force of landing is always taken on one
leg, putting great strain on the whole leg

CONTENTS

LAMENESS INVESTIGATION

What is Lameness?

Lameness is the visible evidence that a horse is taking its weight unevenly on one or more legs because of pain. There is, however, a grey area between a sound horse and a lame horse. In most cases if someone tells you that a horse is 'not lame but just going a bit short' they mean that the horse is lame but they don't want to admit it. Similarly if someone refers to a horse being 'just bridle lame' they mean that the horse is lame but they are not sure why or where and hope it will go away. There are horses which for a variety of non-painful reasons have a very uneven gait; the most easily understood of these would be a horse which has lost a shoe. However, in the following investigations lameness will usually be considered to be associated with pain.

Which Leg is it Lame On?

We detect lameness in two ways: by observing a horse's head nodding when a foot hits the ground (see Fig 1); and by observing one of the hindquarters sinking when a foot hits the ground. We cannot detect anything other than severe lameness at the walk, and we cannot reliably detect lameness at all at the canter, although pain in a horse's back may affect how the horse moves at that gait. All lameness assessments are therefore carried out at the trot, because only at the trot does the horse normally put exactly the same amount of weight on first the left and then the right leg, and lameness is all about such a comparison. If a horse has the same amount of pain in both front feet, which may be the case in navicular disease, for example, it will not appear lame because there is no difference to compare.

When a horse puts a painful front foot to the ground, it does not put its full weight on that foot; instead it puts more weight on the next front foot to hit the ground. When a front leg takes such extra weight, the horse's head nods down. Detecting front leg lameness is all about watching for the horse's head to nod as it trots towards you, deciding which leg is hitting the ground when this happens, and therefore pinpointing the other front leg as the painful one. Of course, the elementary mistake which many people make is to suggest that it is the lame leg which hits the ground when the horse nods. Detecting hind-leg

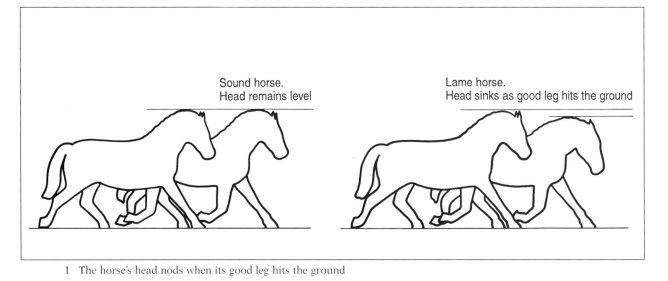

Sound horse.
Head remains level

Lame horse.
Head sinks as good leg hits the ground

1   The horse's head nods when its good leg hits the ground

2   A horse being trotted up for lameness

lameness is all about watching the horse's hindquarters and the base of the tail as the horse trots away from you, deciding which leg is hitting the ground when this happens, and therefore pinpointing the other hind leg as the painful one.

When a horse is being assessed for lameness it should be trotted in hand with about 45cm (18in) of loose rope between the horse and the groom's hand (Fig 2), and the examination must be carried out on a smooth, hard surface; a field is very rarely suitable for this purpose. Although lameness may be obvious when a horse is ridden, it is not a good thing to try and assess lameness in a ridden horse because few riders are perfectly balanced on the left and the right, and this can distort the situation. When watching the horse trot up, it is necessary to discipline oneself to watch only the hindquarters when the horse trots away in a straight line, and to watch only the head when the horse is trotting directly towards you.

In certain circumstances it may be useful to trot a horse in a tight circle on a lungeing rein. As a general rule this exacerbates lameness when the lame leg is on the inside of the circle because this inevitably makes the horse take more weight on the inside legs. When the lameness is associated with movement of the leg and length of stride, then it will also be worse (compared with trotting in a straight line) when the affected leg is on the outside of the circle, because the outside strides have to be longer than the inside strides. There are those who suggest that lungeing a horse in a tight circle on a hard level surface such as concrete carries a risk of injury if the horse should slip. We have to set against that risk the fact that such lungeing may show up lameness in an otherwise sound-looking horse which is bilaterally lame.

Very occasionally a horse will send out misleading signs at the lameness examination, and this almost always involves the diagonally opposite leg because of how the horse moves at the trot. It is also more common for horses to appear to be lame on the front leg when they are actually lame on the diagonal hind leg, rather than the other way around.

Grading Lameness

It is often useful to grade the degree of lameness shown by a horse in order to assess its progress

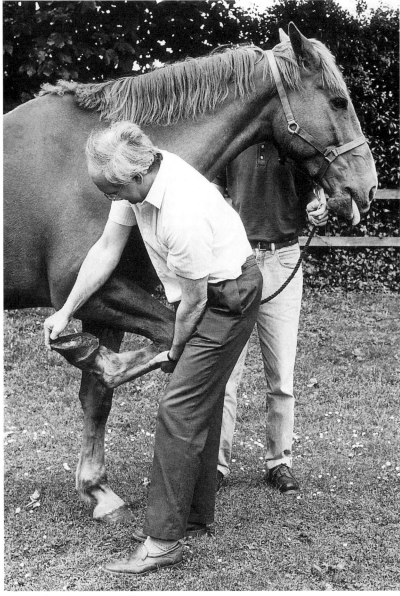

3a and 3b Administering flexion tests

with treatment. Sometimes lameness is scored on a 0–10 basis, and sometimes on a 0–5 basis. In both cases 0 means no lameness is present at all, and the highest score means that the horse will not take any weight on the leg, even when standing. Inevitably there will be variations between the degree of lameness attributed to any one horse by different observers, but lameness scoring is intended to compare like with like, ie the same horse and the same observer but on different occasions, rather than allowing us to place any significance on a change from a 5/10 score from one observer to a 6/10 score from another observer.

Flexion Tests

Flexion tests are a somewhat controversial part of the physical examination of a horse, to detect lameness. Such a test consists of holding a leg so that a particular joint or joints are firmly bent, or flexed (see Fig 3), and then after a period of time releasing the leg and immediately trotting the horse away. A positive flexion test is one which either causes lameness in a previously sound horse, or which markedly increases an existing lameness. There are discussions among vets about how long the leg ought to be flexed, and the majority opinion appears to be that it must be flexed for 30–60 seconds. Of course not all vets exert the same amount of pressure when flexing the leg, so results will vary because of that. Perhaps the most obvious difficulty with flexion tests concerns the duration of the lameness afterwards. If a horse has had a leg flexed for a whole minute, it seems reasonable that it might be lame when it first uses that leg. But how many lame strides is a horse allowed before it becomes a positive test? Again, majority opinion seems to be that only two to three lame strides are normal. If the response continues after that, then it is abnormal.

Because of the way the horse's leg is constructed, it is often not possible to flex one joint without flexing others and for this reason flexion tests rarely provide a precise location for a lameness. A flexion test carried out on a hind leg is often called a spavin test because it may show the existence of a condition known as spavin in the hock, but a positive reaction may just as well be due to stifle problems. Flexing the front fetlock may cause a reaction due to fetlock problems, but it may also cause a reaction in a foot condition such as navicular disease as a result of increasing the blood pressure in the foot.

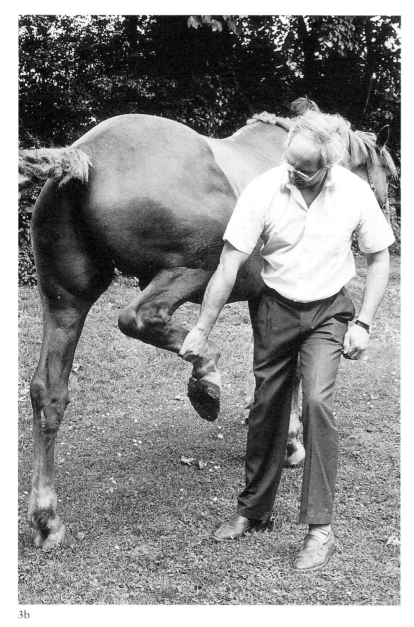

3b

The Gaits

Surprisingly few owners know what a horse does with its legs anyway, whether it is sound or not. At the walk the horse puts a front foot to the ground, then the opposite hind leg, and only then the opposite front leg; there are always three feet on the ground (Fig 4). All this is less than ideal for lameness evaluation. At the trot, on the other hand, there are only ever two feet on the ground at the same time, one of which is a front foot and the other the diagonal hind foot. The front feet (or the back feet) hit the ground consecutively and should bear the same amount of weight (Fig 4), and that is why it is so easy to detect lameness at the trot.

The canter and the gallop have some significant differences. First there is the question of speed: a horse automatically changes to the gallop in order to go faster. Second, the way the feet hit the ground is slightly different at the two gaits: at the canter the left front foot hits the ground, then the right hind foot and finally both the right front and left hind feet simultaneously. At the gallop, however, the right front and left hind feet are not linked as tightly, and the left hind foot hits the ground slightly before the right fore foot (Fig 5). The two gaits have two even more important similarities: the first is that they both have a suspension phase, a fraction of time when no feet are touching the ground at all (Fig 6), which occurs immediately after the leading foreleg has

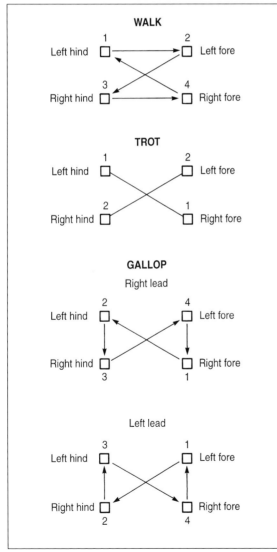

4 The gaits of the horse, showing the order in which it puts its feet to the ground

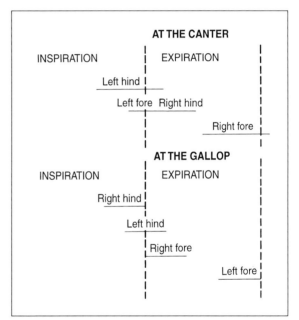

5 The timing of the footfalls at canter and gallop

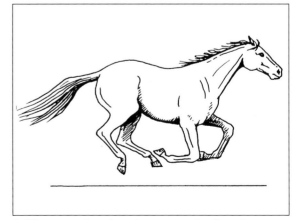

6 The suspension phase in canter and gallop when no legs are touching the ground

left the ground. If a horse changes its lead leg during this suspension phase it will put its other foreleg to the ground and then have another suspension phase. In other words, it will have only used energy to move two legs, but will have covered proportionally more ground ie it will have saved some energy without sacrificing any speed. That is why a horse which is tiring at the end of a race but is being urged to maintain its speed will change its lead leg. The other important point about the canter and the gallop is that they are linked to the horse's breathing. The stride rate is the same as the respiratory rate. As the lead leg hits the ground, the horse breathes out. Most of the time it is the leg movements which control the breathing, but if a horse has severe breathing difficulties, this may restrict the way it moves its legs, as well as any effect the lack of oxygen from the lungs has on speed.

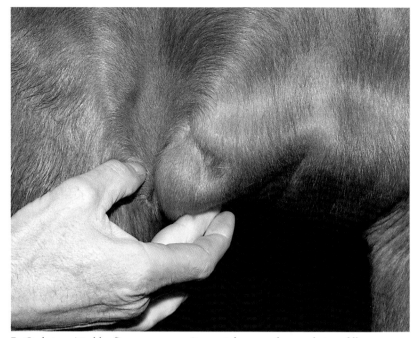

7   Oedema pitted by finger pressure; it may take several seconds to refill

Examining the Leg

Having decided which leg the horse is lame on, the next stage is to carry out a detailed examination of it. The opposite leg should also be examined because it may be a bilateral lameness, or the other leg may be starting to show physical evidence that it is having difficulty in supporting the extra weight. This physical examination is aimed at detecting any of the classic signs of inflammation, namely heat, pain or swelling.

The detection of increased warmth in a leg needs to be assessed critically if it is not to prove misleading. A clipped leg will always feel warmer than a hairy leg. A leg which has been bandaged will feel warmer than one which hasn't. A warm hoof indicates that there is reduced blood circulation in the foot rather than the opposite, because the longer the blood stays in the foot because of poor circulation – for example in laminitis – the more opportunity there is for it to heat up the overlying hoof.

Swelling may take two forms. Oedema is swelling due to the accumulation of tissue fluid in the tissues, causing them to act rather like a sponge; when a finger is pressed firmly into an area of oedema and removed, it leaves a depression which takes several seconds to refill (Fig 7). Oedema can occur for several reasons: it may be associated with infection, for example the swelling that can occur with mud fever. It can also occur due to circulatory problems. So if a joint such as the knee is very swollen, and this causes pressure on the veins which drain the blood from the lower leg, then oedema may well occur in the lower leg. In this situation fluid is escaping through the blood-vessel wall into the surrounding tissues due to pressure in the vein. The other type of swelling is a much more specific and localised reaction to inflammation, such as a swollen joint capsule when the joint is inflamed, or a swollen tendon sheath when the tendon has been sprained.

Even when a horse is quite markedly lame it may be very difficult to find the painful area. This is when it would be so helpful if horses could talk! When an area is found which appears to elicit a pain response to pressure, it is important to check that this result is reproducible – that the horse always reacts that way when you press there, and that it doesn't respond in the same way when you press the same area on the opposite leg. There are often red herrings – areas which respond to pressure but are not the seat of the pain. Many horses, for example, will react to firm pressure in the mid-tendon area of the cannon: if it responds by starting to rear away, then it is more likely to be significant than if it just snatches the leg away.

Nerve Blocks

At this stage, even the most experienced horse owners will have reached the limit of their ability to investigate lameness, and any further investigation requires specialist veterinary techniques. The first of these is the use of nerve blocks. Anyone who has had a tooth filled at the dentist will probably first have had the area numbed by an injection of local anaesthetic over the nerve, and this same technique is used on horses, too. The local anaesthetic removes all sensation, including pain, from the area supplied by the nerve. As lameness is all about pain, the nerve block also removes all lameness associated with structures in the area supplied by the nerve. Nerve blocks are almost infallible – if a horse goes sound after a nerve block, then the site of the lameness must be in that area. There are some factors which a vet has to consider when a nerve block does not affect the lameness: first, he has to be sure that he has allowed a long enough period of time to elapse for the full effect of the drug to be exerted. Second, he has to be sure that the local anaesthetic was injected in the right place and did affect the nerve. This is usually assessed by pressing an object such as a ballpoint pen firmly into the skin over the area which should have been desensitised; if the horse makes no reaction then he can be sure that it can't feel anything. Even then a horse will occasionally have a different nerve distribution and will respond differently.

A so-called palmar digital nerve block should remove sensation from just the heel region of the foot (Fig 8); a cause of lameness which lies in this region only, such as one involving the navicular bone, will be abolished by this block. An abaxial sesamoid nerve block removes sensation from the whole foot, and possibly the lower pastern as well. A four-point palmar nerve block removes sensation from the fetlock joint and below. These nerve blocks are common to all four feet, and relatively reliable. It is also possible to perform nerve blocks to remove sensation from the knee and hock areas. The removal of sensation lasts one to two hours.

Nerve blocks never pin the diagnosis down to a specific structure, just to a general area. Local anaesthetics can be more specific when they are injected into a particular joint. Such an intra-articular block only removes pain affecting the surfaces of that joint, be they cartilage, bone or joint capsule.

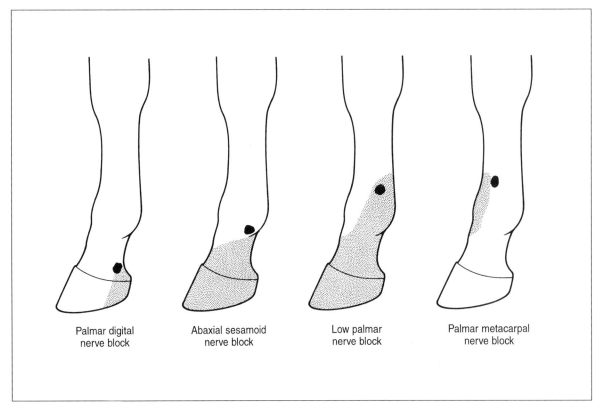

| Palmar digital nerve block | Abaxial sesamoid nerve block | Low palmar nerve block | Palmar metacarpal nerve block |

8 Areas of the leg desensitised by nerve blocks

The Use of X-Rays and Their Limitations

Many lameness investigations involve taking x-ray pictures of the bones of the affected area. The x-ray machine head sends out a diverging beam of electrons; these pass through the target tissues and hit the x-ray film behind. Bone blocks out the x-rays, and so shows as a white image. Air is the opposite; it does not absorb any radiation and shows as black on an x-ray. When x-raying horses, intensifying screens are often used on either side of the actual x-ray plate. These screens contain crystals which emit light when irradiated, and this light is also recorded on the x-ray plate, intensifying the image. The use of such screens has markedly reduced exposure times for horse x-rays, enabling vets with even relatively modest equipment to take good x-rays of the front leg up to the elbow, and the hind leg up to the stifle. X-rays of the horse's shoulder, its pelvis, its neck and its spine all require extremely powerful x-ray machines which are only usually found in one or two specialist clinics (Fig 9).

■ Preventing Exposure to Radiation

Precautions should be taken to prevent exposure of people to radiation during radiography. Owners should never hold a horse's head during radiography unless they are wearing a full lead-impregnated protective apron. If there is any chance of them being pregnant, they should not be present at all. If they are holding a leg or an x-ray cassette holder in place, then they should wear lead gloves as well. They should never hold an x-ray plate in place just with a hand.

■ The Limitations of Radiography

Radiography is a very valuable technique, but it does have its limitations. X-rays never diagnose a problem, they are only an aid to diagnosis. Also, the more horses that we x-ray, the more bone abnormalities we find in clinically normal horses; we therefore have to resist the temptation to make a diagnosis from an x-ray without adequate confirmation that there really is a problem. So it might not be wise to put too much importance on seeing x-ray evidence of new bone having being formed on the dorsal processes of the horse's spine, for example, unless we are able to tell by using other techniques whether the bone is active or not.

Another limitation is that although we often want to x-ray joints, neither the cartilage nor the joint capsule of those joints will show on x-rays; we may be able to make guesses about them, but not actually to visualise them. So if the wear and tear of competition has damaged a localised area of articular cartilage but not the underlying bone, then nothing will show on x-ray. Only if sufficient cartilage has been lost for the distance between the two bones to have been narrowed will we see anything (Fig 10).

Frustratingly, x-rays only travel in straight lines. Where that straight line passes through more than one bone, or even through both sides of the same bone, the resulting overlapping of images can mask defects. For this reason it is often necessary to take a number of different x-ray views at either different angles or different exposures before one can be sure that no abnormalities are present.

It is important to realise that x-rays are historical rather than up-to-date documents. Bone changes its density and sometimes its shape all the time, but the x-ray image only picks up these changes after a certain point. It is not possible to 'age' accurately the changes we see on an x-ray. By the time significant changes are visible in areas such as the navicular bone, the underlying pathological changes have probably been present for at least 4–6 weeks. On the other hand, there is nothing about new bone which has been present for several months which distinguishes it from bone which has been present for several years.

■ Ownership of X-ray Plates

One point which may be of interest to the owners of competition horses, which often change hands for large sums of money, concerns the ownership of the actual x-ray plates. It is generally assumed that an owner can either commission a vet or radiographer to take some x-ray plates, which are then his property; or he can pay a vet for a professional opinion, in which case the plates remain the vet's property. Merely 'allowing' a vet to x-ray your horse does not make you the owner of the x-ray plates. The clearest example of this is when a vet travels some distance to examine a horse prior to purchase. A local vet may be paid to x-ray a significant part of the horse, but he gives no opinion of what might be visible and sends them to the prospective purchaser. The purchaser's vet gives

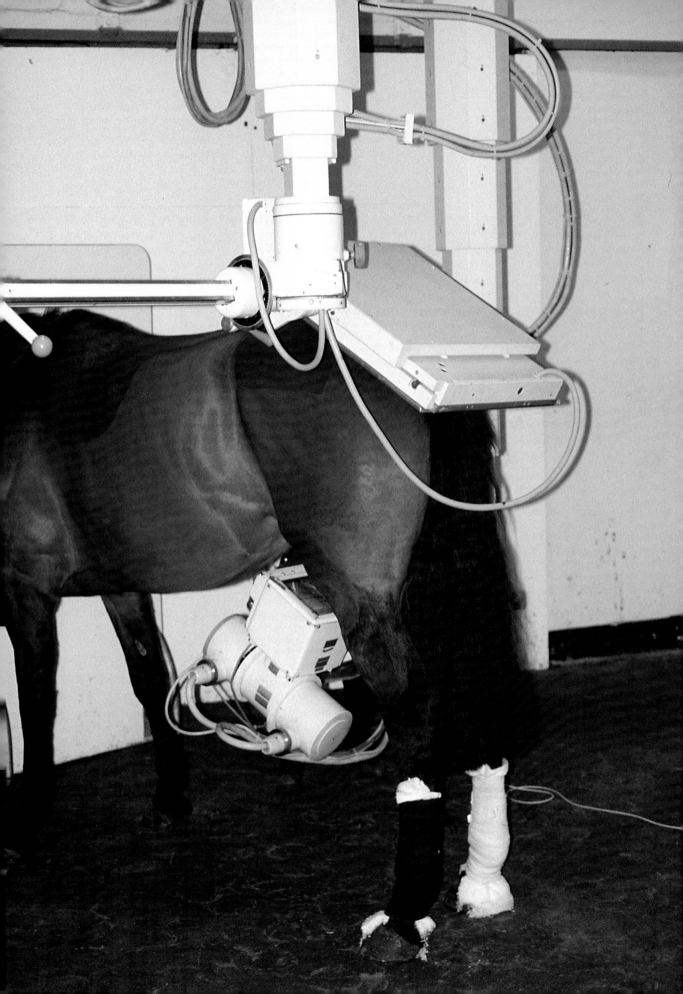

New bone shows.
The amount of new bone seen on an x-ray does not necessarily correlate with the amount of pain or lameness shown. New bone can be seen on x-rays around the joints of perfectly sound horses

Articular cartilage between bones does not show.
The diagnosis of DJD and OCD cannot therefore always be made from an x-ray alone. Arthroscopy may be necessary to view the articular cartilage directly

Tendons attached to bones do not show.
Swelling associated with the tendon sheath at this point may give the false impression that it is the joint which is affected. An ultrasound scan will be necessary to show any tendon damage

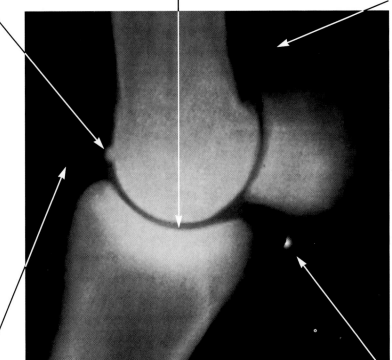

Joint capsule does not show.
Damage to the joint capsule affects the quality of the joint fluid. This affects its lubricant qualitites and ultimately the health of the cartilage which receives so much nutrition from that joint fluid. It may be necessary to obtain a sample of joint fluid via a sterile needle and check this for both the presence of any infection and for its molecular weight (or lubricant value) of the hyaluronic acid it contains. The ultimate confirmation that lameness is due to a joint problem is to replace some of the joint fluid with local anaesthetic and then see whether the horse goes sound

Loose bone in the joint shows.
These so-called 'joint mice', or small fragments of bone, are thought to be new bone which formed at the edge of the joint and was broken off during joint movement. The larger the piece of bone the more likely it is to be the cause of lameness. The bone can be removed arthroscopically

Opposite: 9 A large x-ray machine x-raying the spine   Above: 10 What shows on x-ray in joints, and what does not

an opinion on what significance, if any, the x-rays have and thus whether the horse is suitable for purchase.

■ Multiple X-ray Views

In some countries there is a tradition of taking multiple x-ray views of different parts of the horse prior to purchase. In my opinion there is little point in doing so. First, there is the question of how to decide what to x-ray: do you x-ray just the feet, or the feet and the knees, or the feet and hocks, or all four legs up to the knee and the hock? If you choose the final option, do you take one view of each part, or two views at 90° to each other, or four views? Second, there is the fact that although no x-ray changes might be visible in a joint at the time of x-ray, that does not mean that there are no pathological changes present. The worst scenario might be a horse which had its feet x-rayed 'clear' at purchase, developed clinical symptoms of lameness four weeks later, which by 6–8 weeks after that could be seen as typical navicular changes. Was the horse normal at purchase? Almost certainly not. But if a legal case ensued, those clear x-rays should prove a double-edged sword because although taken for the purchaser, they would be used by the vendor. The real role of x-rays at purchase is to provide additional information about doubtful features: lumps and bumps, and joints which give marginal responses to flexion tests, for example.

Other Techniques

Radiography was the first non-invasive investigative technique to be used by vets, that is, it is a way of seeing what is going on inside a horse without resorting to surgery. Nowadays we have a number of such techniques.

■ Ultrasound Scanning

Just as x-rays are used to look at bone, ultrasound scanning looks at the soft-tissue structures above the bone. The technique may involve a hand-held probe placed in direct contact with the skin (a contact improved by clipping the hair and applying a special gel to the skin) in order to send out a beam of ultrasound waves. These are partly reflected by the underlying soft tissues, but are completely reflected if they hit bone. The probe

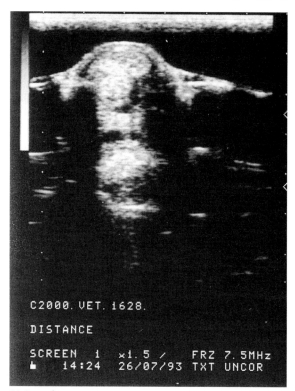

11 A tendon scan

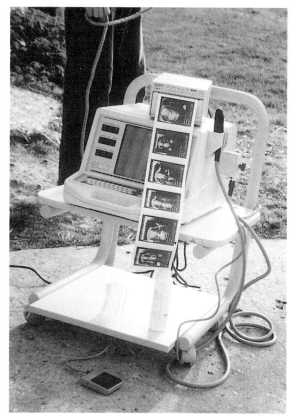

12 Ultrasound scans of a horse's tendon can be carried out at the stable using a portable scanner

receives the reflected waves and uses them to build up a picture that is a cross-sectional view of the underlying tissues (Fig 11). Tendons show as white areas on the black-and-white image. Fluid, such as the clot that forms in an area of badly sprained tendon, shows black on the image. It is also possible to turn the scanner head through 90° and look at a longitudinal slice rather than at a cross-sectional view. This is particularly useful for checking the alignment of tendon fibres, which in healthy tendon are parallel but in damaged tendon have a very irregular pattern.

Ultrasound scans can be useful in a variety of situations. From the performance horse point of view, the most common use is to investigate tendon problems. Because the scan results in a computer image, that image can be printed, and precise measurements made automatically – even the area of any lesions can be calculated automatically . Ultrasound scans can also be the only way to see inside the horse's heart whilst it is beating, showing any physical abnormalities and measuring the blood flow through the valves.

■ Nuclear Scintigraphy

Another type of diagnostic picture is that taken by a gamma camera in a technique called nuclear scintigraphy. The horse is injected with a solution of radioactive technetium. The isotope spreads throughout the body, with more being taken up by areas of active inflammation or bone activity than by normal tissues; the amount of radioactivity present is then measured using either a hand-held Geiger counter holder or a gamma camera. With the hand-held probe, the string of readings has to be fed into a computer to provide a comparison between the two sides of the horse, a lengthy process. With the gamma camera, an image is produced which is rather like an x-ray but which shows the so-called 'hot spots' where extra isotope has been taken up (Fig 13).

The low levels of radioactivity involved have no effect on the horse, but Health and Safety regulations require it to be kept in special stabling for a short period afterwards whilst the radioactivity levels return to normal.

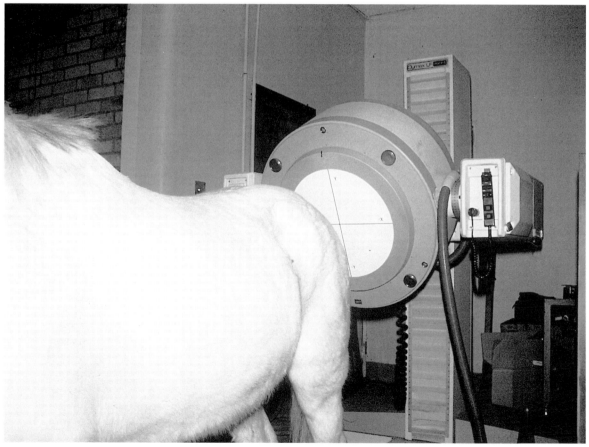

13 Gamma camera

Nuclear scintigraphy is better at showing where a problem is than at saying what it is. In a lameness investigation, it is often used to pinpoint a site of inflammation for further investigation by other techniques in cases where we have failed to find the site of the lameness by other means. We cannot, for example, x-ray every part of a leg, but nuclear scintigraphy can assess the whole leg. Whereas x-rays may miss early changes because the bone density has not yet changed significantly, scintigraphy picks up early activity but not the old, inactive bone.

■ Arthroscopy

There can be a very fine line between investigating the cause of lameness and its treatment. This is certainly the case with a technique called arthroscopy. This keyhole surgery technique consists of inserting a lens directly into a joint and using optical fibres both to look through that lens and to illuminate the fields of vision with light. In order to improve the fields of vision, the joint is distended by large volumes of water during the procedure (Fig 14).

Arthroscopy enables us to see areas of cartilage damage and suchlike in a joint, sometimes confirming what an x-ray has suggested and sometimes providing a definitive diagnosis where there wasn't one before. However, having done so, the surgeon will often want to continue and, using tiny instruments and power tools which have to fit down the same tube as the fibre optics, to treat the problem. Arthroscopy is an invasive technique, but it is far less invasive than just opening the joint right up surgically. Although a general anaesthetic is usually given, the horse can return to exercise surprisingly quickly after the procedure.

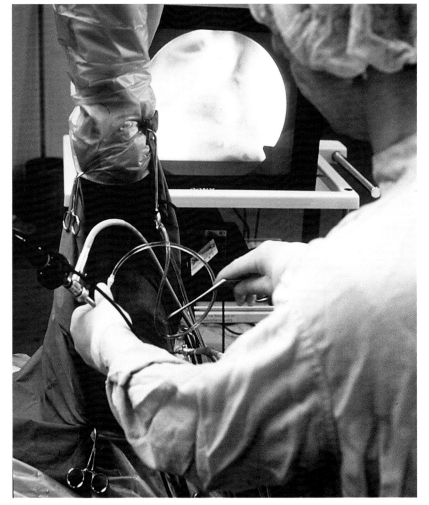

14 Arthroscopy, the keyhole surgery technique. The joint is distended by volumes of water in order to improve the fields of vision

■ The Force Plate

The ultimate electronic gadget used in the assessment of lameness is a force plate. This is an extremely expensive piece of equipment that is more to do with physics than veterinary science. It consists of a number of extremely sensitive sensors underneath a metal plate. When a horse's foot hits the plate, its velocity and the direction of the forces which are controlling the leg, are measured continuously. So the mechanical force exerted vertically downwards, as well as any sideways or forward forces, are all measured. This means that with sufficient skill in interpretation, abnormalities of movement are picked up in apparently 100 per cent sound horses. The force plate looks a little like a miniature long-jump pit, with the force place extending onwards from what would have been the take-off board.

THE TREATMENT OF LAMENESS

It is the aim of this section to provide background information on the most commonly used forms of treatment for lameness problems. In many cases a choice has to be made because more than one type of treatment would theoretically be effective. There tend to be fashions in treatment, and the same fashions do not always prevail with vets as they do with horse owners. By and large owners prefer machines, such as lasers, which anyone can buy, to drugs whose use is restricted to vets.

Poultices

A poultice is designed to raise the temperature of a localised area of the body. Most people also consider that poultices draw infected discharges out of wounds; certainly a poultice dressing that has been on an infected wound will have some pus and discharge on it. However, so would an ordinary dry dressing. There is actually no scientific evidence that any kind of poultice draws pus out, but that may only be because nobody has researched the subject well enough.

■ Types of Poultice

The simplest kind of poultice is a **bread** or **bran poultice**. The bran (or bread) is mixed with boiled water to make a stiff paste, and when it is cool enough it is applied as a thick layer over the affected part. A dressing of some kind then holds it in place. Bran has no effect other than as a warm mass of material; once it has cooled down it has no effect at all.

Then there is the **Animalintex** poultice. This consists of a piece of dressing material impregnated with boric acid and tragacanth powder; it has an outer polythene membrane to keep in the active ingredients as the dressing is prepared: it must be soaked in hot water, allowed to drain, cooled to blood heat and then applied to the affected area. An Animalintex poultice is light and easy to store beforehand, and easy to cut to size

and activate by soaking when needed. However, it does not really stay hot any longer than a piece of wet gamgee covered with polythene would do.

Kaolin clay poultices are usually more messy to apply. The wet clay material has to be heated up either by immersing the whole tin in boiling water, or by somehow heating only the required amount of kaolin on a piece of gauze (possibly in a microwave) or in foil (possibly in boiling water or an oven). Foil envelopes of kaolin are available which can be quickly heated in water. However, although easy to apply, they provide only a thin layer of kaolin; really a layer of kaolin 13mm (^{1}/2in) thick is needed, because this will keep its heat for quite a long time. Kaolin poultices should never be applied directly to the skin; a piece of gauze should be put over the area first. A piece of aluminium foil on the top of the poultice will reflect radiating heat back into the poultice.

■ Using a Poultice Properly

If one assumes that poultices do work – that by increasing local blood flow they bring more white blood cells to the area to kill off bacteria – then they need to be used properly. As I have mentioned, they have no real effect once they have cooled down, despite some manufacturers' claims, so they need to be replaced frequently. Horse owners are usually reluctant to change a poultice more than twice a day, but most, if not all, should really be changed more frequently than that. The poultice must cover a reasonable area, certainly extending 5–7cm (2–3in) away from the wound.

When the poultice is changed, all the old material should be removed. In the case of an Animalintex poultice this includes all of the gelatinous material which has exuded from the dressing into the wound. In the case of kaolin it includes all the clay – not an easy task. A wound should not be poulticed for more than 48 hours unless on veterinary advice because the hot, wet conditions, and the chemicals, will kill the skin edges around the wound making later skin healing more difficult. In any case, once the body's defences have been attracted to the area, they will continue their work unstimulated.

■ Applying a Poultice

It can be difficult to hold a poultice in place. Normal bandaging will be sufficient on the horse's leg, but it can be very time-consuming to bandage a poultice in place on a horse's foot every few hours. Various types of poultice boot are available to enable foot poultices to be changed quickly and easily, and to prevent the poultice coming off due to soggy, torn bandages. These boots range from an all-enveloping plastic or rubber 'wellington boot', to a relatively cheap plastic shoe which covers the toe and sole and is tied in place (Fig 15). I would certainly recommend using the latter since its ease of use encourages poultice changing rather than discouraging it.

15 A simple plastic boot to hold poultices and other dressings in place

■ Tubbing a Foot

An alternative to poulticing a foot is tubbing. This means simply immersing the foot in a bowl or bucket of hot water. Obviously not all horses are patient enough to stand still with their foot in a bucket, so although cheap and easily obtainable, the technique is not always practical. It is usually recommended to put a handful of Epsom salts in the water as well. This prevents the horn softening too much during prolonged or repeated immersion.

The Use of Cold

Whatever doubts there may be about the effects of hot poulticing, the effects of cold applications are undisputed. Cold is one of the most vital treatment regimes for athletic injuries. Indeed, whenever there has been any physical injury apart from a skin wound, the immediate application of cold will probably be beneficial. The rationale of the treatment is that cold constricts the blood vessels and reduces the blood supply to the area. This means that it reduces the effects of inflammation – heat, pain and swelling – because fewer white blood cells reach the area. Cold also reduces pain by physically affecting the nerves, and slowing down the speed at which they pass pain impulses along.

Although it is not possible to apply cold too early, it is possible to apply it for too long. After the initial inflammatory reaction, injuries need to heal, and they need repair material from the bloodstream to do this. Continuing application of cold may slow this down. Perhaps the commonest situation where owners are tempted to apply cold for too long is with sprained tendons, where after 10–14 days the acute inflammatory response is over; but people may continue hosing and so on to cool the leg. Cold applications are also not appropriate when an infection is present, for example an infected wound, because they reduce the number of white blood cells available to kill the bacteria.

■ Hosing and Hosing Boots

Cold can be applied in a number of ways. Hosing the affected area with cold water has some cooling effect, especially in the winter when the tap water is at its coldest; it also has a massaging effect to disperse oedema. However, it is time-consuming. A variation is to use a hosing boot (Fig 16): this fastens around the cannon area and has a hosepipe attached to it. Some nervous horses will not tolerate being tied up with a hose attached to their leg, although many will. The hose boot has no massaging effect, but it does maintain a flow of water over a reasonably wide area. From time to time hydrotherapy becomes fashionable. This consists of a large boot into which the horse's leg is placed; a motor then makes the water in this envelope pulse rhythmically from the toe upwards. In this case there is little cooling effect, but the massaging effect will help to disperse oedema.

■ Ice

Ice is obviously a more effective way to apply cold than the use of tap water, and cools the leg quite quickly. However, it should not be used continuously for too long a period because near-freezing

16 Hosing boot; it has no massaging effect, but it does maintain a flow of water over quite a wide area. Note the attachment for the hose

temperatures will damage living tissues. The insuperable disadvantage of ice is that it melts: this means that if you incorporate ice cubes into a bandage dressing, that dressing becomes looser as the ice melts. Take care never to have ice in direct contact with the skin; there should always be at least one layer of bandage or gauze in between.

Gel Packs

A variety of gel packs is available to take the place of ice; the chemicals they contain stay frozen longer than ice, and so they stay cold longer. It might be worth pointing out at this point that any steps which are taken to keep the cold in by insulation will mean that once the dressing has returned to body heat, it will start to apply heat

rather than cold. So cold dressings need replacing at intervals: they do not stay cold forever. If one of the frozen gel packs is not available, a packet of frozen peas is the accepted substitute, and will fit around the leg quite well.

Chemical Applications

A variety of chemical applications is available to cool legs down. I have reservations about their use in an injury situation, although they may be of some value after exercise, because the cold they provide is not as intense as that obtained from ice. This must be the case, because it is not practi-cable to keep applying the product and then removing it, as one does with ice. If there are any cuts or abrasions, the chemicals may cause a degree of inflammation in their own right. Perhaps the biggest drawback is that it is difficult to assess when the effectiveness of the product is wearing off; only the horse can really tell us that.

The Bonner Bandage

Perhaps the most intense cold is that obtained by using a Bonner bandage. This is a thick bandage like a stable bandage which is designed to remain flexible even after it has been soaked in water and frozen. Precisely because it is so effective, such a bandage should only be left in place for 3–4 minutes; it should then be removed for a short period before it is reapplied.

Rest and Convalescence

Rest and exercise are two vital parts of the treatment of lameness, and it can be very difficult to decide when to rest a horse and when to work it. There is certainly no point in resting a lame horse unless one knows what the problem is, because the chances are that when the horse is exercised again, the lameness will return and that time will have been wasted. This is the case with spavin, for example. It is now realised that degenerative joint disease (DJD), or arthritis, is not necessarily helped by rest. Just as human doctors advise old people with arthritis to keep on the move, so vets have also realised the advantages of regular exercise in this situation. The secret is that it has to be a relatively constant amount of exercise, and it has to be seven days a week, fifty-two weeks a year. The horse will often adapt to such exercise to the extent that painkillers can be reduced or withdrawn.

There is some evidence to support a claim that rest helps to *cause* DJD! It is certainly true that if a horse is rested because of injury, the incidence of DJD during the following months is much increased. A survey of horses which had developed navicular disease, for example, showed that a large majority of them had been laid off from work because of another lameness problem during the six months before the navicular disease first became apparent.

Care has to be taken when resting physical injuries such as wounds or tendon sprains. The healing process may result in the formation of fibrous adhesions linking structures which should move freely, and once such fibrous adhesions have matured, they represent a permanent restriction on movement. Indeed, in many cases the long-term lameness following such injuries is solely due to the adhesion. Walking the horse in hand for 10–15 minutes twice a day will help to prevent adhesion formation. In the case of tendon damage especially it will also help to ensure that new fibrous tissue is formed in the direction of pull when the horse moves the leg, rather than in a haphazard fashion, and this will have a beneficial effect on the strength of the repair.

Do Alternative Medicines Have a Role to Play?

In recent years a wide range of 'alternative' or 'complementary' therapies has become available for the treatment of horse ailments as well as human ones. The common factor for all of them is that they are not controlled by legislation, and so unfortunately can be carried out by anyone without formal training. As a result, their practitioners owe as much to their salesmanship as to any independently proven ability, and the result is that sometimes horse owners are 'taken for a ride'. That is not to say that the therapies themselves are necessarily worthless, but much of the antagonism that does exist between vets and alternative medicine practitioners stems from the fact that due to ignorance, such practitioners sometimes make demonstrably untrue statements about the nature or cause of a problem, and this overshadows the fact that the treatment may be of value.

Manipulation

Perhaps the commonest example of this is in the field of manipulation, where ridiculous claims about bones being displaced and suchlike overshadow the ability of manipulation to relieve muscle spasm and so relieve pain. In most cases manipulation achieves this by causing all the muscles in a system to contract sharply and then relax; when expertly done, the muscle which was previously in spasm will relax with the others (Fig 17). The disadvantage of manipulation is that where the spasm is merely a response to some underlying problem – for example, spasm of the back muscles because of the horse's attempt to redistribute its weight away from a painful hock – then the problem returns at a later date. In my experience, where owners are aware of a real problem and seek manipulation, repeated treatments over a long period are always necessary. Only when a symptom-less horse has been diagnosed by the manipulator as having a problem does one treatment put things right, and it is possible to draw cynical conclusions from this.

There is some evidence that manipulation carried out on an anaesthetised or sedated horse is more successful than that carried out on a conscious horse. Presumably this is because it is possible to exert a wider range of movement on the relaxed muscles.

My advice would be to look on manipulation as one would aspirin: a useful means of pain relief. Of course it has the added advantage for the performance horse that there are no problems with dope testing following its use.

Acupuncture

Acupuncture is another therapy which can provide valuable pain relief. I am totally unconvinced that acupuncture affects the course of a lameness problem – that is, it does nothing to reverse or slow down the pathological processes – but it can give visible pain relief. One significant factor here is that whether the so-called acupuncture points are stimulated by needles (Fig 18), massage, laser or whatever, the effect is just as genuine. The other point to note is that acupuncture is far less successful in affecting diseases that are not obviously painful, for example respiratory disease. It is likely that if the effects of stimulating the acupuncture points had not been

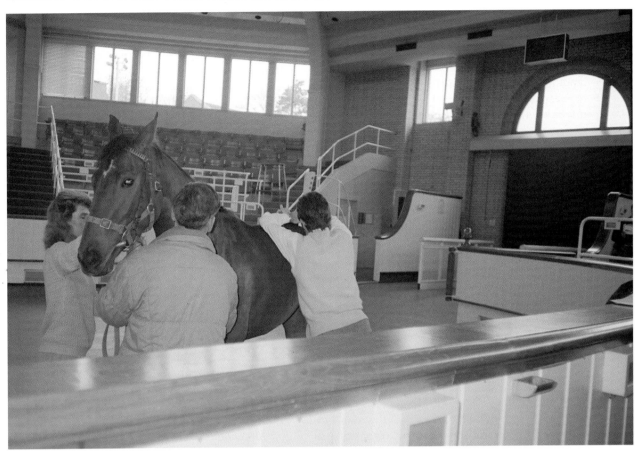

17 Manipulation relieves muscle spasm and therefore pain

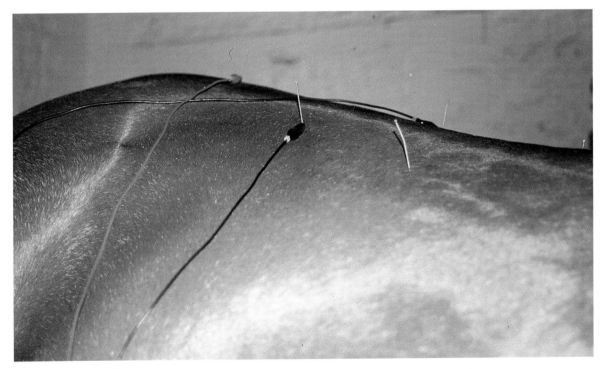

18 Acupuncture needles

discovered until now, their use would receive widespread support from all doctors and vets. It is the explanation of how the therapy works, which dates back thousands of years, that blinds us today. If some alternative practitioners would be prepared to accept that such explanations might be wrong (just as we no longer believe that the earth is flat), then more vets would accept that the treatment itself does actually work.

Homoeopathy

I am afraid that I personally cannot accept that homoeopathy works at all. Our whole concept of the structure of the universe has been based on the concept of the molecule as being the smallest 'building brick' which has a specific identity. So an electron from an oxygen molecule is the same as one from a hydrogen molecule, but the two molecules are different and individual. Homoeopathy is based on the concept of using liquids that contain no molecules at all of a substance, but which are claimed to act as if they did contain the active substance. I think that many people consider homoeopathy to be just about using 'old-fashioned' or 'natural' remedies, and do not realise the leap of faith required to imagine how the diluted-to-nothingness preparations could work, even if the original remedy was effective anyway.

Ultrasound Therapy

Inevitably a certain amount of confusion has arisen between ultra-sound used for lameness assessment, and ultrasound used for treatment. In the latter a probe is held in contact with the skin, helped by an application of gel to ensure that there are no air bubbles between the two. The beam of ultrasound waves which is directed into the soft tissues such as muscle causes what might best be described as 'molecular vibration'. This 'shakes loose' the pockets of tissue fluid which collect in inflamed tissues, and which are responsible for much of the swelling associated with such inflammation. It also stimulates the opening of tiny blood vessels which can usefully bring healing elements into the centre of the tissue and carry away fluid and undesirable by-products of tissue damage; these tend to be shut down by inflammation.

Ultrasound therapy is easy to use, but it is not easy to use beneficially. If too much ultrasound

energy is directed into an area, it gets hotter and hotter, and can even start to cook! Training is needed both to ensure success and to safeguard the horse's welfare. This whole question of physiotherapy needs to be more controlled. Just because a person has bought an ultrasound machine and is prepared to make a business of treating horses does not mean that he or she is a physiotherapist. Many of them have spent no more time studying than the few minutes spent perusing the machine's instruction manual, and no more time training than as little as a morning spent with another unqualified therapist. Yet there are properly trained, chartered physiotherapists who specialise in the treatment of animals and who can bring a great range of expertise to the field. One of the reasons why they may have a lower profile than some of the 'quacks' is that they don't break the law. Most countries have laws which forbid anyone who is not a vet diagnosing what is wrong with an animal, whilst allowing people such as qualified physiotherapists to carry out the treatment in conjunction with the vet. Qualified physiotherapists face discipline from their professional body if they break the law, but 'quacks' do not.

All owners of competition horses should seriously consider what they would do if treatment by an unqualified person delays healing or makes the condition worse. If the horse is insured, they will have invalidated the policy and so may receive nothing. And if the quack subsequently proves to have been seriously wrong, they may well find that they have no redress because the quack has no assets worth suing: he or she will certainly not have any insurance cover to protect himself.

Faradic Stimulation

Faradism is the application of a pulsing electric current to a muscle in order to stimulate its contraction (Fig 19). A base electrode is attached to the horse's body, usually in a special roller, and a hand-held probe used to complete the electrical circuit. Water and gel under the electrode help to ensure a good electrical contact. Controlling the frequency of the stimulation and the strength of the current alters the frequency and force of the contractions. Faradism can be very painful in unskilled hands, not least because the muscles which are being stimulated are often injured.

The technique has several roles: it is diagnos-

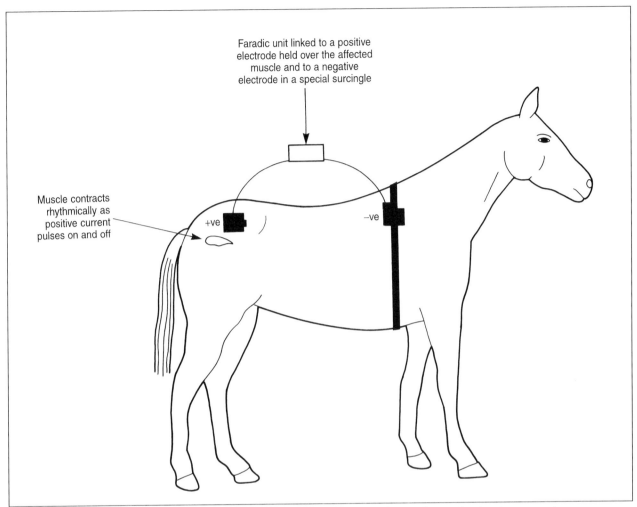

Faradic unit linked to a positive electrode held over the affected muscle and to a negative electrode in a special surcingle

Muscle contracts rhythmically as positive current pulses on and off

+ve   –ve

19 How faradism works: the application of a pulsing electric current to a muscle in order to stimulate its contraction

tic, because careful stimulation can reveal a stronger contraction from the particular muscle which has been damaged; it enables inflammatory fluids to be squeezed out of the muscle by contraction; it also prevents shrinkage (and thus weakening) of the muscle after injury when pain is stopping the horse using the muscle normally. Indeed faradism can be a useful way to build up muscles after injury or to help reduce the loss of muscle fitness if a horse has to be rested for some reason.

Laser Therapy

Cold lasers (as distinct from the cutting lasers used in surgery) use light energy to stimulate the horse's natural anti-inflammatory response. It is thought that they do this by stimulating structures called mitochondria within the cells. Laser therapy can look like magic, because no direct contact is needed between the crystal which emits

the laser light and the target area. The effect of lasers has been shown to increase the activity of cells vital to the healing of structures such as tendons and skin, even in strict laboratory conditions. Laser therapy has also been shown to increase dramatically the levels of the horse's natural anti-inflammatory hormones such as cortisol and seratonin, which circulate in the bloodstream. These may reach up to 300 per cent of normal levels by four hours after treatment, and then slowly decrease back to normal over the next 3–4 days. The value of laser therapy is therefore twofold: it has an anti-inflammatory effect without having to use drugs which would affect dope-testing, and that effect lasts some time. So whereas manipulation might relieve back spasm now but the condition will return within hours, laser therapy will relieve it now and prevent its return for several days, thus allowing the tissues involved to settle down.

Magnetic Field Therapy

Magnetic field therapy has had some wide-ranging claims made for it over the years. Its origin lies in the use of pulsed electromagnetic fields on either side of a broken bone to stimulate fracture healing where it had not occurred before (Fig 20). An effect was proven in the human field, and the technique transplanted to the horse. Along the way some of the equipment became bowdlerised, ending up as blankets covering the whole of the horse's body which are littered with electromagnetic coils. In my practical experience, it might be worthwhile to use electromagnetic fields to promote bone healing in the cannon region, and to stimulate activity in chronically sprained tendons which have healed so far but not further, but in other circumstances the strength and alignments of the fields are just not proven to have any effect.

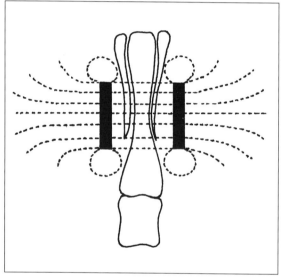

20 Magnetic therapy, where electromagnetic fields are used to promote bone healing in a horse's cannon

Iontophoresis

Iontophoresis, or ion transfer, uses electric current to introduce drugs applied to the skin into the deeper tissues such as tendons. The current involved is only small – 4 milliamps – so the horse does not feel any unpleasant sensation. The drugs have to be water solubles, such as corticosteroids. The technique is sterile and enables the overall dose of the drug used to be around only 1 per cent of that which needs to be given by injection to produce the same tissue level.

Drugs Used in the Treatment of Lameness

■ Steroids

Earlier I mentioned the naturally occurring anti-inflammatory hormone, cortisol. The synthetic version, cortisone, was the first real anti-inflammatory drug, and a number of such steroids (so called because of their molecular structure) are now available. Steroids have little or no pain-killing effect, but they can reduce the effects of inflammation. Nevertheless, their use in the horse is very limited nowadays, for a number of reasons: all steroids can have long-term side effects on the heart, but in both horses and ponies there are also short-term side effects which can produce laminitis; for this reason the systemic use of the drug – use by injection or tablet so that levels circulate throughout the whole body – must only be contemplated when no other treatment is possible, and restricted to short periods.

Steroids have also been used by injection directly into joints affected by degenerative joint disease (DJD), and here the effect can be miraculous. The horse may return to soundness within a couple of days, and in some cases may remain sound for long periods. However, there is a price to be paid. The steroid affects the structure of the surrounding bone, and at some time in the future (which may be months or may even be a couple of years) the bone may start to demineralise and lose all its density and hardness. This change is irreversible and usually results in a horse being much worse off than it was in the beginning. For this reason steroids should not be injected into joints unless all other forms of therapy have failed. Of course some unscrupulous owners use steroid therapy to return a competition horse to soundness and then sell the horse, leaving a time bomb ticking away in the joint. Always ask for, and write down, a full veterinary history of any new purchase. If the vendor fails to disclose that a joint received steroid therapy it may be easier to obtain recompense if the joint disintegrates later.

■ Non-Steroidal Anti-Inflammatory Drugs

The next class of drugs to be developed were the non-steroidal anti-inflammatory drugs (NSAIDs). These have a number of common properties. Their low acidity helps the drugs to accumulate in areas of inflammation, an obvious advantage. Less desirable is the fact that a high proportion of the drug becomes bound to proteins in the blood and consequently inactive; this means that relatively large quantities have to be given, although if the horse is also receiving another protein-binding drug, then there will be less protein available and so more active drug – *ie* a normal dose will result in an abnormally high amount of active drug. The various NSAIDs act at varying stages of the inflammatory cascade. This cascade is a series of chemical reactions which change a substance called arachidonic acid into various prostaglandins. It is these prostaglandins which produce the classic symptoms of inflammation, and which increase the sensitivity of pain receptors.

It will now be apparent that NSAIDs are not centrally acting painkillers in the way that morphine is, for example. However, by blocking the release of prostaglandins they prevent the increased sensitivity of the pain receptors. We might use the analogy of a tooth which is hyper-sensitive to pain because of an abscess. Thus a warm drink might feel excruciatingly hot, but cure the abscess and the tooth won't register any pain. So stop the increased sensitivity and the condition will no longer be painful and the horse no longer lame. We sometimes refer to NSAIDs as masking problems. This might be unfair, but it does emphasise the separation between the anti-inflammatory and the pain sensitivity effects of these drugs. Neither is actually a direct antidote to the original pathological disease or injury.

NSAIDs have naturally been used to enable injured horses to compete, either to enable healing to be completed before the competition or to make the horse temporarily sound for the competition. The attitude of the authorities to the use of such drugs varies, but all competitions now involve the possibility of samples being taken from competing horses and tested for the presence of prohibited substances. Most NSAIDs are broken down in the liver and ultimately removed in urine or bile. Testing urine samples is therefore a particularly sensitive way to detect such drugs; certainly they will be present in urine for longer after their administration than they will in a blood sample. Of course the ability or otherwise to detect NSAIDs in either blood or urine is not the ultimate test as to whether a drug is still active in the body or not. Because they are protein-bound, some of these drugs will remain bound to proteins in the tissues after they have disappeared elsewhere (Fig 21). That is why their 'pain-relieving' effect persists for so long after their administration has been stopped.

There are people who consider that there should not be any restrictions on the use of NSAIDs in competitions, on the grounds that they merely restore performance to normal – they do not improve on what it used to be. Such are the pressures of modern competitions that relatively few horses can reach the top without wear and tear; allowing the use of NSAIDs would widen the spread of horses at the top, thus reducing the pressure on each one. There is also the question of how to treat horses which sustain a minor injury during a competition, and which otherwise might not be allowed to continue the competition after treatment.

On the other hand, many people consider that the use of NSAIDs should never be allowed in competitions because they result in abnormal demands being made on horses which would otherwise be in pain. They consider that medication may result in horses breaking down in competition, or at least the underlying condition deteriorating. Finally they argue that if treated animals win, we may end up selecting horses for breeding which have an inherited unsoundness.

At present the trend is to restrict the use of drugs rather than to relax the controls during competition. There are, however, some parts of the world which allow the use of phenylbutazone, or bute, in racing because there are not enough sound horses. Moreover modern analytical techniques allow the detection of minute levels of drugs, and this dramatically prolongs the time after administration during which the drugs can be detected. Not all competitors think that this increased sensitivity of testing is fair.

■ Bute: its Advantages and Disadvantages

Bute was the first NSAID to be used in the horse, and it is still employed far more widely than any other. It is most commonly given by mouth, although its bitter taste can present problems; paste formulations or injections get over this. The timing of administration of drugs such as bute can be very important. If bute is given in the morning on a more or less empty stomach, then more of it is absorbed in the small intestine. The more food there is in the stomach, the slower the stomach empties and the longer the delay before

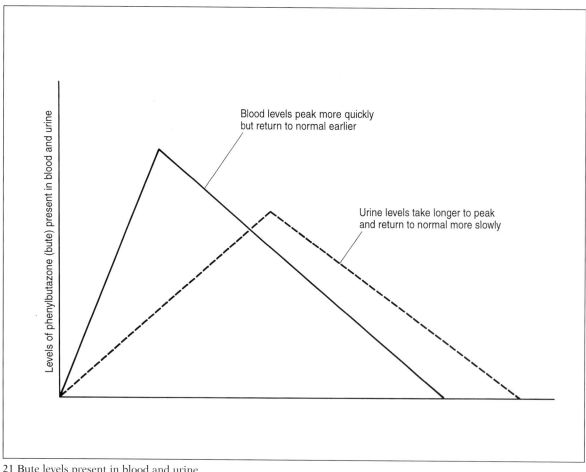

Levels of phenylbutazone (bute) present in blood and urine

Blood levels peak more quickly but return to normal earlier

Urine levels take longer to peak and return to normal more slowly

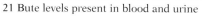

21 Bute levels present in blood and urine

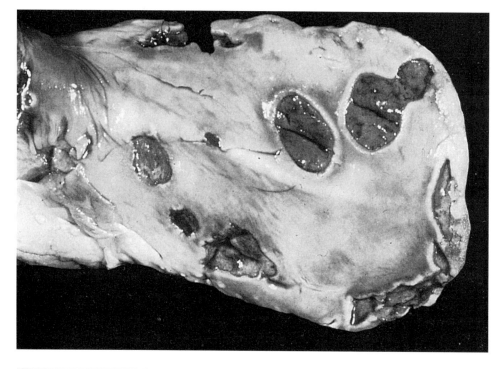

22 Ulceration of the tongue. An overdosage of bute can result in ulceration of parts of the mouth and digestive tract

the drug reaches the intestine. Ponies have a relatively small stomach; their stomach-emptying time is therefore short, and so they absorb relatively more of any bute that has been given.

Bute is far and away the cheapest NSAID; it is also the only one which is licensed for long-term use. Unfortunately there can be toxicity problems in ponies, for the reason already explained: the drug affects the intestinal lining, especially along the large colon, causing it to become permeable to proteins. So the horse loses protein and therefore fluid accumulates in its tissues because the protein is no longer holding that fluid in the bloodstream. These effects can be fatal.

■ Naproxen

Naproxen is not at present available in the UK, but it is interesting to compare this anti-inflammatory drug with bute. It is only available in powder form, but this is quite palatable for horses. Whereas bute is particularly effective in relieving bony conditions, naproxen is at is most effective in treating muscular conditions. Because the drug is rapidly eliminated from the horse's body, it has to be given twice a day in order to maintain effective levels. This is in contrast to the situation with bute where no more than once a day or every other day dosage may be possible once the system has become saturated with the drug.

In a very interesting piece of research, young Quarter Horse colts in training were given a low dose of naproxen every day, and were then compared with colts who only received treatment for any clinical problems. The naproxen horses only lost 3 per cent of their training days because of musculo-skeletal problems, compared with a 13 per cent loss in the other colts. The continuously medicated colts also raced more often afterwards and had fewer clinical illnesses.

■ Meclofenamic Acid

Meclofenamic acid is another NSAID available in powder form. Plasma levels of this drug reach a peak 4 hours after the first dose and decline over 24 hours, so daily dosing is required. However, the chemical effect may not be seen until 36–96 hours after the first dose, which is a little confusing. Meclofenamic acid is claimed to be up to twelve times more effective than bute at reducing inflammation; it is particularly effective at relieving the inflammatory symptoms of laminitis.

■ Flunixen

Flunixen can be given as a powder, paste or injection. It is particularly effective at counteracting the pain associated with colic, indeed so much so that some clinicians are concerned that its use gives a false sense of security in colic cases which should have been receiving surgery. This relief of colic pain occurs within minutes of an intravenous injection; the relief of pain associated with lameness, however, will not occur until 12–16 hours after initial dosing.

■ Ketoprofen

Ketoprofen is an NSAID which can only be given by intravenous injection, which limits its use. It is an effective painkiller in both colic and musculo-skeletal problems, but there seems to be an element of doubt as to where it works in the inflammatory cascade.

Drugs which Affect the Joint Fluid

Unlike the NSAIDs, **hyaluronic acid (sodium hyaluronate)** is a naturally occurring substance. It is the most important constituent of joint fluid, following synthesis by synoviocyte cells in the synovial membrane lining the joint capsule; it provides the lubricant properties of joint fluid; it is also a component of articular cartilage, and plays a role in the nutrition of that cartilage. This is in addition to some standard anti-inflammatory properties.

The original practice was to take joint fluid containing healthy hyaluronic acid from one joint of a horse and to inject it into a joint with DJD. Hyaluronic acid forms complex polymers of high molecular weight around water molecules, which normally provides a very viscous lubricant; but joint fluid removed from a damaged joint is much less viscous and contains hyaluronic acid of low molecular weight. So the rationale was to replace the lubricant for the joint by injecting hyaluronic acid of high molecular weight, in the belief that the higher the molecular weight of the hyaluronic acid polymers used, the more effective they would be. This concept has been dealt a blow by two discoveries. The first was that the hyaluronic acid injected into the joint only survives for 36–96 hours, but the effect lasts much longer than that.

So the high molecular lubricant is not a major factor. The other discovery was that intravenous injection of hyaluronic acid could be just as effective in the treatment of acute joint problems as injection into the joint. This only emphasised the wider role of the drug other than lubrication; indeed it is being used increasingly to reduce the inflammatory response in sprained tendons.

Another approach to the treatment of DJD in horses is the use of **polysulphated glycosamino-glycans (PSGGs)**. Again, there is a naturally occurring PSGG in articular cartilage. Inflammation causes the loss of this substance and the degeneration of the cartilage, but injecting PSGG into the joint will prevent this process because the new PSGG will go directly to the damaged cartilage. PSGG also has conventional anti-inflammatory effects.

It now seems to be accepted that in cases of acute degenerative joint disease and trauma, hyaluronic acid should be given as early as possible. However, in more long-standing cases of DJD the administration of PSGG is more likely to be beneficial. (It is perhaps of practical importance to point out that both of these drugs are relatively expensive to use.)

Antibiotics

Although we do not use antibiotics to treat lameness as such, there are a number of situations when killing infection is a vital part of restoring the horse to soundness. There are actually very few antibiotics licensed for use in the horse: penicillin and streptomycin, trimethoprim, metronidazole and ceftiofur. As a result, vets occasionally have to resort to using human drugs. People are sometimes surprised to learn that antibiotics are prohibited substances as far as competitions are concerned. What is the harm in giving an antibiotic when a horse sustains a wound? they ask. The answer is that some antibiotics are combined with other drugs which do affect performance. For example, penicillin is often given as a procaine salt, and procaine is a local anaesthetic. Analytical laboratories cannot distinguish between procaine used as a local anaesthetic to hide lameness, and procaine given with penicillin, and the only way to stop the former is to stop the latter as well. However, there is now a trend to allow the use of non-procaine bound antibiotics in animals taking part in competitions.

If an infection is not responding to an antibiotic, owners sometimes ask for a 'stronger' drug. There is no such thing: there are only effective and ineffective drugs, and lack of success may be due to the ability of the particular bacteria involved to resist the antibiotic. That resistance may develop even in mid-treatment, so that the antibiotic starts off effective but ends up ineffective. It hasn't become weaker, but has become ineffective. If it is possible to obtain samples of the bacteria and culture them in a laboratory, antibiotics can be tested and their effectiveness assessed.

LEG WOUNDS

Horses involved in competitions invariably suffer superficial wounds to their body, especially their legs. These are particularly frequent when the competition involves jumping, but there are other aspects of competing which carry an increased risk of injury, such as travelling in the horsebox to and from competitions. Three-day event riders in particular tend to put a thick coating of grease over the front of their horses' legs in an attempt to decrease the risk of skin wounds. I don't know whether any statistics have ever been collected to prove whether this works or not, but it is worth bearing in mind that such a coating of grease can have a significant effect on preventing heat loss when the horse tries to cool down after the competition, because it inhibits sweating.

Mud Fever

Mud fever is not a skin wound at all, but inexperienced owners see the scabs which form on the skin as a result of mud fever and sometimes confuse them with small skin wounds. In particular the horizontal line of cracked skin and scabs which often forms across the back of the lower pastern may be mistaken for an overreach. Mud fever is caused by a surface infection with *Dermatophilus congolensis*. These bacteria destroy the superficial layers of skin to leave a raw place which forms a crusting scab. This scab in turn prevents the underlying infection from advantageously drying out, and also the beneficial effect of ultra-violet rays. The name 'mud fever' comes from the fact that muddy, wet conditions soften the horse's skin and make it easier for the infection to establish itself. In some parts of the world the condition occurs in hot dusty conditions where dust constantly abrades the surface of the skin, leaving breaks in the surface through which the infection can gain entry and establish itself.

Treatment

The first step of treatment is to soften every single scab on the horse's body and legs with a good antiseptic shampoo, and then to remove them. This exposes the bacteria to drying. Antibiotic ointment or aerosols can then be applied to the whole affected area in order to kill the *Dermatophilus*. Every day the scabs have to be removed, although the skin may only need to be shampooed every third day. These scabs are infective and so should be disposed of carefully. After shampooing, great care must be taken to dry the skin completely again, making sure not to damage the skin further by using a harsh towel. Sometimes the infection not only involves the skin surface but also spreads under the skin, producing a cellulitis which is recognised by the presence of oedema. If such a swelling does occur the horse will need systemic treatment with antibiotics, via the body as a whole, rather than just by applying more antibiotics to the wounds. Penicillin or trimethoprim preparations are usually effective. The 'cracked heel' *Dermatophilus* causes chronic problems because its situation ensures that any healing of the skin surface only takes place slowly.

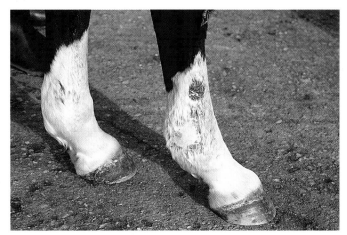

23 Mud fever, a skin infection caused by *Dermatophilus congolensis*; it particularly affects the lower legs and underbelly, and is caused by prolonged exposure to mud and wet conditions. Thin-skinned horses are especially vulnerable

Over-reach

An over-reach is a skin wound on the back of a front leg caused by the toe of a hind leg. Unfortunately in cutting the skin, the back hoof also causes appreciable bruising around the wound, and this slows healing.

24 The over-reach boot has been designed to allow complete freedom of movement of the foot, whilst always protecting the heel region

Treatment

Wounds of any size should still be stitched, because this helps to stabilise the two skin edges. The back of the pastern can be difficult to stitch and then to immobilise with bandages, but immobilisation is vital if the wound is to stand even a reasonable chance of healing. If the horse has to return to fast work before the wound is completely healed, an over-reach boot should certainly be fitted to protect the wound from further injury.

General Considerations regarding Wound Care

There are some general points to consider when looking at any skin wound:

- Straight wounds heal better than wounds with jagged edges.
- If a wound results in a V-shaped flap, the point of the flap rarely heals as well or as quickly as the rest of the wound.
- Vertical wounds usually heal better than horizontal wounds because in the latter, the edges are pulled apart when the horse takes its weight on that leg or uses the underlying muscles.

- Wounds above the knee and hock heal better than those lower down the leg.
- Proud flesh, or exuberant granulation tissue, is more likely to develop at wounds below the knee and hock than at wounds further up the legs.
- Skin flaps contract very quickly so it may look as if a piece of skin has been lost when in reality the skin can still be pulled across the gap; so do not rush to the conclusion that a wound is gaping too much to be stitched.
- Skin wounds should be stitched within an hour of their formation. They will heal if stitched up to 6–7 hours after formation, but the success rate for healing then falls rapidly.
- Stitched wounds may appear to be healing perfectly at first, but around the eighth day they may pull open again.

Skin wounds can be stitched using monofilament nylon thread, although this means that at some future stage the stitch will need to be removed. Dissolvable materials are used to stitch wounds where, perhaps because of the horse's temperament, it will not be easy to examine the wound again, and in such situations the sutures will dissolve on their own after a minimum time that depends on the material used. Increasingly vets are using metal surgical staples to stabilise skin wounds. These cause very little reaction in the skin and do not cross into the subcutaneous tissues in the way that sutures do. A special implement is needed to remove surgical staples from wounds.

One of the reasons why a wound may fail to heal is that an infection has established itself in it; this is always associated with a fluid discharge that is thick and creamy rather than clear and watery. The availability of antibiotics has drastically reduced the incidence of wound infections, but it has not abolished them completely. Applying antibiotic aerosols or creams to the skin surface has only very limited effect on bacteria deep in the wound, and antibiotics really need to be given by injection or by mouth so that they reach the whole body. As long as a wound is discharging or the skin is broken then there is a potential way for new bacteria to get into the wound, and antibiotic treatment needs to be continued until this risk no longer exists. One injection of antibiotic given on the day a wound occurs is often quite inadequate to prevent infection.

When wounds which have been stitched open up again after several days, it is not due to any inadequacy of the suturing: it is because the skin edges have failed to join together. This process is normally complete by the fourth day and it takes the tension off the stitches. If it does not occur, then movement will eventually pull the stitch through one side of the wound. The less movement there is around a wound, the less likely this is to happen. Wounds which break down in this way *will* heal eventually: the gap between the skin edges becomes filled with granulation tissue, which is to a large extent a mixture of fibrous tissue and blood vessels, and skin cells will slowly spread over the top of this and seal the wound.

Unfortunately the horse has a great tendency to continue producing granulation tissue long after the wound gap has been filled. Thus instead of producing a level surface which will heal over quickly with skin, this results in raised granulation tissue, or proud flesh, that skin will never cover. Although other animals do produce such proud flesh, none does it so often or so exuberantly as the horse. Wounds of the lower leg are far more likely to produce granulation tissue than those on the body itself, and such tissue will not heal or go away of its own accord: it has to be removed so that the skin surface is flat before healing may occur (Fig 25). There are two ways in which this is done: the extra granulation tissue may be surgically removed, or it may be destroyed chemically, most commonly using copper sulphate powder. Surgical removal may need to be repeated a number of times for a large wound where the granulation tissue is growing quickly, but it does give quicker results than chemical methods. Returning a horse to work too soon after it has suffered a wound may precipitate granulation tissue development because movement encourages the formation of granulation tissue and slows wound healing.

Dealing with Wounds at an Event

Three-day events pose a particular problem because if a horse injures itself during the cross-country phase there is just one night to get it sound again before the veterinary inspection on the morning of the third day. It is advisable to have a routine to follow during that time in order to minimise the chances of elimination at the veterinary inspection.

The first step is to ensure an adequate cooling-down period at the trot immediately after the cross-country phase. Besides ensuring the removal of lactic acid produced as the muscles recover from their exertions, this helps to maintain a good blood circulation to injured areas in order to bring blood cells and so on for initial healing. Adequate cooling down can prevent much of the general stiffness so often present on day three.

Next, a thorough examination is needed for any small skin wounds, each of which should be carefully cleaned with an antiseptic such as chlorhexidine. A decision has to be made as to whether to have any wounds stitched, bearing in mind that if they are not stitched at this stage then it will not be possible to stitch them successfully after the event. The biggest single factor here is the horse's temperament, because this will decide whether it is possible to stitch a wound without sedation and/or local anaesthetic. Some horses will let you stitch or staple small wounds with only a twitch for restraint, whilst others object violently. By and large stapling of skin wounds causes less reaction from the horse than actually stitching the wound.

Check the horse's back in the way described in the section on back problems, and if there does appear to be any muscle spasm then attempt to

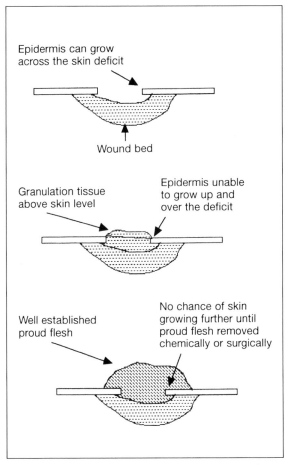

Epidermis can grow across the skin deficit

Wound bed

Granulation tissue above skin level

Epidermis unable to grow up and over the deficit

Well established proud flesh

No chance of skin growing further until proud flesh removed chemically or surgically

25 Effect of proud flesh development on wound healing

relieve it by manipulation or by laser therapy if this is available.

I would suggest applying cold to the tendons overnight even if there is no evidence of a sprain or other injury. It is better to prevent oedema developing around the tendon if you possibly can, not least because it will draw people's attention to the fact that the horse might be likely to be lame. If localised heat and swelling are evident, then you have to be prepared to lose some sleep. If therapeutic ultrasound or laser therapy is available then a session as soon as possible and another four hours before the inspection is ideal. Niagara therapy can be used every couple of hours whilst there is any swelling. Remember how quickly cold applications heat up, and replace them frequently. If you use a block of ice on a localised area then 20 minutes on and 10 minutes off is the pattern to follow.

Trot the horse up about an hour before the inspection. If it is sound, then rest it until your number is called. If it is stiff, however, then start walking it around continuously, interspersing five minutes' trotting every twenty minutes. If it goes sound as a result it is important that you continue the exercise right up until your number is called, because otherwise there is the risk that the horse will stiffen up again, even in a short time such as five to ten minutes.

A higher-than-average number of horses will have colic on the night after the cross-country phase. The problem is when to abandon hope of continuing in the competition by using drugs to relieve the pain, and when to persevere without using painkillers. A rolling horse in a stable with a thick bed and someone on hand in case it gets cast will not usually come to any harm. So if the horse starts rolling don't panic. Try to persuade it to eat a warm bran mash (having made sure that some bran was included in the provisions you take to the event for just this eventuality); this will encourage normal bowel movements. If it rolls for more than twenty minutes then seek veterinary help, and sooner if the rolling is violent even earlier than that. Do not embark on a night-long walking expedition in an attempt to stop the rolling: a twenty mile walk is certainly *not* going to help, but it may well leave both the horse and the owner very tired.

26 A look at what happens during a heavy fall shows that even if the horse gets straight to its feet afterwards, its musculo-skeletal system will be bruised and injured and is likely to need the attention of a vet

THE FOOT

Every veterinary book about the horse repeats the phrase 'no foot, no horse'. It is certainly true that the vast majority of lameness problems either involve the foot, or are affected by the foot; for example, a poorly balanced foot will cause abnormal strains on the structures higher up the leg. So when a vet examines a lame horse and finds no obvious cause for the lameness, then it is the foot that has to be eliminated as first suspect, nerve blocking it and assessing whether this significantly reduces the lameness or not.

The Hoof Wall: Sandcracks

Sandcracks are cracks in the hoof wall (Fig 27). They may be merely superficial, extending only partly through the wall, in which case the effect will be solely cosmetic. If, however, the crack extends right through the hoof wall to the sensitive laminae underneath, it will cause lameness because the laminae will be pinched during movement. Sandcracks usually start at the ground surface of the hoof and extend upwards, and those that reach as far as the coronet will cause further problems because not only is the shearing movement that then occurs at the coronet painful, it also prevents normal horn being formed at that point. The sandcrack is therefore self-perpetuating because horn cannot grow across a damaged, moving coronary band.

■ Treatment

The hoof wall consists of vertical tubules of horn that are held together by chemical bridges; when these chemical bonds are torn apart by force, or when they are weak for metabolic reasons, a

27 Severe sandcrack

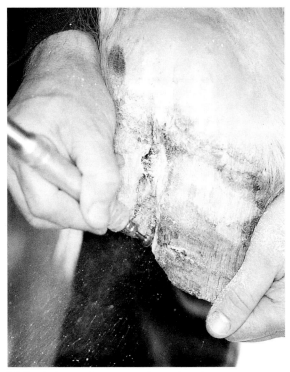

28 Vertical grooving to remedy sandcrack

sandcrack appears. Obviously substandard horn cracks more readily, so it is sensible to try and improve the quality of the horn when even one crack appears. We have to remember that any steps we take in this direction will only affect new horn that is formed, not the existing hoof. It will be six months before the majority of the hoof benefits from any changes we make, and in that time other cracks may continue to appear. The principal chemicals involved in forming the chemical bridges which stabilise the horn tubules are biotin, methionine and calcium. Feed supplements containing high levels of these may therefore be of value in improving horn quality. Except in those rare cases where exceptional physical conditions have dried out the horn so much that it cracks, rubbing anything into the horn will have no benefit at all. Likewise there is not really any scientific evidence to indicate that applying mild irritants to the coronet will stimulate the production of better quality horn.

A variety of techniques are used to prevent a sandcrack from extending further. These include making a deep horizontal groove in the horn just above the crack, or making vertical grooves on either side of it to reduce the tension forces on it (Fig 28), or hammering horizontal nails or staples across it. Once a sandcrack reaches the coronet, the only way to deal with it is to immobilise it completely until new horn is being formed and has extended right down the hoof. This is achieved by cleaning out the crack (the hoof often becomes secondarily infected) and then filling it with a hard synthetic horn substitute which is stabilised by metal sutures and plates across the crack.

The hoof wall sometimes shows horizontal ridges or rings. These may merely reflect differences in nutrition over the months that the hooves were forming. However, similar rings can occur when a horse has had laminitis. When buying a horse it is not possible to distinguish between the two causes, but at least it will prompt a careful examination of the rest of the foot for confirmation one way or another.

Balancing the Foot

Throughout this section, reference will be made to the correct shape of the foot. This is of vital importance: if the shape is right, the percussion forces that occur every time the foot hits the ground will be transferred up the leg properly. If the shape is wrong, then so will the forces in the foot and leg be wrong. It is rather like hitting a nail with a crooked hammer – the nail will not go in straight unless the percussive forces are straight.

In this connection we refer to the hoof/pastern axis. This requires us to draw an imaginary straight line up the centre of the hoof and to continue it upwards. It should pass up the front of the pastern, and be parallel to an imaginary line drawn down the centre of the pastern (Fig 29); if the two lines either converge or diverge, then the horse is said to have a broken hoof/pastern

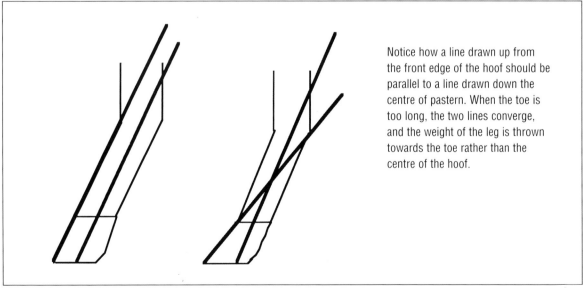

Notice how a line drawn up from the front edge of the hoof should be parallel to a line drawn down the centre of pastern. When the toe is too long, the two lines converge, and the weight of the leg is thrown towards the toe rather than the centre of the hoof.

29 The hoof/pastern axis: if the foot is correctly balanced, the percussion forces will be transferred up the leg properly

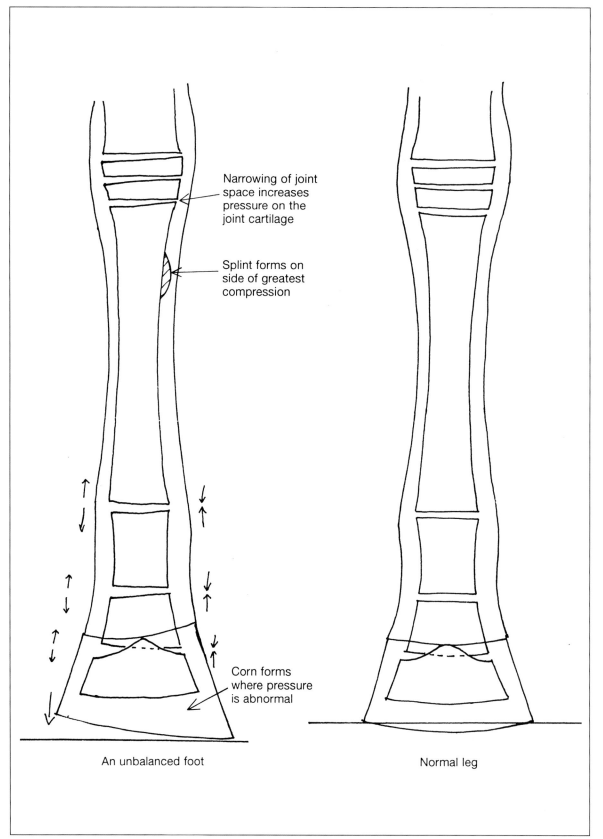

Narrowing of joint space increases pressure on the joint cartilage

Splint forms on side of greatest compression

Corn forms where pressure is abnormal

An unbalanced foot

Normal leg

30 An unbalanced foot causes normal forces in the leg, leading to splints and joint problems

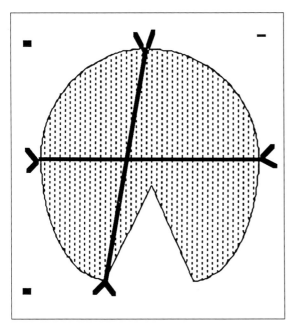

31 The balanced foot

axis. Most commonly the lines converge when the toe of the hoof has grown too long and/or the heels are too low. This means that the horse's weight, which is represented by that central line, falls on the heel region instead of the centre of the foot. The extra pressure on that region leads to a number of problems because the heel is not completely encased with rigid horn. Compression of this area reduces the blood supply to the navicular bone and associated structures, and this predisposes to navicular disease. Such a hoof shape also puts extra pressure on the two branches of the horseshoe and if these are too short they, too, may predispose to the development of corns. Another result of the long toe/short heel shape is that it increases the tension in the ligaments and tendons higher up the leg. Correction involves the removal of a wedge of hoof from the toe extending backwards towards the heel.

The hoof itself should be symmetrical so that the medial, or inside wall is exactly the same height as the lateral, or outside wall. When we look at the sole of the foot, a line drawn from the frog/wall angle to the centre of the toe should be the same length as the maximum width of the foot (Fig 31). When the toe is left too long, that measurement is greater than the width of the foot.

If a horse's feet do not meet these criteria, the farrier should be asked why they do not. If after two shoeings they still do not do so, and there is no explanation offered, then a change of farrier might be called for. A farrier should always be chosen for the quality of his work rather than on price, or whether the shoes will stay on for months on end.

Corns

Bad shoeing is one of several possible causes of corns. Abnormal pressure from the heel of the shoe on the seat of corn causes bruising; this shows as blood-tinged fluid seeping into the horn under that area (Fig 32), which is painful to pressure. Shoes pressing on the sole rather than the wall of the foot, and heels which have been cut too short, are the main causes of corns. Farriers tend to blame the horse for corns, but in many cases the blame is really theirs. Obviously factors such as long periods of roadwork and the thickness of the horse's sole also have a role to play. There are also some horses whose faulty bone conformation results in extra pressure on one or other of the seats of corn – even when standing perfectly square, such horses do not have a vertical cannon and fetlock when viewed from directly in front. If the lower leg deviates outwards it is known as a *valgus* deviation; if it deviates further underneath the horse then it is known as a *varus* deviation.

A horse with corns is lame. It will put its toe to the ground first, rather than taking weight on the heel. The medial heel is most commonly

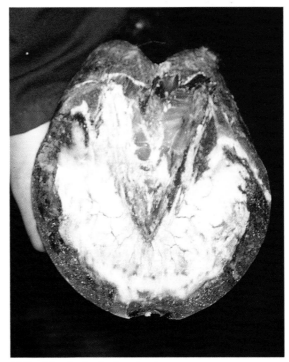

32 Bruising in the heel region known as corn

affected because it takes more weight than the lateral heel; as a result the horse's leg or legs tend to be held further under its body so that the lateral part of the hoof takes more weight.

■ Treatment

Once a corn has formed, the discoloured horn should be pared away. The pain stems from the fact that inflammatory fluid has produced pressure because there is no space for it to go; removing the horn over the corn relieves that pressure. Tubbing the foot or poulticing it for forty- eight hours may be advantageous before the horse is re-shod. The shoe fitted should have its ground surface cut away for 2cm (1in) or so from the affected heel or heels (Fig 33), so as to reduce percussion on that area. Of course exercise on hard surfaces such as roads should be avoided.

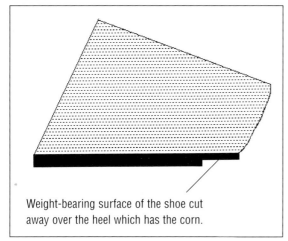

Weight-bearing surface of the shoe cut away over the heel which has the corn.

33 Remedial shoe to alleviate corn

Solar Bruising

Similar bruising can occur elsewhere on the sole and this may be difficult to diagnose. If it is near the junction between the horn of the wall and that of the sole, called the white line, the pressure may force the fluid into the white line and it will then be visible (this can be seen in the laminitic foot shown in Fig 35, page 186). In other cases, though, there will be nothing visible on the sole. The hoof will be painful on pressure with hoof testers, but there is no specific test for bruising under the sole; the diagnosis tends to be made by default, rather than by anything we can see.

■ Treatment

Because the pressure cannot be relieved in this case, it can take weeks of resting for the horse to recover. Painkillers tend not to be very successful in removing the pain, although this is not such a bad thing because it removes the temptation for owners to work the horse before this inflammation has subsided. Covering the sole with a protective vinyl pad, held in place by the shoe, may reduce percussion when the horse does return to work, but this should be a temporary rather than a permanent measure as it does produce some abnormal stresses in the hoof itself. Foam filler, which hardens on contact with the air, should be used under the pad to prevent mud or grit penetrating under there.

Pus in the Foot

One of the most dramatic lamenesses is that seen when the sole is punctured by a sharp object, such as a nail or flint, and infection is introduced to the sensitive laminae. As the bacteria multiply, the pressure builds up, and like the abscess over the nerve to a tooth, the pain can be intense. Characteristically the horse is very lame very quickly; often it will not put the foot fully on the ground if made to move, and rests it when standing. The hoof wall may be warm to the touch, but this is not always the case. Sometimes the lower leg may become swollen as infection spreads out from the foot, and this can distract attention from the real cause.

■ Treatment

With pus in the foot, treatment and diagnosis are almost the same thing because once a reservoir of pus is found, the pressure will be released. Usually careful examination of the sole will reveal a dark mark where the puncture occurred, and cutting down this mark with a hoof knife will lead to the pus. Occasionally the collection of pus will only be located on x-ray. When it is found it may spurt out under pressure, and may have formed a surprisingly large cavity in the foot.

The pain relief once the pus is able to escape can be almost instantaneous. The foot is generally poulticed for a couple of days afterwards to allow the pus to drain out completely, by which time the horse is usually sound again. Antibiotics will be needed to control any infection which has entered the sensitive tissues, especially if there was any swelling up the leg. Because the bacteria involved are often anaerobic – meaning they can flourish in the absence of oxygen – it may help to flush the cavity with an antibiotic such as metronidazole, which is effective against anaerobic bacteria. Before the horse returns to work, the cavity in its foot should be plugged with cotton wool soaked in either metronidazole or an antiseptic, to prevent soil being packed into the cavity. Because the horn of the sole is relatively thin, it is replaced quite quickly and the hole will soon 'grow out'.

A Pricked Foot

Because owners often have horses shod ready for a competition, these are susceptible to problems that arise during shoeing. The most dramatic is if a farrier 'pricks' the horse, when the nail penetrates the sensitive tissue whilst it is being inserted. This is immediately painful, and so the farrier knows what has happened and repositions the nail. Unfortunately that is not normally the end of the problem because it may take twenty-four hours for the inflammation to subside, during which time the horse will be lame. It is also possible for infection to be introduced, in which case the injury will become pus in the foot, as already described. A more insidious problem is nail bind, where one or more nails are close enough to the sensitive structures to put pressure on them, but have not penetrated them. The result is a low-grade lameness after shoeing, which usually settles down after a few days but which can affect performance.

Seedy Toe

The pus which forms in the foot is often unlike pus that develops elsewhere. It may not be liquid, but instead be more like a dry black paste, and this is especially the case with a condition known as seedy toe. This involves infection travelling up the white line at the toe, presumably because the laminae have separated or been slightly damaged; it can penetrate a surprisingly long way up towards the coronet. Although the foot may not feel warm, and may not be very painful when compressed by hoof testers, the horse is lame.

■ Treatment

This kind of pus will not drain out and must be physically removed, and unless every last bit of it is cut out, the problem will tend to recur at a later date; this may mean cutting a deep hole up the inside of the hoof wall. Once all the infection has been removed, it is best to fill the hole with a synthetic horn replacement in order to prevent any gravel, mud or grit being pushed up into the cavity. It is important to avoid a long toe/short heel in these horses, as this contributes to tearing of the laminae, thus enabling infection to reach the deep tissues.

What is Laminitis?

Laminitis is the degeneration of the laminae that provide the junction between hoof and pedal bone. In fact there is no physical link: it is the surface tension between the thousands of tiny folds that keeps the link rigid, and the horse's weight is suspended from the laminae, rather than supported by the frog or sole. So there is always the potential for tearing (Fig 34), and as already

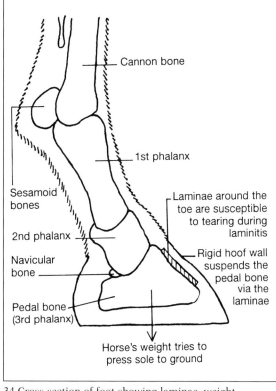

34 Cross-section of foot showing laminae, weight direction and tearing forces

35 Bruising of the sole. There is also some separation between the hoof wall and the sole, possibly indicating the beginnings of laminitis

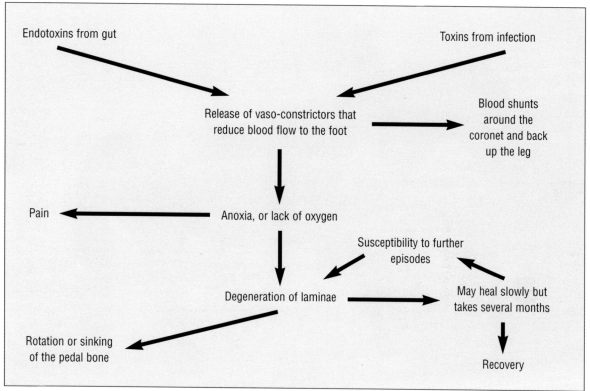

36 The story of laminitis: how anoxia leads to degrees of laminitic degeneration

mentioned, a long toe/short heel conformation will increase the tearing forces. The cause of laminitis always lies away from the feet. Toxins released from degenerative tissues elsewhere – for example, a mare with a retained placenta, or from bacteria in the gut after a carbohydrate overload of the stomach – affect the blood vessels to all four feet, although not all will show symptoms. The blood vessels to the actual foot close down, and instead the blood shunts around the coronet. This results in a period of anoxia, or oxygen starvation, in the sensitive laminae, and this in turn causes pain (see Fig 36).

■ Symptoms

Laminitis is a multi-foot lameness. It can be sudden in onset, and the pain may be so intense that the horse will not be willing to move at all, or it may just look like a generalised stiffness. The horse often tries to take its weight on its heels to avoid the toe tearing any more laminae (see Fig 37). There is a common misconception that the feet are always hot in laminitis, but this is not so; when it does occur, it is because the blood is pooling in the foot, rather than because of increased circulation. During its longer stay in the foot, there

is more opportunity for the blood to lose heat to the horn, which therefore feels warm.

Ponies are much more likely to suffer laminitis than horses, especially laminitis associated with dietary overload. Ponies with a pronounced crest may be more at risk of developing the condition. Once a horse or pony has had one attack of laminitis, it is more susceptible to the condition until the laminae have completely healed; this may take from one to two years, even though outwardly everything looks, and feels, normal during that time.

In severe laminar degeneration, the pedal bone may lose all its support, and it then sinks vertically downwards. In other cases the laminar support at the toe is lost, and the deep flexor tendon pulls the heel upwards and backwards; the pedal bone rotates, presenting its sharp toe to push down through the sole (see Fig 38). Both these abnormalities can be seen on x-ray, although the former requires some experience to spot. X-rays may also show the dark shadow at the front of the pedal bone where the laminae have separated and there is an air gap.

■ Treatment

Until recently, horses with laminitis were kept on

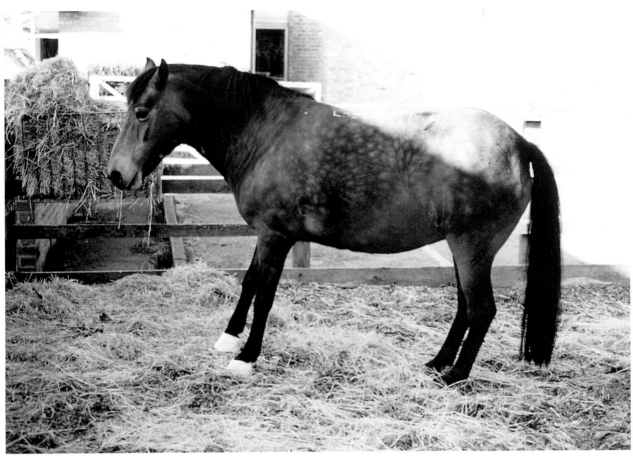

37 Typical stance in the laminitic horse

the move to keep the circulation to the foot ticking over. However, now that we appreciate the significance of laminar instability in the condition, we realise that they should be box-rested. Even farriery should be delayed until the laminae have settled down, because trimming the foot can occasionally make things worse if it disturbs some degenerating laminae. Whilst the horse is being rested, a deep sand bed is best; this can be up to 30cm (12in).

Obviously we must give the horse as much relief from pain as we can, realising that the pain in laminitis comes from anoxia in the tissues rather than anything else. Nevertheless, if the pain stops, it does not mean that the feet are back to normal, with stable laminae. Phenylbutazone, meclofenamic acid, flunixen and ketoprofen are all used, but because of the duration of the condition there may be problems in maintaining pain relief. Only phenylbutazone is really marketed for long-term use, and even that can be toxic in small ponies at anything more than low therapeutic doses.

Where laminitis is associated with a recent overload of food such as lush grass, it is worth giving a purgative, such as liquid paraffin by stomach tube, to speed up the emptying of the gut. Horses with laminitis should not be starved, even if they are overweight, as this can cause metabolic problems such as hyperlipaemia. Instead they should be allowed maintenance quantities of hay. Repeated bran mashes are not necessary.

Once the feet start to settle down, we can turn our attention to them. Rubber 'lily pads' (see Fig 39) fixed to the foot with adhesive tape will provide support via the frog for the bony column to prevent further tearing of the laminae. The aim of farriery is to restore the hoof shape to its normal relationship with the pedal bone. Where the pedal bone has rotated, this may involve removing much of the front wall of the hoof; in some cases the whole front wall is removed in what is called a hoof-wall resection. This must not be undertaken lightly. Having ensured that the pedal bone is back to its normal position, remedial shoes are usually fitted. Heart-bar shoes (Fig 40) may help to stabilise and support the structures of the foot, but if not correctly fitted they can cause more problems. The frog support must not press on the sole at all, and the pressure it exerts must not be too great or the horse will be in great pain. Whatever farriery is undertaken, regular 3–4 weekly monitoring will be necessary.

■ Prevention

There are certain aspects of management that owners should continuously bear in mind to prevent laminitis occurring:

- Do not overfeed. Fat, 'show condition' animals are much more likely to develop laminitis than thin ones.
- Avoid marked variations in the amount of concentrate or lush grass fed.
- Keep the feet properly trimmed. A broken hoof/pastern axis results in extra tearing forces on the laminae.
- Seek prompt veterinary treatment for toxic conditions such as a retained placenta after foaling, because these can lead to secondary laminitis.

Fractures in the Foot

Despite the protection provided by the hoof, both the pedal bone and the navicular bone which lies behind it can be fractured. Naturally this results in lameness, although some horses with fractured pedal bones are not severely lame after the first week or so, and as a result the severity of the problem is not recognised until x-rays are taken. Fractured pedal bones may heal themselves: the hoof acts as a splint, and further stability can be provided by a shoe with toe clips. Healing will take approximately six months, and the horse must be rested until x-rays show that the fracture line has healed, rather than relying on the return of soundness as an indicator of healing.

Some fractures may be suitable for repair by screwing the fragments together. To do this, small windows are made in the hoof, and screws inserted into the bone; these may remain in place for the rest of the horse's life. Screwing can provide a better repair than conservative treatment, and so will warrant consideration if it is hoped to return the horse to competition. Screwing can also be used to repair fractured navicular bones, but this is a very difficult operation which does not have

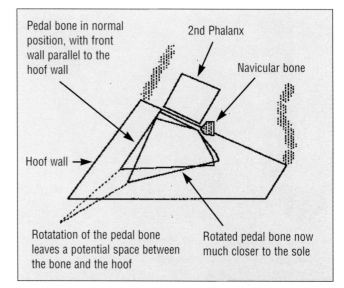

Pedal bone in normal position, with front wall parallel to the hoof wall

2nd Phalanx

Navicular bone

Hoof wall →

Rotatation of the pedal bone leaves a potential space between the bone and the hoof

Rotated pedal bone now much closer to the sole

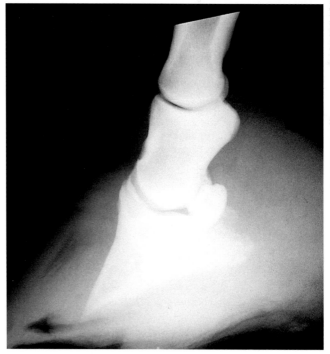

38a&b   Rotation of the pedal bone

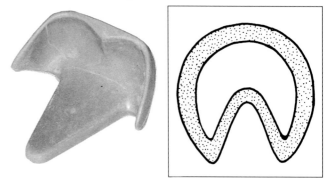

39 A rubber lily pad   40 A heart-bar shoe

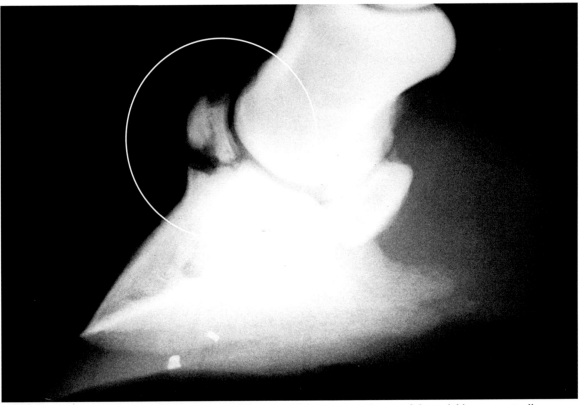

41 X-ray of pyramidal disease, an inflammation of the pyramidal process on the top of the pedal bone; eventually new bone forms on the site

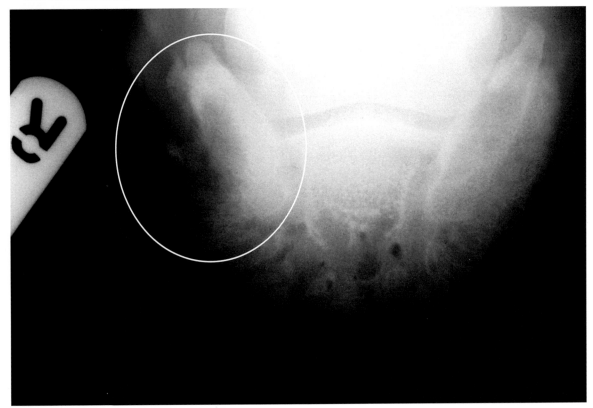

42 X-ray to show pedal osteitis

such a high success rate. Unfortunately fractured navicular bones rarely heal with rest.

Pyramidal Disease

Pyramidal disease is an inflammation of the pyramidal process on the top of the pedal bone where a tendon attaches to the bone. It is caused by tension on that attachment, and, in time, new bone forms around the site. Like most new bone, it is painful, and in this case, x-rays are needed to make the diagnosis (Fig 41); unfortunately in some cases they may also show that the process has fractured and become detached from the pedal bone.

Rest will usually enable the problem to settle down, although there is always the possibility of it flaring up again. Some horses become permanently lame and can only be ridden using painkillers. When a fracture occurs it may be possible to fix it back in place using a screw if the bone fragment is large enough.

Pedal Osteitis: Does it Exist?

It has been said that pedal osteitis is a radiographic diagnosis, by which is implied that the x-ray changes are not really significant but that it is convenient to blame them for the horse's lameness. The changes may include an apparent loss of bone around the edge of the pedal bone, making it look as if something has been nibbling it (Fig 42), and there may also be areas of reduced density in the bone itself. The problem is that these changes occur in almost as many sound horses as they do lame horses, so it is difficult to say that they represent inflammation or degeneration of the pedal bone. Vets have sometimes clung to the name as a last resort, when they find nothing else wrong. One of the problems with accepting it as a specific disease entity is that we have difficulties in explaining what disease process has caused such generalised 'changes' in the pedal bone. It is probably safest to consider such cases as a form of navicular syndrome (see below) which just happen to show these 'normal' x-ray changes as well.

What is Navicular Disease?

Navicular disease is the commonest cause of chronic lameness in the riding horse; it is also the most puzzling, so much so that there is a tendency to use the term 'navicular syndrome' rather than 'disease' because there are different symptom patterns that all appear to have a common link. Classic navicular disease causes chronic lameness in one or both front feet. Nerve blocks prove that the pain is located in the heel region, and when the foot is x-rayed there are characteristic x-ray changes in the navicular bone. However, the range of symptoms we see includes horses with the characteristic x-ray changes but no lameness, and horses with chronic heel pain but no x-ray changes at all.

Much has been written about the predisposing factors for navicular disease, and which horses are most at risk of developing the problem. It usually affects horses at the height of their competitive life, at 8–10 years old. Thoroughbred-cross horses are said to be most susceptible, perhaps for conformation reasons. Usually in the majority of cases the horse's feet will have been poorly balanced, with the long toe/short heel conformation particularly common. Perhaps because of the effect of shoeing or because of the amount of work the horse carries out, navicular disease often surfaces 6–8 weeks after a horse has been purchased, or even after it has just moved stable yards. There is also evidence that if a horse is box-rested for some reason, perhaps because of some other type of lameness, then navicular disease is more common in the succeeding months.

■ Symptoms

The onset of navicular disease may be very gradual. The horse may be lame when it first comes out of the box in the morning, but the lameness quickly wears off with work. Alternatively it may be sound at work, but if, for any reason, it is trotted a half to one hour later, it appears lame. Some horses are not lame as such but start stumbling when ridden. However, there are other cases where the onset of lameness is sudden: the horse comes out of its box noticeably lame one day and remains so. Perhaps one of the factors in this variation is that navicular disease does affect both front feet, so the pain in one can cancel out the

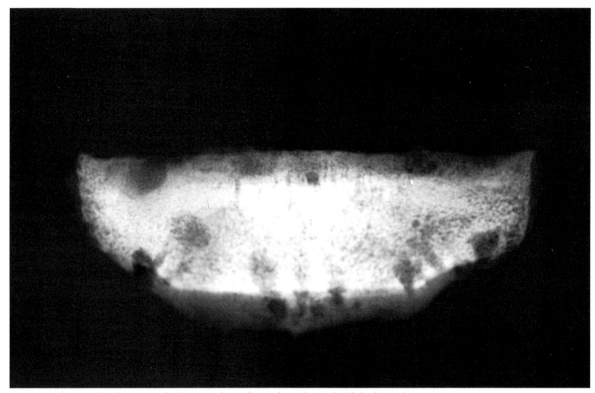

43 X-ray of navicular disease including new bone formed on the ends of the bone, known as a spur

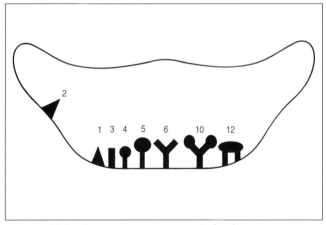

44 Scoring system to assess navicular disease

pain in the other and will make the horse appear sound. If one foot is nerve blocked, though, the horse may be very lame on the other foot. Similarly it may be sound when trotted in a straight line, but lame when trotted in a circle on one or both reins.

Flexion tests can be useful in the diagnosis of navicular disease: hold the leg with the foot flexed as much as possible for one minute, and then trot the horse off immediately – this may reveal a surprising degree of lameness. Flexion tests may well be positive even before any clinical signs have been spotted. They are not specifically diagnostic for the presence of navicular disease, but they do sound a loud alarm bell for its presence.

THE ROLE OF X-RAYS

X-rays play a vital role in the diagnosis of navicular disease. There are three types of x-ray change that occur: first, there are changes to the nutrient foramina, the channels through which blood vessels pass supplying the shuttle-shaped navicular bone; these may increase significantly in numbers or complexity. Second, one or more areas of the body of the bone degenerate, which on x-ray results in a black shadow inside the bone. Third, new bone forms on the ends of the bone where the collateral ligaments attach; this new bone is referred to as a spur (Fig 43).

Most horses with navicular disease show the first type of x-ray change, but this is also the most difficult to interpret. An attempt has been made to award points for different shapes of nutrient foramina and their numbers, and thus to produce a total score for that particular horse (Fig 44). Scores under 10 are insignificant, scores over 15 are definitely significant, and scores between 10 and 15 may be significant. Not everybody, however, is convinced of the validity of this system.

There is no real link between the severity of the x-ray changes and the degree of lameness, and there is little we can tell from the changes we see in individual cases except to confirm the diagnosis. One thing which owners often ask is, 'How long has the disease been present?' This has a particular significance when the horse has only recently been purchased, but unfortunately it is not possible to answer the question. It is probably safe to say that it takes 4–6 weeks for changes such as I have described to become obvious on x-ray, but it is not possible to go any further back than that and say that the problem has been present for three months, a year or any particular period.

Owners very often want to know whether navicular disease is hereditary, because they are considering retiring an affected horse for breeding. It is certainly true that most lists of hereditary diseases, such as those used when deciding whether a stallion is suitable for breeding, include navicular disease on them. However, it is probably more likely that it is the predisposing confirmation which is hereditary rather than the actual disease. As such, if a horse with navicular disease has good conformation then breeding from it might be considered.

X-ray changes are not directly associated with the production of pain, so if a horse responds to treatment and becomes sound, the changes apparent on the x-ray will still be present, and will not have 'improved'. Presumably the horses which have such changes but no lameness represent those which are naturally cured. So if we x-ray a horse on any particular day – for example, prior to purchase – we can tell very little about its future with regard to navicular disease. If there are changes present, they may be entirely historical and represent no threat for the future. If there are no changes present, there is no way of forecasting whether both changes and/or lameness will or will not arise in the future. In my opinion therefore, such precautionary x-raying is pointless. The difficulty is that once the x-rays have been taken, you either act on them and refuse to buy an apparently sound horse, or you ignore them and buy an apparently sound horse which is probably uninsurable.

X-rays can, however, be useful in deciding the significance of one possible feature of navicular disease, namely a contracted foot. It has often been noticed that affected horses have one foot narrower than the other, and that this foot becomes progressively more upright and box-like. At one stage it was thought that this predisposed to navicular disease but it is now thought to be the result rather than the cause. Anyone who is considering buying a horse with one foot narrower than the other, or has a horse which starts to develop a contracted foot, should ask for x-rays to be taken so as to look for evidence of other changes indicative of navicular disease. On the other hand, some horses are born with asymmetrical feet and they are not at any increased risk of developing the disease.

■ Treatment

SHOEING

The first and most important step in the treatment of navicular disease is to ensure that the feet are properly balanced. As a minimum the horse should be shod with shoes that have a rolled toe set slightly back from the front edge of the hoof (Fig 45), and with heels that extend slightly behind the back of the hoof. Egg-bar shoes (Fig 46) are better because they provide even more protection for the heel region. Some horses do occasionally tread on the heels of egg-bar shoes with their hind feet, and pull them off, but this is a small price to pay for the valuable job which they do. Pads have no role in the treatment of navicular disease, and wedged heels should only be used as a last resort when the heels are originally so low that it is not possible to balance the foot properly just by trimming. Remedial shoeing alone will return many horses to soundness; this is a slow process, however, which may take up to two years and so occupy much of the horse's potential competitive life.

DRUGS

The first drug to be used in the treatment of navicular disease – rather than just masking the pain associated with it – was the rat poison known as warfarin, an anti-coagulant whose effect is to ensure a better blood supply to the bone. Unfortunately over-dosage is toxic and puts the animal at risk of fatal haemorrhages, so the horse's blood-clotting time has to be checked regularly throughout treatment. More recently the vasodilator isoxsuprine has superseded warfarin as the

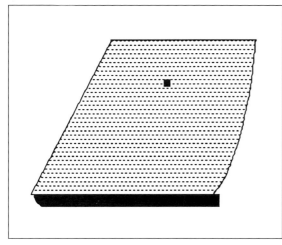

45 Lateral view of a foot shod for navicular disease. Notice how the rolled toe is set very slightly back from the toe of the hoof, whilst the heels of the shoe similarly extend fractionally back behind the hoof

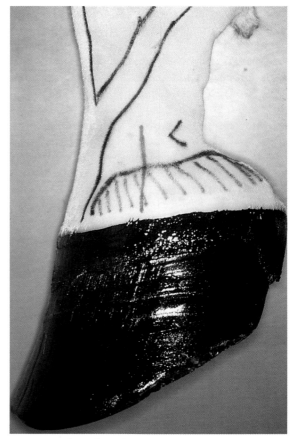

47 Cutting the collateral navicular ligaments

drug of choice to improve the navicular bone's blood supply. It is non-toxic, and its effect can usually be seen within 6–12 weeks.

There is some discussion about whether isoxsuprine actually 'treats' navicular disease because the x-ray changes remain, and the lameness may return in 1–3 years. In my opinion it is treating the condition, although it is not removing the predisposing factors which made the horse liable to the problem in the first place. After all, the horse ends up sound without the need for continual medication so it is not masking the existence of the disease. Neither isoxsuprine nor warfarin have any painkilling effect.

SURGERY

Surgery is also an option. Over the years many horses have had the nerves to their feet cut to remove the pain of navicular disease, an operation called neurectomy. However, apart from any ethical questions this raises, it brings only temporary relief, and during that time any other foot problem, such as pus in the foot, can have disastrous

46 Egg-bar shoe

consequences. More usefully the navicular bone's collateral ligaments can be cut surgically (Fig 47); this allows the bone to re-position itself slightly into a less painful, or more effective position. The operation allows a rapid return to work – indeed, its success depends on regular and consistent exercise in the early period after the operation. In many cases horses which have had this operation can be detected by a fibrous thickening or hard swelling over the operation sites.

■ Will the Horse Compete Again?

All the treatment methods outlined above will return a percentage of otherwise chronically lame horses to soundness, and the overall success rate of each treatment when assessed a year later is surprisingly similar: around 60 per cent. The treatments are not exclusive, and all of them can be used in the same horse. Unfortunately some horses do not respond to treatment at all, and even the use of painkillers such as phenylbutazone may not enable some cases to become sound. Indeed it is often the very horses which do not respond to painkillers which do not respond to any treatment for navicular disease, and there is something to be said for trying a horse for a short time – say, 5–7 days – on bute early on in order to find out whether it has a minimum future ability to be used for hacking.

Because the development of navicular disease involves problems with the blood circulating in the foot, rest is very much contra-indicated once the disease has been diagnosed. Apart from anything else, if a horse goes sound with rest it is often not really cured and goes lame again so soon as it returned to work. The horse should be given twenty minutes walking and trotting in hand twice a day even if it is lame. This is continued until the first assessment after six weeks. If a horse receiving isoxsuprine is sound at that stage, and has been for at least two weeks, then the drug is withdrawn over a further three weeks. If the horse is not sound, then the dosage of isoxsuprine may be increased by approximately 40 per cent. If the horse then responds and goes sound, the drug can be withdrawn. A small number of horses will remain sound whilst on continuing isoxsuprine, but will go lame whenever it is withdrawn.

Owners often seem to be in an indecent hurry to abandon the therapeutic shoes which have so recently helped to return their horse to soundness. I would recommend that such shoeing be continued for the rest of the horse's competitive life – why risk allowing the problem to return? One of the commonest reasons why a horse which has become sound after navicular disease will go lame again is that the strict attention to balancing and shoeing the feet has been forgotten.

Once the horse has remained sound for three weeks after the isoxsuprine has been withdrawn then ridden work can recommence, and there is no reason to limit what that work entails, although obviously it will have to build up gradually over a period of time.

Rehabilitation following surgery to cut the collateral ligaments is very similar. Twenty minutes in-hand walking exercise twice a day starts on day one after surgery. When the wounds have healed, trotting is included, and once the horse has been sound for three weeks then ridden work can commence.

TENDONS

What Do Tendons Do?

There are, of course, many tendons and ligaments throughout a horse's body, but when we talk about a horse having sprained a tendon we are referring to the structures which lie behind the cannon bone (Fig 48). There are two flexor tendons, which in this region lie one on top of the other: the superficial flexor tendon transfers tension from the muscle higher up the leg to the pastern; and the deep flexor tendon flexes the foot, attaching to the pedal bone. It is a feature of the horse that there are no muscles below the knee or hock; the structures of the lower leg are all moved by tendons from muscles in the upper leg. Because the flexor tendons pull the leg backwards, and because the leg is bearing weight when it does so, they are vital for movement but unfortunately are all too readily injured.

Running from the back of the knee to attach to the tendons about a third of the way down the cannon bone is the check ligament, whose role is to prevent too much movement of the tendons; in particular it prevents the fetlock collapsing down to the ground when the horse lands over a jump.

Finally there is the suspensory ligament which originates at the back of the knee at the top of the cannon bone. About three-quarters of the way down the cannon it divides into two branches, each of which originally attaches to a sesamoid bone at the fetlock. The suspensory ligament provides an elasticity to the fetlock and, almost like a spring, restores it to its normal position after every stride.

Because of the widespread use of ultrasound scanning to assess tendon injuries, it is important to be able to relate the structures described above to what is seen on a scan. In the top third of the cannon there are three blocks of tendon immediately visible. On closer examination the block immediately below the skin consists of both the superficial and the deep flexor tendons. Below them is the check ligament, and below that the suspensory ligament. Halfway down the cannon there are two structures visible, the flexor tendons and the suspensory ligament below them. Finally, three-quarters of the way down the cannon the suspensory ligament can be seen dividing into two, branches lying underneath the flexor tendons (Fig 50, p198).

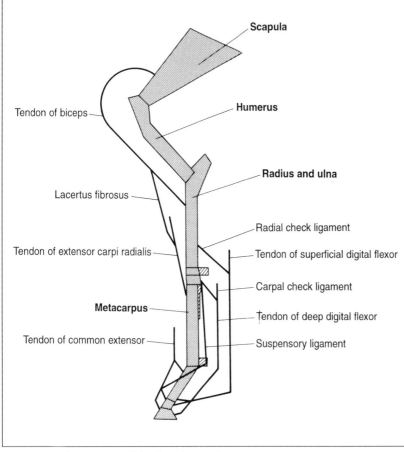

48 The anatomy of the front leg tendons

Scapula

Humerus

Radius and ulna

Tendon of biceps

Lacertus fibrosus

Radial check ligament

Tendon of extensor carpi radialis

Tendon of superficial digital flexor

Carpal check ligament

Metacarpus

Tendon of deep digital flexor

Tendon of common extensor

Suspensory ligament

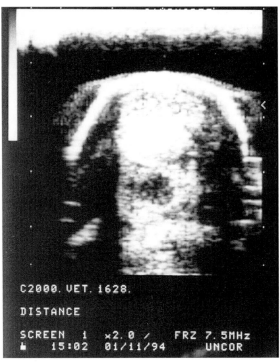

C2000. VET. 1628.

DISTANCE

SCREEN 1 x2.0 /   FRZ 7.5MHz
  15:02 01/11/94   UNCOR

49 Scan of damaged tendon showing a black 'hole' in the middle of the tendon where the disruption has occurred

Even when moving at a controlled pace over level ground the horse's flexor tendons have very little safety margin. Mechanical measurements show that the maximum force they can withstand without significant disruption is 25–50,000 N, and it has also been calculated that the average Thoroughbred has a force of around 22–33,000 N on a single leg at times when galloping; so it needs only the slightest lack of co-ordination to take that force over the danger level.

How Does a Tendon Heal?

When a horse does sprain its tendon, the fibres are torn and cells migrate from the outer membrane of the tendon into the damaged area. These cells, and cells from blood leaking out of damaged blood vessels, are responsible for the healing process; by the end of the first month after an injury the whole area will have been filled with granulation tissue. This has large numbers of cells, in contrast to healthy tendon tissue which has very few cells, and the sprained area may be thickened up to twice its normal thickness. Ultrasound scans taken during these early stages after injury reveal the characteristic 'black hole' where the disruption has occurred (Fig 49).

New tendon fibres then start to be formed, consisting of a protein called collagen, but unfortunately the initial fibres are formed in a very higgledy-piggledy fashion and do not lie in the direction of pull along the tendon as the normal fibres do. Over the following months, more and more fibres are formed to replace the granulation tissue, and the fibres come to be more normal in their layout. By six months after the initial injury the tendon begins to look more like normal, with the collagen fibres lying along the lines of stress.

This does not mean that healing is complete. The early collagen fibres formed after injury are not the normal mature form of collagen, which is called collagen type I, but a much weaker, immature form called collagen type III; even 12–14 months after the injury, many of the fibres may still be type III collagen. One significance of this is that type I collagen fibres are not straight but have 'crimp' in them which enables them to stretch slightly like elastic. The type III collagen has little or no crimp. As the crimping is the major factor which allows tendons to stretch under stress, recently healed tendons will have a greater tendency for further injury. It is *not* the case that the thickened, healed tendon is stronger than the original, which is what some people expect.

During initial repair of a tendon injury the horse is obviously having to manufacture much increased amounts of protein. By the six-months' stage, protein manufacture has returned to normal. However, by nine months after the injury both the injured leg and the normal leg are manufacturing protein at a significantly increased rate again. Why? This time levels will not return to normal until 12–24 months after the injury. The assumption is that at the time when horses are often returning to work with an apparently healed tendon, both the injured *and the non-injured* legs are under such stress that they need to increase the amount of protein they manufacture. This appears to be confirmed by the fact that when tendon tissue from the non-injured leg is examined under a microscope it is found to be far from normal, and contains increased numbers of cells just as an injured tendon does in the initial stages of healing. This explains why, when a horse sprains a tendon in one foreleg, it is more likely to sprain the tendons of the other foreleg when it returns to work.

It is obvious that the healing of any injured tendon must be complete before the horse is returned to work, and assessment by the hand

and eye is not reliable in establishing this. The ultimate test is to use a sophisticated (and very expensive) piece of electronic equipment called a force plate. This is basically a metal plate which is mounted in the ground, so that the horse can be trotted over it; when the leg in question hits the plate, the machine measures how much force has been applied, not only in the vertical direction but also in a forwards and sideways direction as well. The force plate is so sensitive that it can detect minute abnormalities in the horse's action which do not show as lameness because the rest of the body is compensating for them. The force plate also confirms that the horse's action is usually back to normal by six months after the original injury, but that at around nine months after the injury, the time when the changes in

protein manufacture are occurring, marked abnormalities are again present in the horse's action as a result of strain put on the 'good' leg, even though these cannot be detected clinically.

A good response to tendon injury would be as follows:

3 months: lameness, pain on palpation, heat and swelling all absent
6 months: no clinical symptoms or thickening of the tendon
9 months: horse in full work

And a fair response to tendon injury would be:

3 months: lameness, heat and swelling absent
6 months: only slight thickening remains
9 months: ready for full work

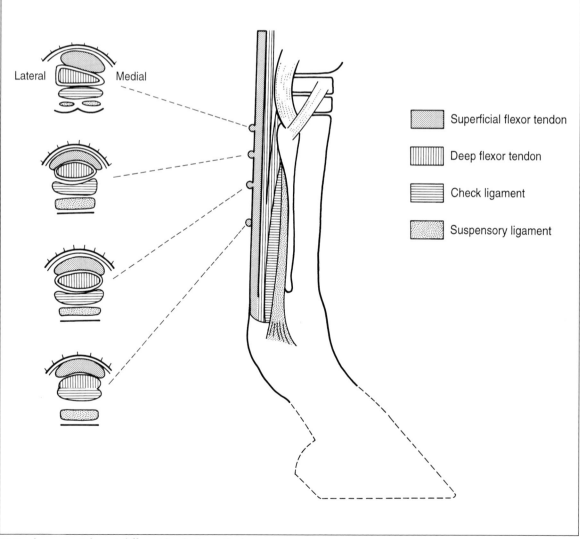

50 Tendon scans taken at different levels down the leg

Tenosynovitis

The tendons are surrounded by a thin-walled tendon sheath containing a small amount of fluid; this allows easy movement of the tendon. In a mild injury such as a knock on the leg, the only symptom may be an increase in the amount of this fluid and a corresponding soft swelling of the sheath. The horse may still be sound and the tendon may not appear to be painful at all. However, it is important that such injuries are not ignored because all too often they prove to be the forerunner of a much more serious situation, where the tendon may actually be damaged even though it feels normal. An ultrasound scan may well pick up areas of damage deep in the tendon tissue. It has been suggested that almost all serious tendon injuries are preceded by warning signs such as temporary swelling of the tendon sheath, if only the person looking after the horse is thorough enough to spot them. Even in large training yards the successful trainer is often the one who sets aside time every day specifically to check the horse's legs. This attention to detail always ultimately pays off.

■ Treatment

Mild injuries such as this may only need a reduction in the horse's work in order to settle down; thus it might still be possible, for example, to do an hour or so of walking exercise even though fast work is stopped. Fitness does not disappear overnight: even with complete rest, musculo-skeletal fitness will be maintained for about a fortnight, and although the horse will not get any fitter in that time of course, nor will it lose any fitness. So reducing work levels when a swelling is found around a tendon will not have serious fitness implications. Many of the details of treatment have already been discussed in an earlier section. Cold applications are useful, even though there may be little or no increase in the temperature of the area over the tendon. Gel containing sodium heparin and salicylate may be rubbed into the skin to help reduce the underlying inflammation, and di-methyl sulphoxide (DMSO), with or without a corticosteroid such as flumethasone, can also be applied to the skin. In the human field of sports medicine an increasing use is made of Feldene applied topically. This is an NSAID and can be effective in horses too, although so far no manufacturers have licensed such topical products for equine use. Before any of these products are used it is necessary to clip the leg to remove the hair. This prevents the product being wasted on the hair, but more importantly it makes sure that it really does reach the skin.

Tendon Sprains

When a more severe tendon injury occurs, we will see marked swelling of the leg and the whole area around the back of the cannon may be swollen and oedematous. We may no longer be able to feel the actual tendons precisely, and the oedema (recognised as swelling that remains pitted when we press a finger firmly in and then remove it) may extend around the sides of the cannon as well. The area will be warm, and the leg will be

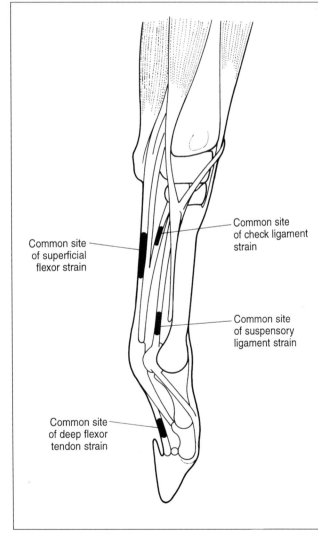

51 Common sites of tendon sprain

painful. This is the classic sprained tendon, and it is one of the most serious sports' injuries of the horse.

There are three sites of sprain that perhaps deserve a special mention (Fig 51). A sprain of the check ligament is usually a chronic jumping injury, because the check ligament's role is to limit movement of the flexor tendons when they are stretched on landing. Because it is not under great tension except during such activity, the check ligament can heal quite quickly. This brings its own problems, however, because owners often return the horse to work too soon after a check ligament injury, only to find that problems return at a later date.

The commonest site of tendon sprain is approximately halfway down the cannon and involves the superficial flexor tendon, and there has been much discussion as to why this is so. It has been shown that because the blood supply to the tendon comes down from the knee and up from the fetlock, it is less effective in this area. Against that, however, is the fact that the area of sprained tendon immediately becomes a mass of clotting blood, so there doesn't appear to be any practical shortage of blood supply to the area.

A sprain of one or both branches of the suspensory ligament, just above its attachment to the sesamoid bone, can have serious implications for a competition horse. The resulting scar tissue occupies a relatively high proportion of the short branch, leaving little normally functioning ligament. Healing of suspensory ligament sprains is usually slow.

Ultrasound Scanning to Assess Healing

Ultrasound scanning enables us literally to see which tendon or ligament is involved, and the extent of the injury along that tendon. The picture on the scanner screen, or its print-out, is of a cross-section of the tissues between the scanner probe on the skin and the bone, which reflects all the ultrasound waves. Areas of tendon damage consist of blood clot and fluid, and initially these show as black holes. As the collagen type III fibres are formed during healing, the injury looks rather speckled; by the time healing is complete, with the collagen type I fibres reasonably aligned, the area will be dense white again on the scan.

Ideally a horse should not be returned to very hard work after a tendon sprain until healing with type I collagen is complete. Unfortunately this takes months, and horse owners tend to be impatient people. One of the difficulties is that by 6–8 weeks after the initial injury the horse may be sound and the swelling gone, leaving a leg that looks almost as well as it is ever going to look. However, a scan at that time may show that healing is far from complete, and owners who work the horse too soon must be aware of the risk they are taking. It will be 6–9 months before a severe sprain will be healed completely.

Treatment

■ Firing

In the nineteenth century and before, the treatment of sprained tendons was hijacked by the red-hot firing iron. Treatment consisted of either repeatedly inserting a red-hot needle-like iron through the skin and into the body of the tendon, or of making a series of partial cuts through the overlying skin with a firing iron. The idea was that this would stimulate an active healing response to the firing, which in turn would also heal the sprained tendon. An added effect was said to be the production of a fibrous support around the skin over the fired area. A great deal of folklore and mystique grew up around firing. Some people felt that one type of firing iron was more effective than another, others that one pattern of lines or pin marks was better than others.

There is no doubt that some fired horses compete very successfully afterwards, but it is open to question whether that is because of the firing or in spite of it. The suggestion was made that firing is painful for the horse and makes little or no difference to the rate of healing. In 1983 the controversy over whether the gains from firing justified the pain came to a head with the publication of the so-called Silver Report. This showed that immediately after line firing, considerable amounts of tissue fluid ooze from the burnt skin. At times this acute reaction leaves behind adhesions between the skin and underlying tissues. In some cases the amount of protein manufactured in the tendon is increased for a couple of weeks after firing, but unfortunately this protein is not the vital collagen which is really needed. Firing does not affect the rate at which the thickened tendon returns to a more normal size. Pin firing right into the tendon tissue results in cores of fibrous tissue which never return to properly aligned collagen fibres. Firing does not speed up the return of the horse to soundness either, and it leaves behind a thinned, weakened skin rather than a strengthened support.

Following the publication of the Silver Report, the research was strongly attacked by traditionalist vets who fired large numbers of horses, whilst others called for the treatment to be banned. The body controlling ethical matters in the UK, the Royal College of Veterinary Surgeons, first condemned the use of firing and then tried to ban it altogether. That ban has only been a partial success, but it has resulted in a great decrease in the numbers of horses with sprained tendons which are fired.

■ Tendon-Splitting Operations

Another treatment for sprained tendons which was examined by Professor Silver was the tendon-splitting operation. This involves inserting a scalpel into the tendon and making a series of cuts parallel to the direction of the tendon fibres through the damaged area. The idea is to allow the healing process better access to the damaged tissues. Professor Silver found that tendon splitting actually slows the rate of healing, slows the return to normal size of the tendon, and slows the return to soundness; in short, he considered the operation to make the condition worse rather than better. Despite these findings there are some experts who carry out the operation today. The difference is that whereas Professor Silver was evaluating an operation carried out weeks after the injury, supposedly to help long-term healing, nowadays the operation is carried out one or two days after the injury and the aim is to enable some of the blood and fluid to be almost squeezed out of the injured area.

■ Surgical Options in Tendon Care

One idea which has attracted surgeons is of operating to install an implant of some kind that will either provide support for the damaged tendon or help ensure more normal healing by stimulating the collagen fibres to be laid down in a proper way. Despite a vogue at one time for the use of carbon-fibre implants to achieve the latter, so far it has not been a success in the long term.

Surgery to cut the accessory ligament of the superficial flexor tendon represents a completely different approach to tendon problems in that it is not concerned with the injury itself, but with what happens functionally when the horse returns to work. The accessory ligament extends from the radius bone to the superficial flexor tendon just below its muscle, and limits the amount of strain that can be transferred up to the muscle, concentrating it instead in the tendon. When the tendon is injured, the amount of healthy tissue left to withstand any strain is reduced, and the amount of force per unit length of normal tendon is increased. By cutting the ligament, the strain is borne more evenly by the muscle and the tendon, and the amount of force per unit length of the whole system is reduced.

A recent research study showed that 82 per cent of horses raced again after this surgery, a high percentage of them (69 per cent) more than five times. Horses that had already raced before the injury actually achieved faster times after the surgery than they had done before – although owners tended to race them in less prestigious races and they earned less money per start than they had done originally. The surgery is carried out soon after the original injury, and on average the horses were back on the racetrack within forty weeks of surgery.

■ Medical Options in Tendon Care

The medical treatment of a sprained tendon may involve a number of the treatment modes already discussed: cold applications, a range of anti-inflammatory drugs and laser therapy have all been used, but it is speed which is of the essence here. Even half an hour's delay between the actual injury and applying a cold pack or injecting an anti-inflammatory agent into the injured area (or into the body as a whole) can make a significant difference to the recovery rate.

It has been suggested that the main effect of firing for sprained tendons was that it ensured that the horse had sufficient rest to allow recovery. Another treatment that might fall into this category is blistering, which involves rubbing an irritant – for example, mercuric iodide – into the clipped skin over the injury. The result is fluid-filled blisters over the treated area which ooze clear fluid; the skin is thickened and there is oedema underneath the skin. The idea behind blistering is that it leaves behind a thickened and so strengthened skin to support the tendons. As it has never been shown that the skin's relative thickness has any effect on the incidence of sprained tendons, it is unlikely that blistering has any real preventive effects. In any case the increasing restrictions on drug licensing have almost driven the treatment underground.

Both sodium hyaluronate and polysulphated glycosaminoglycan are used to reduce the inflammatory response. They may be injected into the actual area of damaged tendon, but they appear to work just as well when injected intravenously or intramuscularly respectively. A new drug called bapten, which was isolated from the wild sweet pea plant, appears to have great potential for treating sprained tendons and is currently undergoing trials. It is injected into the injured tendon and prevents the stabilisation of the initial higgledy-piggledy collagen fibres; this makes it much easier and quicker for the horse to lay down the permanent collagen fibres in a properly organised pattern. Although bapten appears to speed up the return to soundness after tendon injury, its main value is that the healed tendon has a much better quality of repair, so the cross-sectional area of the tendon and the tendon fibre pattern both return to normal.

At one time horses with sprained tendons were confined to complete box rest. In part this followed on naturally from the restriction of movement – including the use of a 'cradle' to restrict head movement – necessary after blistering and firing. The pain which follows these treatments can otherwise lead to self-inflicted trauma, and with blistering there is the added need to prevent the horse's tongue coming in contact with the chemical and being blistered itself. Now, however, it is normal to walk the horse out in hand for a time twice a day, even in the early post-injury days, because this helps to ensure that the new collagen fibres are laid down in the direction of stress that they will be required to withstand. It also helps to disperse fluid.

After a tendon injury, horses should *not* be given prolonged box rest because the healing tendon needs some tension on it to show the new fibres which direction they need to follow. Turning the horse out in a field is also bad because this carries an equivalent risk to riding it. The best course of action is box rest with a slow build-up of work. Given below is an example of a tried and tested rehabilitation programme.

Injury	1st month	2nd month	3rd month
Mild	Walk in hand 15 mins twice daily	40 mins twice daily	Walk, ridden 20–30 mins
Moderate	Walk in hand 15 mins twice daily	40 mins twice daily	Walk, in hand 60 mins
Severe	Walk in hand 15 mins twice daily	Walk in hand 30 mins twice daily	Walk in hand 40 mins

The horse is then assessed and graded as having made good, fair or poor progress:

Progress	4th month	5th month	6th month
Good	Walk, ridden 30 mins	Walk, ridden 45–60 mins	Add 5 mins every 2 weeks
Fair	Walk, ridden 30 mins	Walk, ridden 45–60 mins	Walk, ridden 60 mins
Poor	Walk in hand 60 mins	Walk, ridden 20–30 mins	Walk, ridden 60 mins

6 months after the injury the horse's progress is assessed again:

Progress	7th month	8th month	9th month
Good	Add 5 mins every 2 weeks	Continue cantering	Full flat work
Fair	Add 5 mins every 2 weeks	Continue cantering	Continue cantering
Poor	Make decision whether to continue		

The Annular Ligament

One problem involving the deep flexor tendon which requires immediate recognition and treatment occurs when the tendon is damaged where it passes under the annular ligament of the fetlock. Because this ligament does not stretch, any swelling of the tendon results in a great increase in pressure which can cause further damage in the tendon. At one time it was believed that this problem was caused by contraction of the annular ligament, but it is now thought to be basically tendon-related. It is recognised by the 'step' which is apparent where the swollen tendon sheath is suddenly restricted by the annular ligament (Fig 52).

■ Treatment

Treatment consists of surgically cutting the annular ligament and so relieving the pressure. This must be carried out as soon as possible after the initial injury. Even so there is no guarantee of a successful outcome because the initial tendon injury may still be sufficient to prevent a return to soundness. The danger is that even if veterinary attention is sought immediately after the injury at the competition, it might not be apparent then and by the time it is re-examined it may be too late for treatment to be of real benefit.

■ Complete Tendon Rupture

Sometimes tendons are stretched beyond their limit and become completely severed. This may also occur as a result of a blow which also cuts the skin. The crucial result from the point of diagnosis is that when the horse stands square, the fetlock of the affected leg sinks down compared with its opposite number. If the deep flexor tendon is severed the fetlock may reach the ground, and the toe come off the ground.

■ Treatment

Although in some selected cases, especially where the tendon is cut rather than over-stretched, it is possible to stitch the severed ends together with stainless steel wire or nylon, the success rate is not high. In view of the great pain suffered by the horse and the poor chance of relieving that, euthanasia is often carried out in such circumstances. Certainly there is no significant likelihood

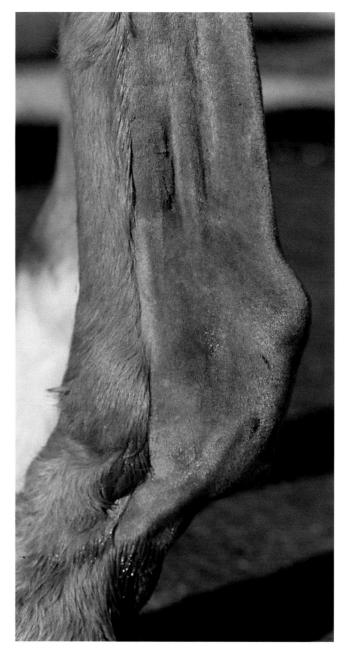

52 Constriction of the annular ligament

of the horse returning to competition afterwards.

The extensor tendon runs down the front of the leg. It is involved in pulling the leg forwards whilst the leg is off the ground and it does not bear any weight. As a result, if the tendon is injured or even severed, the implications are very much less gloomy than when the flexor tendons are involved; in fact the horse will usually make a complete recovery – nor does the resulting scarring and thickening of the tendon generally result in an increased risk of further damage.

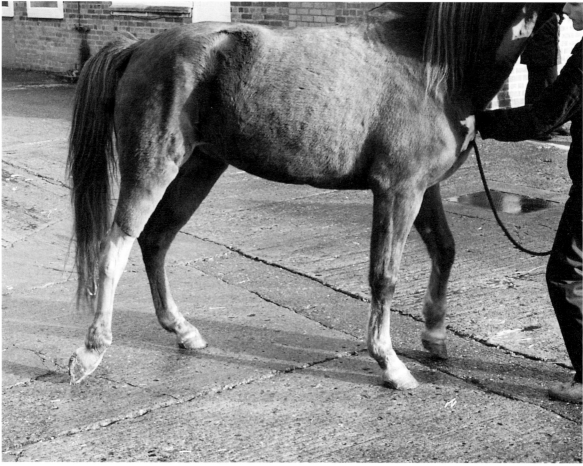

53 Upward fixation of the patella

The Stifle Ligaments

The horse is susceptible to a specific problem involving the ligaments of the stifle joint, which is the equine equivalent of our knee joint. The horse can 'lock' the joint as part of the 'stay' apparatus which enables it to doze on its feet without falling down: the patella, or knee-cap, has three ligaments that attach it to the tibia; when the horse stands still, it pulls the patella upwards until the medial patella ligament becomes hooked around a protuberance on the bottom of the femur. This effectively prevents the joint from moving. When the horse does want to move, it pulls the patella up sufficiently to free the system.

In a condition often referred to as 'locking stifle', or upward fixation of the patella, the ligament remains hooked up: if the horse moves, it must drag the straight, unbending leg behind it. As such the condition is quite easy to recognise. Of course, *we* cannot pick up the foot of the affected leg, either. The problem can occur any-where, even out at exercise, leaving the horse stranded (Fig 53), and there are certain reasons why it should happen. First, if the horse has been in poor bodily condition for some time, the medial ligament shrinks or contracts slightly, and this makes it difficult to free the patella. Second, if the ligament is injured, either by a blow or by stretch, then it will also shorten slightly. Furthermore, in some horses there may be a genetic component because the bony spur is slightly mis-positioned and this makes it more difficult to free the patella. Not surprisingly this situation occurs rather more in youngstock.

■ Treatment

It is usually possible by massage and manipulation to free the patella, perhaps helped by slight sedation of the horse. Unfortunately the condition may recur, and in such cases surgery may be considered to cut the ligament, an operation called medial patellar ligament desmotomy. The hope is that the ligament will eventually heal, but it will then be longer because of the fibrous tissue bridging the gap and so will no longer lock the joint. Recently some doubts have been expressed about the true success rate of the operation and its involvement in future degenerative joint disease in the joint, so vets are being more selective in the cases they do operate on.

Problems with the Ligaments of the Hock

The tendon of the digital flexor muscle at the hock can also be involved in functional difficulties during exercise. It runs over the tip of the calca-

neus bone (Fig 54) which acts as a fulcrum, and it is held in place by short ligaments. During strenuous exercise, one or both of these restraints may be ruptured and the tendon can then slip off the calcaneus when under tension as the horse bends the joint. The result is a very unstable joint rather than a painful one, although the horse may still be quite lame.

■ Treatment

It is possible to repair or replace the restraining ligaments surgically, and in some horses they become stabilised if the joint is just held rigid in a cast. The prospects for a return to competition are not good, however.

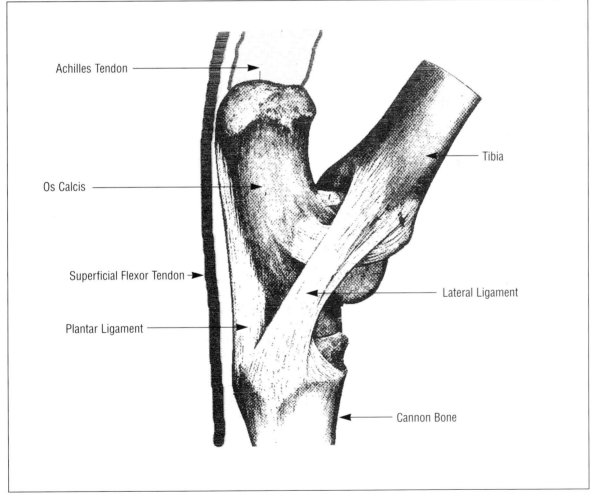

54 Lateral view of the ligaments of the hock

JOINTS

How Joints Work

Before considering any specific joint problems it is necessary to understand the structure of a normal joint. Each joint has two bone surfaces which are in contact with each other, and the greater the degree of movement that occurs between them, the smaller the relative amount of contact. So some of the small bones in the knee or hock joints have very little movement, because their major role is to disperse shock over their surface area rather than to allow movement. The whole of the joint surface may well be in contact with the adjacent bone in this situation. With the joint between the tibia and the hock, however, there is a considerable amount of movement and in this situation only a small area of the articular surfaces will be in contact and bearing weight at any one time.

If the moving bone surfaces *were* in direct contact with each other, they would soon wear away, because bone is designed for structural strength rather than to absorb friction. These surfaces are therefore covered by a layer of artic-ular cartilage (Fig 55) which reduces friction and protects the bone. Articular cartilage has few nerve fibres compared with bone, so whenever cartilage is lost over part of the joint and bone is exposed to wear and tear, there is a dramatic increase in the amount of pain.

The articular cartilage is supplied with nutri-ents and is also lubricated by the joint fluid. This is a fascinating substance. Its main component is a substance called hyaluronic acid, the molecules of which can join together to form long, inter-meshing chains. The longer the chains and the more they entwine with each other, the more fluid they trap between them, producing more of a thin jelly than a watery liquid. So the length of the chains of hyaluronic acid (which are actually measured by the relative weight of the molecules)

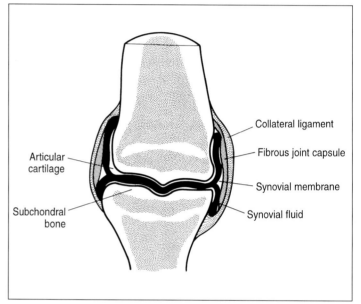

Labels: Articular cartilage; Subchondral bone; Collateral ligament; Fibrous joint capsule; Synovial membrane; Synovial fluid

55 Basic joint anatomy

provides an indication of both the thickness and the lubricating power of the joint fluid.

The joint is enclosed by a joint capsule. There may not be a separate capsule for each and every joint, of course. The knee, for example, contains a number of separate joints between individual bones, but only one overall joint capsule. The capsule itself is a relatively thin membrane, and is responsible for the formation of the joint fluid. So there is a gradient of nutrients and cells from the blood supply to the joint capsule to the joint fluid and finally to the articular cartilage.

Arthritis and DJD

We used to call any wear-and-tear problem with a joint 'arthritis'. Some purists objected to that term, however, because it means 'inflammation of the joint', and in many cases there is actually very little inflammation. The term we now use is **degenerative joint disease**, or DJD. It is impor-tant to realise from the start that DJD can occur at any age, and we must not associate it solely with old horses; two-year-old horses can have their racing career ended by DJD as well.

■ Joint Fluid

There are certain common features of DJD, whichever the joint involved; the most easily detected is that the joint capsule may be swollen because more joint fluid is being produced in an effort to provide cells for repairing the damage. Unfortunately the joint fluid produced at this time has hyaluronic acid of a much lower molecular weight than normal, and so of a much lower viscosity: if we draw a sample of normal joint fluid out with a needle, it will form a 'string' of viscous fluid as it is expelled from the syringe; a similar sample of fluid from a DJD joint will be thin and water-like, readily forming distinct drops as it falls from the syringe. This means less lubricating support for the joint and greater pressure per unit area of the articular cartilage, and the result is almost always a marked increase in the degree of pain. In the longer term, poor quality joint fluid provides reduced nutrition for the cells of the articular cartilage.

When a joint has been damaged by direct injury, red blood cells may be present in the joint fluid, tingeing it pink. Blood is not usually present in joint fluid, and its presence is often associated with pain. If the joint becomes infected, the joint fluid will come to contain large numbers of white blood cells; indeed, the number of white blood cells present is used to determine if an infection is present, because it is a more reliable indicator than the ability to culture bacteria from the joint fluid. Ordinary healthy joints have very little ability to fight infection and bacteria will therefore multiply rapidly, so a joint becomes swollen and painful very quickly – so painful, in fact, that owners are often convinced that the horse must have broken a bone in its leg, it is so lame.

■ The Significance of Cartilage Degeneration

Degenerative joint disease refers more to the degeneration of the articular cartilage than to the bone. Arthroscopy now enables us to look directly into joints, so we can appreciate that all such joints have cartilage changes (Fig 56), although not all will have bony changes. It is important to

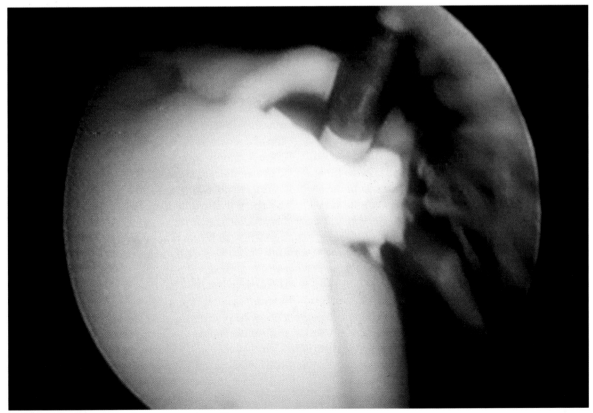

56 Arthroscopy revealing degenerative joint disease

realise that cartilage changes are not visible on x-rays, so such joints do not look very different to normal on x-ray; the only change that is visible is that when sufficient cartilage has been destroyed, the two bones of the joint will be closer together than they would be if there was still a full thickness of cartilage between them.

The presence of degenerating cartilage within a joint ensures that the joint fluid remains of poor quality, and so the cartilage does not heal. If, however, that degenerate cartilage is completely removed, then the self-perpetuating circle is broken, and even if the craters remaining afterwards do not fill with normal cartilage, the joint will still function much better than before. Arthroscopy enables us to see and scrape away such areas of damaged cartilage, thus allowing the joint to settle down. Hopefully the horse will then become sound again.

Eventually, however, DJD joints usually develop bony changes – although we must not link the degree of such changes to the severity of the problem or the degree of lameness. We often radiograph horses which have only recently gone lame but which show evidence of really long-standing bony changes; thus it follows that the bony side of things cannot be directly responsible for the pain. The actual changes we see on x-ray may include new bone being formed, changes in the shape of the bone, or changes in the density and internal structure of the bone.

We are concerned not with finding abnormal joints, but with finding painful joints, and the ultimate proof of this is when we remove some of the joint fluid from a suspect joint and replace it with a local anaesthetic. If the horse goes sound within 20–30 minutes of the injection, then that joint is the sole site of the lameness. It can, however, be difficult to decide which joint we should investigate in this way. Nuclear scintigraphy can be very useful in pointing the way because it highlights areas where this bone activity is occurring now, rather than joints where there has been activity in the past, which is possible with radiography.

When to Rest and When to Work

When we diagnose DJD of a joint, the problem we face is whether to rest the horse or not. Traditionally the view was that continued exercise would only cause more damage. On the other hand, resting the horse solves nothing. If it does go sound with rest, there is a very real chance that as soon as it returns to full work the lameness will return. In human medicine we have accepted for some time that mobility is important for such joints, and we are increasingly coming to appreciate that the same applies to equine joints. Regular fixed exercise levels will sometimes result in a return to soundness without any other treatment, and will certainly make it easier to assess the dose of painkillers necessary to enable the horse to be pain free. This may not enable it to return to competition, though.

There are some competitors who feel that horses ought to be allowed to compete whilst the pain of chronic DJD is controlled by drugs; in certain states of the USA this is even allowed in racing as long as it is declared before the race. On the other hand, in one or two countries it is illegal under the state laws as well as under the rules of the regulatory bodies to use painkillers during competitions. The trend seems to be to set maximum permitted levels for certain drugs in competing horses, but to set that level lower that the normal therapeutic level. The idea is to prevent the long-term use of painkillers to mask DJD, but not to cause the disqualification of horses when modern analytical methods pick up ever-smaller levels of the drug remaining from previous treatments.

■ Medical Treatments for DJD

Although non-steroidal, anti-inflammatory drugs (NSAIDs) do have the latter effect as their name implies, they have little curative influence in DJD. However, injecting hyaluronic acid, or its sodium salt sodium hyaluronate, either directly into the joint or intravenously, can result in a long-term improvement. Although it is easy to understand that replacing the low molecular weight complexes of DJD joint fluid with high molecular weight polymers will restore viscosity, we now know that the injected hyaluronic acid is quite rapidly broken down, over days rather than weeks. Despite this, its effect lasts weeks and months rather than days, almost as if the joint capsule replaces like with like: thus if there is low viscosity joint fluid, it replaces it with low viscosity fluid, but if we restore normal viscosity then any new fluid will also be of normal viscosity. Treatment with hyaluronic acid does not result in an improvement in all cases of DJD, because not all cases have lowered viscosity fluid, but it is a treatment that is safe from a regulatory point of view. If and when symptoms return, treatment can be repeated. Incidentally, taking joint fluid from a healthy joint of the same horse and injecting it into the DJD joint will have a similar effect.

Trauma to Joints

Traumatic injuries to joints, such as knocks received whilst jumping, should be treated by cold applications as soon as possible after the event; this limits the amount of inflammatory reaction which occurs. NSAIDs may be useful in this situation, but their use will be detected if the horse is dope tested at a competition. Laser therapy might be an alternative way to utilise the horse's own corticosteroids, or polysulphated glycosaminoglycan may be effective, given either directly into the joint or by intramuscular injection; it is said to have a cartilage-protecting role. It attaches to and stabilises the inflamed cartilage and so helps to prevent acute traumatic injury becoming a chronic degenerative change.

■ Treatment

As mentioned earlier, haemorrhage into a joint is quite painful. Removing most of the bloody fluid can result in a marked decrease in lameness, but how long this improvement lasts will depend on whether the haemorrhage stops. Sometimes a hypodermic needle punctures a blood vessel on its way into a joint to withdraw fluid, and the resulting haemorrhage can give the mistaken impression that there was previous bleeding. Complete rest is important when haemorrhage is occurring, because any movement tends to disturb the clot that has to form to plug the damaged blood vessel.

I have already mentioned the comparative ease with which infection can establish itself in a joint. Once the diagnosis has been confirmed, a decision has to be made whether to treat the joint conservatively or to opt for surgery. In the former, large doses of antibiotic are given and the horse is encouraged to use the joint, and this may be successful on its own. In many cases of acute infection, though, it is better to flush the joint (usually under a general anaesthetic) with large volumes of sterile saline solution; as much as 5–10 litres (1–2 gals) of saline may be used in an attempt physically to wash out any fibrin strands, pus or inflammatory substances. The result can be a marked improvement in the degree of lameness.

What is OCD?

Quite a number of later DJD cases originate as osteochondrosis dessicans, or OCD, a condition which arises in the first six to nine months of the horse's life. At that time it is growing rapidly, and if the blood supply to an area of a joint fails to keep up with the overall growth, the result is a small area of weak cartilage. We suspect that this is actually a very common situation, which in the majority of horses has no serious consequences. In some, though, a flap of cartilage breaks away at the weak area, and is the seed for future problems. When the horse starts hard work, which may be as a two-year-old if it is a Thoroughbred racehorse, but may not be until it is a four- or five-year-old if it is an eventer, the flap of cartilage comes away completely, leaving an erosion and resulting in a sudden onset of lameness. In some cases where the blood supply failed over a larger area, a piece of bone may be detached with the cartilage, to lie free in the joint.

So OCD is usually a lameness of sudden onset, occurring in horses which are either early into their first training session or have just had an increase in their workload. The lameness often develops overnight whilst the horse is resting in the stable, rather than during the exercise. Almost any joint can be affected, although the frequency is probably stifle, fetlocks, knees and then hocks. The affected joint (or joints because more than one joint can be involved) has increased joint fluid but is not painful to the touch.

■ Treatment

If a fragment of bone has detached from the joint surface, it will be possible to diagnose the presence of OCD radiographically. When only cartilage is involved, however, it is not possible to do so. Arthroscopy will usually enable us to confirm the diagnosis in such cases, and also to treat them. Removal of the cartilage flap and surrounding cartilage will result in the gap being filled with a non-painful 'scar tissue', and the majority of horses then go sound. Where a bone fragment is present it must, of course, be removed. In the case of the stifle joint, these pieces of bone can be surprisingly large, 2–3cm ($^3/_4$–1in) across. Polysulphated glycosaminoglycan may be of value after the surgery.

OCD can only really be treated surgically. If the

condition progresses to degenerative joint disease, then surgery will be less likely to be successful because of the other changes in the joint.

Bone Spavin

Spavin is a specific form of DJD affecting the hock. In the days of carthorses, a visible bony lump often developed on the inside of the hock as a result, but most cases of spavin in riding horses do not show any exterior signs of the bony changes which are taking place. The hock has two rows of more or less rectangular bones which move very little because they have a shock-absorbing role. There are therefore three more or less parallel joints, which are the ones involved in spavin.

The clinical history with spavin is of a gradual onset of lameness, or of an intermittent lameness. In the early stages, forced flexion of the hock for 30–60 seconds (the 'spavin test') will produce lameness for a number of strides in an otherwise sound horse. Even as the condition develops a flexion test will still make the lameness significantly worse. As the horse trots away it will also be noticed that it is pulling its lame leg inwards, towards the other leg, rather than keeping it vertical.

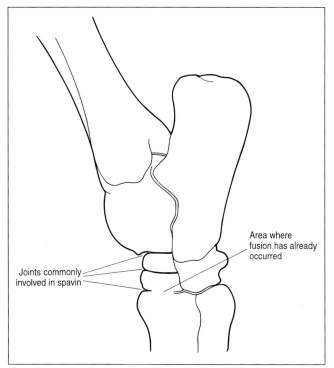

Joints commonly involved in spavin

Area where fusion has already occurred

57 Hock bones showing bone spavin

■ Treatment

X-rays of the hock will show new bone being formed at the edges of one or more of the joints. The lower joint, between the hock and the cannon and splint bones, is the one most commonly affected; if the higher joints are involved, the prognosis is significantly poorer. As more bone is formed, the joint may become fused (Fig 57) and if this happens and only one joint is involved, then the horse goes sound. The aim of treatment is therefore to encourage fusion of the joints. Initially this is done by regular moderate exercise, using painkillers such as phenylbutazone to relieve the lameness. A special shoe with a lateral extension on the heel helps to encourage the horse to keep its leg vertical when hitting the ground, which in turn reduces the lameness. If 3–6 months of exercise does not produce fusion, then surgery may be considered. The success rate for surgical fusion, achieved by drilling into the joint in order to cause more bone activity, is around 70 per cent if only one joint is involved.

Bog Spavin

In the condition known as bog spavin, a soft swelling occurs on the inside of the lower hock. This is actually the swollen joint capsule, which is confined by ligaments around the rest of the hock and so can only bulge out in this one area.

■ Treatment

Horses with bog spavin are not usually lame, and no treatment is necessary; it merely reflects an increased strain on the hock at some stage in the past. If bog spavin occurs as a result of an acute injury, lameness might be present, and anti-inflammatory treatment required.

Windgalls

The fetlock-joint capsule of one or more legs is frequently swollen by an increased amount of joint fluid; this produces a windgall extending up the leg behind the joint. These are painless and not associated with bone or cartilage changes. They may be more common in horses with upright fetlocks which absorb percussion less effectively. As a general rule the presence of large windgalls would not rule out the purchase of a competition horse as long as flexion tests on the joints produced no reaction. If there was any doubt, x-rays of the fetlock would confirm the situation. Fetlocks which develop DJD are no more likely to have windgalls already than are normal fetlocks.

Curb

A curb is a thickening of the short plantar ligament which runs between two lines of bones in the hock. Like any sprained ligament it is hot, swollen and painful at first but usually settles down, and the horse returns to soundness. The injury may be predisposed by the conformation of the hocks, very angled hocks being more susceptible. It often occurs in horses galloping around in the field who have to stop suddenly and brace themselves with their hind legs in an attempt to do so. As such most curbs do not cause any problem to the horse once the initial healing has taken place. Occasionally jumping horses develop a curb as a response to the stresses of jumping and these may flare up on future occasions. Curbs are readily visible when the horse's hock is viewed from the side, and can be felt as a ridge on the back of the leg.

Treatment

No treatment other than rest is usually needed. Laser therapy of newly formed curbs and firing of long-standing curbs have both been said to reduce their size from a cosmetic point of view.

Thoroughpin

A thoroughpin is a painless enlargement of the tendon sheath of the deep flexor tendon above the hock. It does not cause lameness and so does not really require treatment although removing the fluid and injecting some corticosteroid may remove the blemish.

Ringbone

Historically ringbone was the first site of DJD to be recognised, because the new bone which formed in a collar around the pastern joints was easy to detect even without x-rays. Traditionally

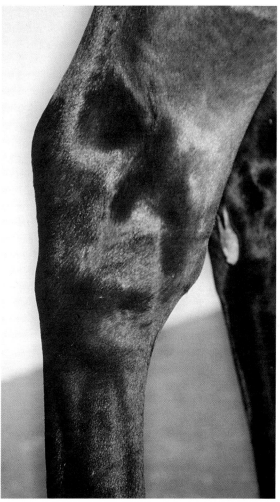
58 Curb

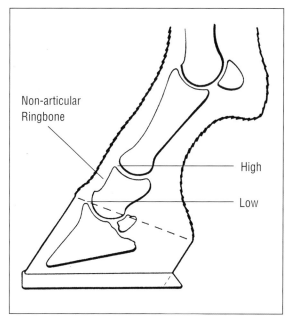
59 Common sites of ringbone

distinctions were made between high and low, and between articular and non-articular ringbone. The former merely refers to whether the problem involves the joint between the first and second phalanx (part-way down the pastern) or between the second and third phalanxes (at the coronet). The distinction between articular and non-articular ringbone is important because non-articular ringbone is not DJD at all: it is often caused by the formation of new bone at the insertion of the extensor tendon onto the bone, and as such a period of rest will usually allow the new bone to become inactive when the lameness will disappear.

Articular ringbone is always bad news. The amount of new bone formed before lameness develops varies enormously: it may be possible to feel the new bone in a horse which is still sound; on the other hand, the horse may be lame with only a small amount of change visible on x-ray – rest may produce a temporary improvement, but the lameness will be back with a vengeance when the horse returns to work.

■ Treatment

No treatment is possible that will realistically return the horse to competition, although surgical fusion of the joint may be possible and may give some improvement.

Bone Cysts

One of the more unusual conditions which may involve a joint is a bone cyst. The stifle joint of young horses is most commonly involved, and the horse becomes lame for no apparent reason. On x-ray an almost round cavity can be seen in the bone near to the joint; this smooth-walled 'cyst' connects with the joint via a small opening, although this may not be obvious on the x-ray.

■ Treatment

With rest the cyst may disappear and the horse become sound. In other cases the horse remains lame and the cyst persists. Surgery to destroy the 'lining' of the cyst and then packing with a bone graft may solve the problem. Once the horse becomes sound it can undertake strenuous work without fear of the cyst reappearing.

The Sesamoid Bones and the Fetlock

DJD of the fetlock joint may also involve the two sesamoid bones which lie behind the fetlock (Fig 60). Sesamoiditis is the result of wear-and-tear stress, and the first detectable signs on x-ray will be alterations to the substance of the bones. In an attempt to reduce the inflammation, the blood supply is increased, and as with the navicular bone (which strictly speaking is also a sesamoid bone) evidence of this is visible on x-ray. In time, the shape of the pyramidal sesamoid bone may become distorted and new bone formed, especially at its summit where the suspensory ligament attaches.

Quite marked changes can occur in the sesamoid bones before the horse becomes lame. To some extent this is due to the fact that as both forelegs are often involved, the slight lameness evens itself out. Eventually the area becomes painful to pressure, and swollen. Flexion increases the lameness.

■ Treatment

The only treatment for sesamoiditis is rest. Moreover it is not enough just to rest the horse until it appears to be sound, because every time it is returned to hard work before the bone has completely settled down makes permanent lameness more likely. Several months' rest, with just 5–10 minutes of walking exercise per day, may represent the best chance of resolution. Care must also be taken over the hoof/pastern axis because a broken axis can increase tension on the sesamoid bones.

60a & b X-rays of the fetlock need to be taken from two angles to check the sesamoid bones and joint.

a) In the x-ray taken from this angle we can see:
1) the joint space between the cannon and the pastern;
2) whether any new bone has formed at the sides of the joint;
3) the outline of both sesamoid bones

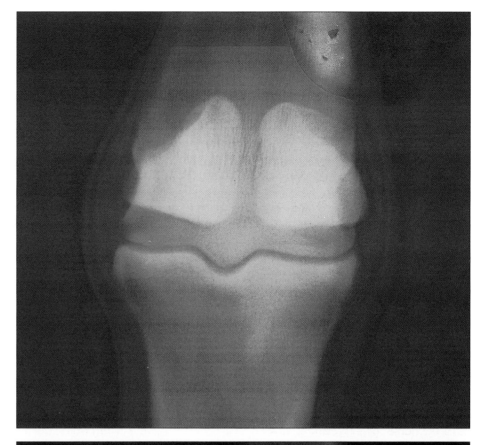

b) In this view we cannot see any of the points mentioned above, but we can see:
1) the rear border of the sesamoid bones;
2) some of the internal structure of the sesamoid bones;
3) whether any new bone has formed on the front of the joint

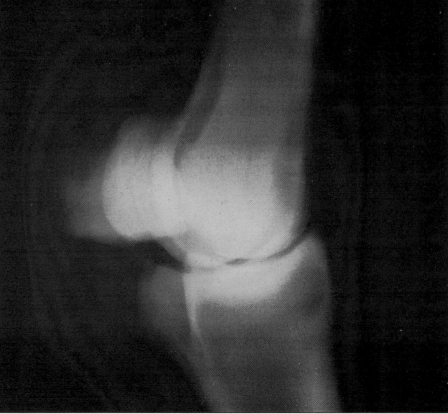

BONE

Bone is not the hard, inactive tissue that many people imagine it to be. It can be trained to withstand greater breaking forces, and research has shown that it needs only short bursts (30–60 seconds) of training to produce this effect, and that it reacts very rapidly, in days rather than months. All the bones in the body are constantly changing, existing bone being dissolved or eaten away and new bone replacing it. In young, growing horses more new bone is formed than is removed, whereas in adult horses the two processes are more or less in equilibrium.

How Bone is Formed

New bone can be formed in one of two ways: by the periosteum, which is the 'skin' on the surface of the bone, or by the endosteum, or bulk of the bone tissue. An insult to the periosteum will tend to result in surface bone formation, so if, for example, a horse is kicked on the front of the cannon bone, then the inflamed periosteum may well form some new bone and so produce a swelling at the site. New bone like this on the surface of the bone is called an exostosis (Fig 61).

Basically, bone consists of a fibrous skeleton within which osteoblast cells lay down dense crystals of a substance called calcium hydroxyapatite. It is these crystals which are being constantly replenished, and that is why the skeleton is such a vital reservoir of calcium and phosphorus: when the horse needs calcium elsewhere in the body, then much less apatite is formed, allowing the calcium which would normally go into its production to be diverted to where it is needed. However, the result is bone which is less dense than normal and so less able to withstand stress. Young horses which are receiving less calcium than they need (31g/1oz per day for a yearling, or 25g/0.75oz per day for a two-year-old) will still grow in size, because the fibrous skeleton of the bone will still grow, but the bone will be less dense. Feeding more calcium than normal to a healthy horse does not produce extra strong bone; the excess calcium is excreted via the kidneys rather than being incorporated into the bones.

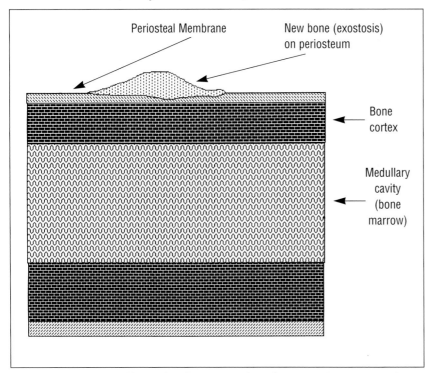

61 Structure of bone, also showing new bone formation (exostosis) on the periosteum

How Fractures Heal

When a bone is broken, the gap between the two fragments is rapidly filled by a blood clot that becomes invaded by inflammatory cells. Fibroblast cells appear and start to lay down collagen fibres to stabilise the fracture. However, such a fibrous repair will not enable the bone to function normally because it is not rigid enough to transmit movement. Gradually apatite crystals are formed around the fibres, until eventually a rigid bridge, or callus, is formed across the fracture. If there is movement of the bone fragments during healing then less apatite is laid down and a bony callus may never form.

■ Defining Fractures

Fractures may be classified as either simple or compound. A compound fracture is one where the bone fragments have broken the skin, and when the fracture consists of several fragments it is classified as a comminuted fracture. These distinctions are of great practical importance, because the more bone fragments there are and the more they are displaced from their original position, the more difficult it is to stabilise them all and so the less likely it is that proper fracture repair will occur. In the horse, compound fractures mean that infection will have had access to the fracture site, as a result of which healing is rarely successful. Indeed it is not usually worth attempting to repair compound fractures of major bones in the horse even when the actual repair would be relatively straightforward, because the chances of success are unfortunately so small.

■ Problems in Recovery

Another of the problems with fracture repair in horses is the recovery from the anaesthetic. During that time the horse wants to stand up, and the leverage exerted by the horse's considerable weight on its long legs places a tremendous strain on the repair. It has proved very difficult to devise splints and plaster casts that will withstand the forces of anaesthetic recovery, especially so above the horse's knee and hock: just as it is difficult to bandage these parts of the leg without the bandage slipping down, so it is difficult to apply a cast that will not move and which will prevent movement of the fracture. Of course casting materials have improved in recent years. Instead of plaster of Paris which takes twenty-four hours to dry and to reach maximum strength, we now have available light but strong glass-fibre or plastic materials that reach their maximum strength within minutes, and which also have the benefit of being waterproof.

Fracture Repair

The secret of fracture repair is to completely immobilise the bone fragments. This is achieved surgically using stainless-steel screws, and in some cases a single screw may be sufficient, using the lag-screw principle (where the hole through the first piece of bone is slightly larger than the screw thread so that when the screw is tightened into the second fragment it can pull the first fragment in tightly). More often screws are combined with stainless-steel plates which are shaped to the contours of the bone. It may take literally dozens of screws and a couple of plates to stabilise a major fracture (Fig 62) and each screw is a potential route for infection to enter the bone.

At the time of writing no one has ever successfully repaired a complete fracture of one of the so-called long bones (the radius and the humerus of the foreleg and the tibia and femur of the hind leg) in the adult horse. Techniques have improved to the point where it seems only a matter of time before it is achieved, but so far it has only been successful in young horses. So the basic rule is that complete fractures above the knee or hock are unrepairable and warrant euthanasia. Fractures below the knee or hock may be repairable, but if they are compound fractures they too may warrant euthanasia.

■ Prognosis for Future Performance

When considering fracture repair in the competition horse the obvious question is whether the horse will ever return to competition afterwards. This has to be assessed in each individual case, but there are two major problems: one is the amount of soft tissue damage which has occurred. If a tendon is also damaged, for example, then the fracture repair might be successful but the horse will remain lame. The other problem involves the adjacent joints, because if the fracture extends up to and into a joint, then even after repair the joint surface will be slightly uneven. Furthermore a large percentage of these joints will develop degenerative joint disease (DJD) later on, so the horse might return to competition initially but become lame later as a result of DJD. It is impossible to guarantee that a fracture repair involving the articular surface of a bone will not at some stage result in DJD of that joint.

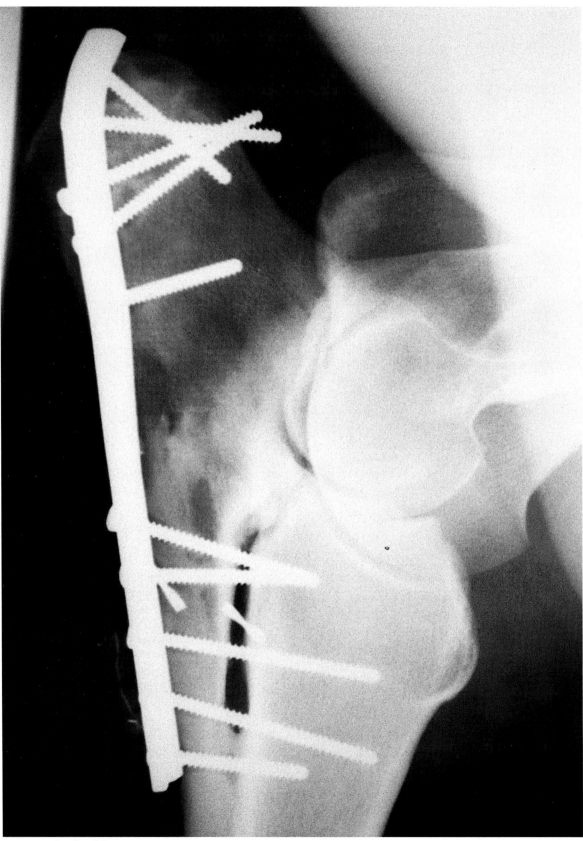

62 X-ray of a plated fracture

Pedal Bone Fractures

A fracture of the pedal bone is a unique kind of fracture, because the hoof prevents the fragments moving away from each other and acts as a splint for healing. The result is that many pedal bone fractures will heal with just rest and shoeing, using a shoe with clips to help stabilise the hoof on either side of the fracture area. The fact that the fracture heals does not necessarily mean that the horse becomes sound, though, and for competition horses a better result can usually be obtained by screwing the fragments together. The screw, or occasionally screws, is inserted exactly at right angles to the fracture, using the lag-screw principle to pull the two fragments tightly together. In most cases only a small window is made in the hoof wall to insert the screw, so it is a relatively quick and easy operation.

As a general rule, screws inserted during fracture repair in horses are left in place even after the horse has returned to normal work. This is in contrast to the situation in human beings, where such screws are usually removed because the greater life expectancy of humans means greater risk of a reaction eventually developing around the screw. Such reactions do occur sometimes in horses and result in resorption of bone around the screw head, leading to renewed pain and lameness. As long as the fracture itself has healed, such lameness will usually settle down once the affected screw is removed. One of the problems with pedal bone fractures is that it can be exceedingly hard to find the screw head to remove it, because the hoof wall will have long grown down, hiding the screw without trace. The result is that a much bigger window of hoof has to be removed to find the screw, than was necessary to insert it.

Fractures through the central body of the pedal bone may involve the articular surface of the coffin joint, and even with good healing the risk of DJD developing later is great in such cases. Indeed, because the horse will probably be rested for something like six months to allow healing, we must make a distinction between horses which do not return to soundness because the fracture fails to heal, and those where the fracture heals but the early onset of DJD prevents a return to work.

Navicular Bone Fractures

The navicular bone is also within the hoof, as is the pedal bone, but fractures here present a very different situation. The navicular bone is in the heel region where the hoof is not rigid, and it is subjected to movement from the deep flexor tendon which runs over its posterior border and holds it in place against the pedal bone. The result is that fractures of the navicular bone do not usually heal themselves. Straightforward fractures of the bone can be repaired with a screw but this is a very difficult operation because the screw has to be inserted from one narrow end of the bone to the other with pinpoint accuracy. Even when this appears to have been achieved, the overall success rate is not good.

The Fractured Pastern

Fractures of the bones of the pastern vary tremendously in their complexity. The simplest form is a major crack or a complete fracture of one bone; at the opposite end of the spectrum, bones may be shattered into multiple fragments. A survey of racehorse injuries showed that, contrary to the expectations of many people, these hopeless multiple fractures were far more likely to occur whilst galloping on the perfectly level turf of a flat racecourse than they were during jumping.

■ Treatment

When there is only a small number of fragments, or just a crack in a 'split' pastern, then surgical repair stands a good chance of success. However, it is vital to immobilise the leg as soon as possible after the injury, because each stride taken carries the risk of converting a simple fracture into a compound fracture, or into even more fragments, with a much smaller chance of successful repair. The application of a 'Monkey splint' before the horse is even removed from the track or arena is vital if there is any suspicion of a fracture, and if a 'Monkey splint' is unavailable, then a Robert Jones bandage must be applied with a suitable splint down the front of the cannon, pastern and foot. This takes longer to apply and there is accordingly more pressure on the vet to move the horse before stabilising the leg.

The repair of pastern fractures may only require the insertion of two or more screws, but especially with the more complicated fractures, stainless-steel plates will have to be bent to follow the contours of the bone. The techniques used are those developed for human surgery, especially skiing injuries. One important feature is that all the holes are pre-drilled and tapped before the screw is inserted, because this lessens the likelihood of reaction around the screw. Metal implants may be able to stabilise a fracture sufficiently for the horse to trot sound soon afterwards, but they are not strong enough to withstand the stress of fast work on their own. A return to work must await x-ray confirmation that healing is complete and that a firm bony bridge is in place, rather than merely a fibrous union.

Chip Fractures

When a joint such as a fetlock, knee or hock is x-rayed, it is relatively common to find small fragments of bone free in the joint. These chip fractures can be found in both lame and sound horses, although they are more common in lame ones. Chip fractures may arise as a result of trauma, when a small piece of normal bone flakes away from the main part; or when a piece of new bone formed during DJD breaks away. The distinction is rather important, even if it is not always very easy to make. If a straightforward chip fracture is causing lameness, then its surgical removal is likely to result in the horse becoming sound. If, however, the chip is part of a degenerative process, then its removal is far less likely to result in a return to soundness because of the other changes in the joint.

■ Treatment

Whenever a chip fracture is seen on x-ray of a lame horse, its significance or otherwise should be confirmed by injecting some local anaesthetic into the joint. If the horse does not go sound, then the chip is not associated with the lameness and is just a coincidental finding. Most chips are removed arthroscopically because this involves relatively little new damage to the joint compared with conventional surgery, and so allows a speedy return to competition.

Fractures of the Sesamoid Bones

Although the two sesamoid bones behind the fetlock joint are relatively small, any fracture of these can have serious consequences. This is especially so if the fracture line is more or less horizontal and therefore at right-angles to the direction of pull from the suspensory ligaments (Fig 63), because this always results in separation of the two fragments by a distance that prevents proper fracture healing. With time the horse may appear sound in the paddock, but as soon as it is returned to work the fibrous repair breaks down again.

■ Treatment

Screw repair of these fractures can be technically demanding because of the difficulties of gaining access to the site where the screw needs to be inserted without causing damage to the other

Stages of fracture repair		
	Natural	*Artificial*
1 Fracture occurs. Movement prevents healing		
2 Initial partial immobilisation	Fibrous callus bridges the break	Robert Jones bandage, or monkey splint
3 Permanent immobilisation	Calcification of the callus as new bone forms	Surgical repair of the fracture immobilises the fragments whilst new bone is formed across the break
4 Return of normal use	Remodelling of the bone to remove the callus and leave a bone more or less the same shape as before	The metal implants may or may not be removed once healing has occurred

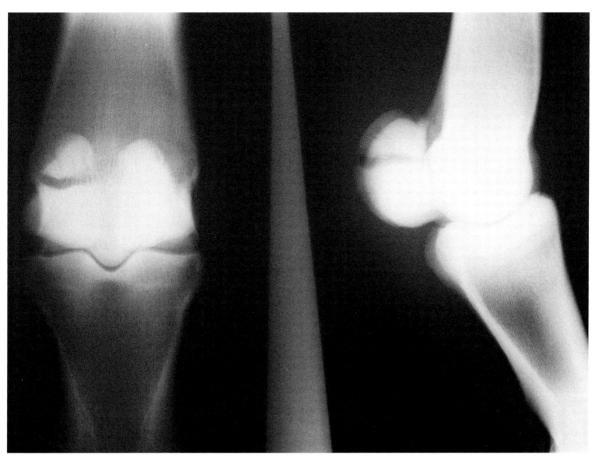

63 X-ray of a horizontal fracture of the sesamoid

structures of the joint. Because there is considerable force on the repair, a force which is being resisted solely by the screw threads in a bone fragment, a relatively high percentage of these repairs break down. Fractures where the break is more vertical than horizontal, although rarer, are much more likely to heal satisfactorily after surgery because the main bone still bridges the ligaments and takes the stress during movement, so there is far less force on the screw or screws during repair.

■ Sesamoiditis

Fractures of the sesamoid bones may be associated with primary sesamoiditis, when a number of changes occur in the bone, caused by repeated stress. The internal structure of the bone changes in an attempt to respond to this stress, but this actually only succeeds in weakening the bone further. For example, its attempts to increase the blood supply to the centre of the sesamoid bone inevitably reduces the mass of bone present to withstand stress. New bone may be laid down

around the insertion of the suspensory ligament into the sesamoid bone. This can be associated with recurring lameness. The existence of changes of these kinds in a sesamoid bone which has fractured further reduces the chances of a successful repair.

Cannon Bone Fractures

The cannon bone is the longest equine bone which is routinely repaired when fractured, but the factors which have to be considered are basically those dealt with for pastern fractures. The cannon may also be subject to stress fractures, very localised areas of surface bone breakdown triggered off either by the percussive forces travelling up the leg, or by a blow. Stress fractures can be difficult to diagnose because they can only be identified on x-ray when the x-ray beam is angled so that it highlights the fracture site on the edge of the bone. Although small, stress fractures still cause lameness and if they are not recognised, that lameness will persist.

■ Treatment

The treatment is rest, and this must continue for some time after the horse becomes sound and before the leg is stressed again. If healing is slow, then electro-magnetic field therapy may speed up the process.

Sore Shins

Sore or bucked shins are particularly common in young horses which are being worked hard. The clinical symptoms are lameness associated with pain and perhaps swelling of the bone on the front of the cannon. What happens is that the percussive forces cause microscopic fractures in the immature bone, and the horse responds by laying down more immature bone from the surface periosteum to act as a support bandage. There may be little to see initially on x-ray until the new bone becomes dense enough to show.

■ Treatment

In their early stages, sore shins may respond to just a decrease in workload, but obviously complete rest is better and may ultimately be necessary anyway. A variety of drugs can be applied to the skin over the shin in an attempt to reduce the inflammation; where it is available, a flumethasone/di-methyl sulfoxide (DMSO) paint is probably the best topical treatment. The DMSO carries the steroid through the skin to the underlying bone. It may be that NSAID gels developed for human sports medicine are more effective when applied topically than are the same drugs given to the horse by mouth. Piroxicam is one such drug available in gel form.

Splints

Certainly the commonest bone 'problem' in the horse is a splint. This is a localised area of new bone formed by the periosteum on the cannon bone anywhere down the line where one or other of the two splint bones is held in place against the cannon bone by the interosseous ligament. The vast majority of splints form on the medial surface of the cannon rather than laterally, and are more common on the front legs than on the hind legs. They vary in size from something which can barely be felt at all, even when the leg is lifted up so that the tendons can be pushed away from the splint bones, to easily visible swellings.

Splints are a response to percussive forces localising in the cannon wall rather than being transmitted along the bone, and as such they are often the response of immature bone to work or to poor conformation; however, adult horses can also develop splints. In many cases a developing splint does not cause lameness, and when it does do so the lameness will disappear once the periosteal inflammation settles down. So although the majority of adult competition horses will have one or more splints, these will not cause any problems after their initial formation. Owners should be aware that the pain can precede the new bone formation in splint development, so the problem of a mystery low-grade lameness may be solved by the appearance of a splint. Splints always look and feel bigger than they appear on x-ray, because not all of the fibrous tissue formed by the periosteum becomes calcified enough to show on x-ray. This also explains why splints sometimes shrink in size after their formation: it is hard fibrous tissue which is being remodelled rather than dense bone.

■ Treatment

Initial treatment for splints is the same as for sore shins. Where the periosteal reaction persists and the lameness continues, it has been claimed that pin firing into the body of the splint will, after an initial acute reaction, resolve the problem. It is possible to surgically remove splints which cause unsightly blemishes in showing animals; the periosteum is peeled back and then replaced after the new bone has been removed. Unfortunately whilst the inflammation of the surgery is settling down there is a real risk that more new bone may be formed.

The splint bones themselves are the remnants of our fingers or toes (with the cannon bone as the middle finger or toe); as such they fit into the knee or hock joint and take some of the weight of the horse's body even though they shrink into nothing lower down. Indeed, the force they absorb from the joint has to be transmitted to the cannon bone via the interosseus ligament. Thus when a splint bone is fractured, the horse will be appreciably lame because the bone, however insignificant we consider it, does 'bear weight' in its own way.

Fractured Splint Bones

Fractured splint bones are often the result of a knock or kick. One result of this is that the skin over the fracture site may be broken, allowing infection to enter and establish itself. It is probable that stress fractures also occur during hard work. Whatever the cause, the fracture may not be recognised as such at first because externally it will feel and behave like an ordinary painful splint. Sometimes such fractures heal themselves with rest, the cannon bone acting as a 'splint' to stabilise them. In other cases the horse goes sound and returns to work, only to go lame again

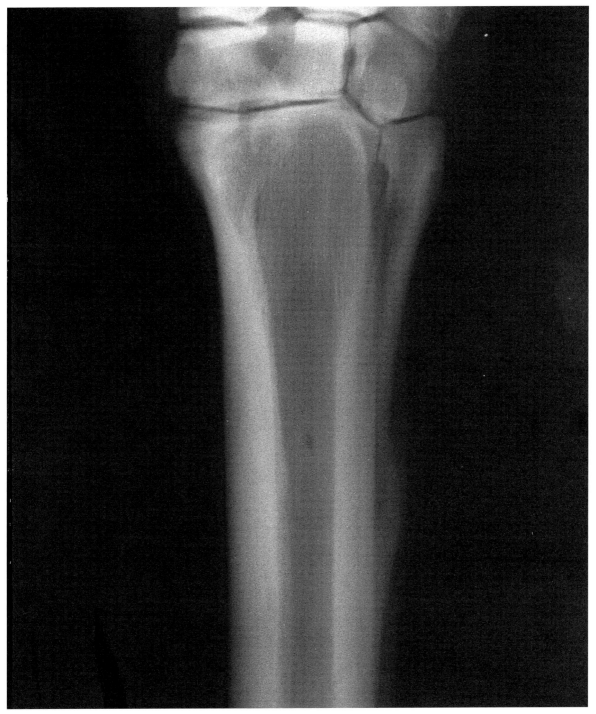

64 Splint

when in really strenuous work just before a competition. This scenario, which may be repeated several times if nothing further is done to promote healing, is caused by a fibrous or false union forming at the fracture site. Just because there is a lump of new bone around the fracture site does not mean that bone actually bridges the fracture gap.

■ Treatment

If healing does not occur with rest, surgery may be necessary. Rather than stabilising the fracture, the furthest fragment is completely removed. If it is felt that this leaves an unstable top piece of bone then this may be stabilised by screwing it to the cannon. If the fracture has become infected, then surgery is the only treatment and should be carried out straightaway, removing too much rather than too little of the splint bone to ensure that all the infected bone has been removed. The further down the splint bone the fracture occurs, the easier it is to deal with and the more likely that the horse will return to competition afterwards.

Other Fractures

Mention has been made earlier of the fact that both the knee and the hock contain a number of small bones which, by providing a larger surface area, help absorb percussion forces. Any one or more of these small bones can be fractured, usually as a result of stress forces rather than a blow. The joint capsule becomes swollen with fluid and painful, but without x-rays it is not possible even to begin to pinpoint which bone is involved; and even with x-rays a fracture is easily overlooked because of the complexity of the joints.

■ Treatment

Surrounding bones may prevent the fragments from becoming displaced, but wherever possible the fragments are screwed together. The horse will often be able to return to competition, at least in the short term.

The os calcis of the hock is a different proposition. If it is fractured, the tremendous force exerted by the tendons on the point of the hock often breaks any metal plates and screws used to repair it. Return to competition is therefore unlikely.

MUSCLES

Muscle fatigue is generally held to be one of the major causes of injury in the competition horse. Movement relies on a balance between opposing forces, and if one of these forces suddenly becomes weak then unco-ordinated movements can occur. Injuries are more likely to happen in the last quarter of a competition than in the first quarter, because fatigue comes into play in its later stages. Surprisingly enough given the large muscle mass which the horse has, primary muscle injuries are relatively rare. However, injuries to tendons, ligaments, joints and bones may all have their origins in muscle fatigue.

Blood Samples Confirm Muscle Problems

The most reliable way to diagnose that significant muscle damage is responsible for a lameness is to take a blood sample before, immediately after, and four hours after exercise. The two enzymes creatine kinase (CK) and amino aspartate transferase (AST), which are basically only found in muscle tissue in the horse, are then measured to see if the levels are generally high, or become raised with exercise. It may then be

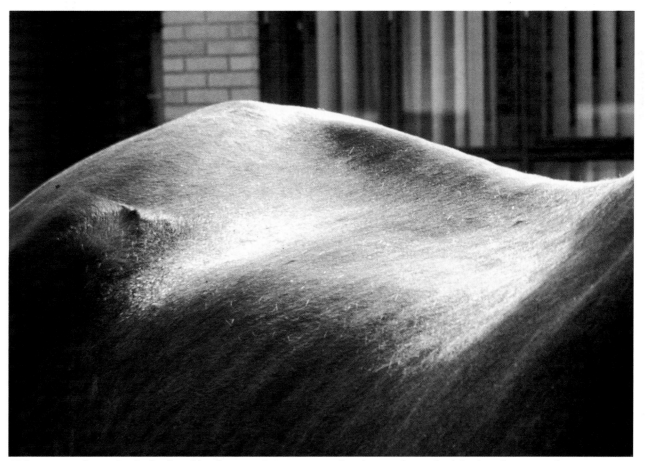

65 Severe muscle wasting in the dorsal lumbar area. It is important that the muscles are built back to their normal mass before the horse is returned to work

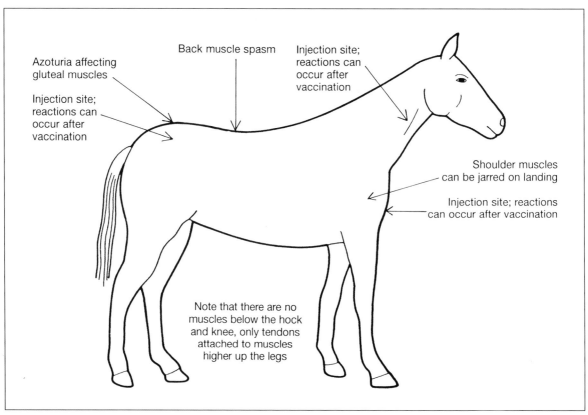

Azoturia affecting gluteal muscles

Back muscle spasm

Injection site; reactions can occur after vaccination

Injection site; reactions can occur after vaccination

Shoulder muscles can be jarred on landing

Injection site; reactions can occur after vaccination

Note that there are no muscles below the hock and knee, only tendons attached to muscles higher up the legs

66 Sites of possible muscle problems

possible to distinguish which individual muscle is involved by assessing its response to ultrasound or faradic stimulation; it is often not possible to pinpoint the problem just by pressing and feeling the muscles themselves. Apart from anything else, the force our fingers can exert just cannot mimic the effect of the horse's weight pulling on the muscle.

Raised muscle enzyme levels show that muscle fibres have been torn open or otherwise had their cell membranes breached, allowing the enzymes to leak out into the general circulation. Any exercise at all is going to make repair of the damage to that muscle cell-wall damage more difficult. On the other hand, muscle damage results in the accumulation of blood, tissue fluid and inflammatory cells, all of which aggravate the problem and really need to be dispersed. Contraction of the muscle is the most effective way to massage those fluids away, so we have two conflicting requirements: rest and exercise.

The Effects of Muscle Damage

When muscles are used less, they decrease in size (Fig 65). Such muscle wastage will occur with any continuing lameness, whether it is a foot problem, a specific muscle problem or any other long-term lameness. This has great significance when the horse becomes sound again, because it means that there is uneven force exerted by the muscle of that leg, or even by a specific muscle in the leg, and this predisposes to further injury. So the aim must be either to avoid wastage occurring in the first place, or to build the muscles back to their normal mass before returning the horse to work; using Niagara therapy, ultrasound, faradic stimulation or plain hand massage, it may be possible to achieve this goal without placing any weight-bearing demands on the leg. Swimming enables the horse actually to use the muscles without them being weight-bearing. As a general rule a horse should not be returned to fast work of any kind until the muscle mass on the affected side is symmetrical with that on the 'good' leg.

The Effects of Nerve Damage

If the nerve supply to a muscle is damaged so that it receives less stimulation than normal, it will also waste away. Techniques such as faradic stimulation may still cause the muscle to contract even though it does not contract during movement. The commonest situation where this occurs is radial paralysis, which usually results from a blow to the radial nerve as it passes over the front of the shoulder. A fall, a kick or a knock from a fence are the common causes of such paralysis, the result being that the horse is unable to pull the leg forwards in a normal manner. Nerves can recover from injury, but they do so slowly. Although stimulation of the muscle is important during recovery to counteract muscle wastage, stimulation of the nerve is even more important. Exercise, as far as the horse is capable, should be carried out on a little-and-often basis, sending repeated impulses down the nerve towards, but possibly initially not arriving at, the muscle.

Healing of Muscle Wounds

Wounds may involve considerable damage to muscle. If the two sides of a wound can be held firmly together, then muscles heal well because of their good blood supply. When it is not possible to hold the two cut surfaces together, the gap between them is called a 'dead space' and its existence slows healing, partly because fluid tends to collect in it and this favours infection. Drains may need to be inserted into muscle wounds to try and prevent this happening. Where muscle tissue has actually been lost in a wound, it can be replaced because muscle tissue will granulate and fill in the gap. The repaired muscle will often include scar tissue, however, and so will have reduced contractibility.

Azoturia

Azoturia, or exertional rhabdomyelosis, is a condition involving muscle damage that can vary from subclinical, where it can only be detected by laboratory tests, to an acute and even fatal degree. In the past everyone thought of azoturia as a feeding problem, but in fact it is more helpful to think of it as a muscle cell-wall problem. The cell wall allows some chemical substances to pass in and some to pass out, nutrients passing in and waste products out. Lactic acid formed during muscle contraction naturally passes out of the muscle cell. It then needs to be removed by the circulation,

because being an acid it can destroy tissue, including the very muscle cell from which it originated. Normally the muscle cell wall is able to withstand the effects of lactic acid, but in azoturia it is not able to do so and therefore suffers damage. Once this happens the muscle cannot contract properly because it relies on electrical impulses spreading evenly over its surface to control contraction, and that system no longer works.

In azoturia the damaged muscle cell starts to leak substances which are normally confined within the cell. We can detect two of these in the bloodstream, the enzymes CK and AST, and raised levels of these are the definitive way to diagnose the condition. The relative permeability of the muscle cell wall to CK and AST varies: in the first few days after acute muscle damage the cell wall appears to be more permeable to CK and so levels of this enzyme are relatively high. In more chronic conditions permeability to AST is greater.

Anything which increases the lactic acid levels around the muscle cells will increase the chances of damage occurring. Thus the classic case of azoturia is a horse which has stored large amounts of glycogen in its muscles during a day's rest when it was still fed a high energy ration. When the horse is next exercised that glycogen is broken down anaerobically and almost to the exclusion of any other energy sources. Large amounts of lactic acid are produced and muscle damage occurs. Anything which reduces the ability of the general circulation to remove the lactic acid produced also increases the likelihood of muscle damage. One of the main reasons for warming up horses before strenuous exercise is to ensure that the muscle circulation is opened up and working properly to remove lactic acid.

Some horses seem to be particularly prone to azoturia, and in many cases this is because their muscle cell walls are not stable, the electrolyte levels that control their permeability being abnormal. We may be able to detect this by looking at the blood levels of the electrolytes sodium, calcium and magnesium, and comparing them with the levels of the same electrolytes excreted in the urine. Although the levels will vary from one horse to another and from day to day, by comparing them with the levels of a relatively inert substance, creatine, we can calculate whether normal levels of electrolytes are present. Experience has shown that horses which are particularly susceptible to repeated attacks of azoturia tend to have abnormal electrolyte clearance into the urine. Correcting this

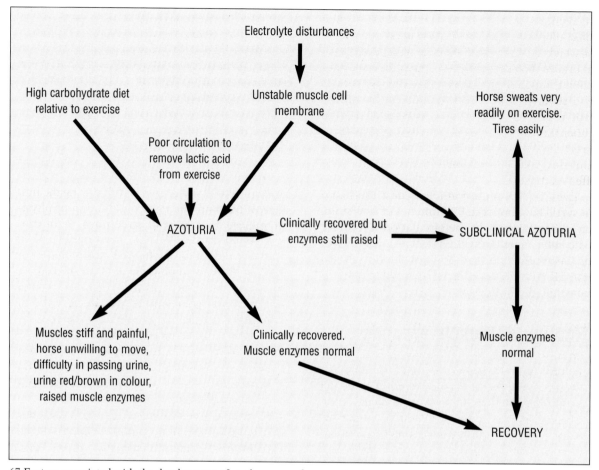

67 Factors associated with the development of, and recovery from, azoturia

by giving the horse more (or less) electrolytes will reduce their susceptibility to azoturia.

The classic form of azoturia, or setfast, is a horse which suddenly seizes up during fast work on the day following a rest day when it was still fed normal quantities of concentrates. For that reason the problem is also sometimes referred to as 'Monday morning disease'. The affected horse has very painful, hard gluteal and back muscles, because these large muscle masses are the major muscle glycogen stores. It may have a raised heart rate and temperature because of the pain, and it may sweat profusely. In severe cases it cannot move, and if it lies down it may be quite unable to get to its feet again.

One important symptom in such cases is the difficulty the horse may have in passing urine. The damage to the muscles releases the pigment myoglobin in the bloodstream, from where it has to be removed by filtration in the kidneys. The sheer quantity of myoglobin released tends to clog the filtering system, and drastically reduces kidney function. Any myoglobin which does get through makes the urine look very dark or brown in colour.

■ Treatment

Maintaining kidney function is to a large extent the most important consideration of treatment for azoturia. It may be possible to open up the filtration system by the administration of diuretics such as frusemide, which increase urine production. In more severe cases large amounts of intravenous fluids may have to be given to flush the kidneys. Corticosteroids help to reduce the inflammatory reaction in the damaged muscles.

If there is any suspicion that a horse is about to develop azoturia then it must be rested immediately. There is no question of walking home, for example, because any further muscle effort may drastically exacerbate the problem. There have even been cases where travelling an affected horse home from a competition, a laudable aim in most circumstances, has resulted in the horse becoming recumbent in the horsebox. Do not forget the muscular effort involved for the horse in bracing its weight as the horsebox goes around corners, or brakes. Massage helps to maintain the circulation through the muscles and so speeds up lactic acid removal. Similarly the muscles should be kept reasonably warm with a blanket or rug, rather than cooled. Cold-water hosing is particularly dangerous because it can cause the shut-down of superficial blood vessels in the affected muscles.

Even as the acute pain subsides, the horse must still have box rest. Five minutes of slow walking in hand may help the circulation to remove toxic substances from the affected muscles, but the basic principle is to box rest the horse until both CK and AST levels have returned to normal, even though this may take weeks. Returning a horse to normal work before the muscles have freely healed is one of the main reasons why it has further attacks of azoturia. A quick return to work is no substitute for having a fully recovered horse which can safely take part in even fast work.

Acute azoturia can also occur in horses which have *not* been rested the day before; which have not been given high concentrate rations; and even in some which have only done a small quantity of fast work. The stability of the muscle cell membrane is the crucial factor. It has been suggested that vitamin E can help affected horses to recover more quickly. This has not been definitely proven, but it may be worth giving vitamin E supplements to affected horses. Increased levels of electrolytes

can be very beneficial. The best supplement for the purpose comprises 4 parts calcium gluconate; 6 parts ground limestone; and 8 parts common salt, all mixed thoroughly. 28g (1oz) twice a day is a reasonable starting dose. If a creatine clearance test still shows abnormalities with such a dose then it can be increased. Even just 28g (1oz) of salt per day in the drinking water can help both to prevent and to treat azoturia.

Subclinical azoturia is extremely common in competition horses. Most horses show significantly raised muscle enzyme levels during the first stage of training due to a combination of physical muscle trauma and subclinical azoturia. Increasing the workload before the muscles have stabilised themselves is likely to perpetuate the problem. The symptoms of subclinical azoturia are dullness and/or a tendency to sweat at the slightest exercise. Owners may be tempted to respond by increasing the amount of high energy food fed, but this is not a wise thing to do. Nor is increasing the workload in an attempt to improve fitness. If the diagnosis is confirmed from a blood sample then rest is the only answer, even though the horse looks well in itself.

The stable management of a horse which has had azoturia is very important. Feeding should be at precise, spaced intervals every day, and the horse should be exercised every single day. 30 to 60g (1 to 2oz) of salt a day should be given in the drinking water, unless a specially balanced mixture is available. Alfalfa hay or nuts can be very beneficial because of their high mineral content.

THE BACK

It is important to understand how the horse's back works: what can move and why it does so. After all, it is the back upon which the rider sits, and which links the front and back legs to provide co-ordinated propulsion. When we talk about the horse's back we usually mean the spinal cord, the thirty-one bony vertebrae which protect it, and the muscles which move those vertebrae.

Although it links the front and back legs there is no substantial joint between the spine and those legs. Indeed there is no contact at all between the front legs, which take 60 per cent of the horse's weight, and the spine, because the spine is actually suspended in a powerful muscular sling between the two legs. There is, however, direct contact with the hind legs via the pelvis. Here the spinal vertebrae and pelvis form the sacro-iliac joints. However, these really only consist of flat areas of contact rather than one articulating joint such as forms the hip. There is a short but power-ful ligament, the sacro-iliac ligament, which holds the spine and pelvis together.

The interconnection of all the structures around the back is emphasised by the concept of the horse's back being a 'bow' which is kept under tension by its 'bowstring' (Fig 68). In this case the bowstring consists of the sternum, or bony breast bone, the muscles of the abdomen, the muscles which pull the front legs backwards, those which

pull the hind legs forwards and the sheets of fibrous tissue, or fascia, which join everything in the midline under the horse's body. The muscles which pull the front legs forwards, those that pull the hind legs backwards and the muscles along the top of the back all tend to straighten out the bow. Nor must we forget two important variables: the weight of a rider and the weight of the abdomi-nal contents. The rider's weight acts to straighten out the bow, whilst the weight of the guts (which of course depends on how much the horse has eaten or drunk during the hours before exercise) acts to bend the bow.

This concept of the horse's back acting like a bow is completely different to the way that our back works, because we have turned our spine through 90° with the ground and removed the anchorage of the weight-bearing front limb. It is pointless to draw analogies between a human back and an equine back because they function entirely differently. Similarly some of the methods used to treat human back problems cannot phys-ically have the same effect on the horse's back.

In the performance horse we are concerned with movement of the back and the problems which arise either to restrict movement or to make it painful. There can obviously be considerable movement in all directions between the spine and the front legs. In contrast, very little movement is possible at the sacro-iliac joint. Unfortunately a whole sub-culture of completely untrained 'back people' has grown up in the horse world, and as a result one frequently hears the suggestion that a horse's pelvis is 'out of alignment', or tilted. In fact these are mostly physical impossibilities. The hind legs are firmly attached to it via the pelvis, and if it were rotated even 2cm (1in) around its axis, then one leg would be pulled off the ground and the other held at an angle under the horse's body.

When we look at a horse's pelvic region from behind and see one side apparently higher than the other, then this merely reflects the different amounts of weight being put on the two legs. The

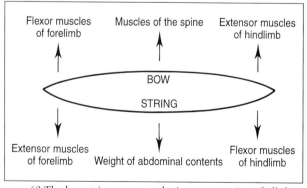

68 The bowstring concept: the interconnection of all the structures around the back are like a bow, kept under tension by its bowstring

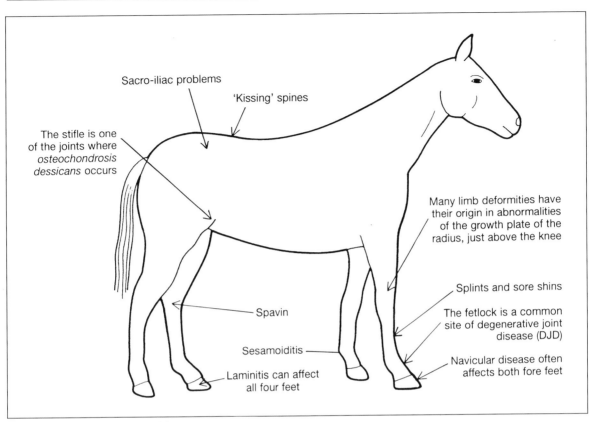

Sacro-iliac problems

'Kissing' spines

The stifle is one
of the joints where
*osteochondrosis
dessicans* occurs

Many limb deformities have
their origin in abnormalities
of the growth plate of the
radius, just above the knee

Splints and sore shins

The fetlock is a common
site of degenerative joint
disease (DJD)

Spavin

Sesamoiditis

Laminitis can affect
all four feet

Navicular disease often
affects both fore feet

69 Sites of possible skeletal problems

spinal column as a whole twists to accomodate this, but as the rotation is spread right along the back, the amount of movement of each vertebra is minute and cannot be seen with the eye. When someone claims to 'put back' a horse's displaced pelvis, what they are really doing is to make the horse take its weight evenly on both hind legs again. A moment's thought will reveal that if the junction between the spine and the pelvis really did allow movement to take place, then it would be unstable at every stride when the immense forces of propulsion applied to the long levers of the legs moved the weight of the horse forwards via just this attachment.

Post-mortem studies have been carried out on the horse's back to find out how much movement can occur and where. The general rule is that movement is more likely to be possible the further along the spine one goes. In other words, the further away you are from that crucial rigid sacro-iliac junction, the more movement is possible. Filming a horse from above has shown that when it bends to the left or to the right then the thoraco-lumbar region, which is the section of the back between the fore- and hind legs, is still basically rigid, and most of the bending takes place around the shoul-

der area. The horse's long neck has evolved to allow the head to be bent or curved to one side in relation to the tail without compromising the thoraco-lumbar region.

Having emphasised the impossibility of the back person's sole diagnosis, namely displacement of the bones of the back, I must immediately state that this does not mean that the horse does not suffer serious back problems; nor does it mean that properly trained physiotherapists and chiropractors cannot help the horse. Back problems can be divided into five groups: muscle spasm, kissing spines, sacro-iliac problems, fractures and imaginary problems. The latter includes lamenesses where the site of the pain has not, for a variety of reasons, been located and so is blamed on the back. It also includes mouth and bit problems that prevent the horse responding to the aids as it is expected to do. Finally it includes those horses whose owners have a falsely high opinion of the horse's capabilities and so prefer to blame its lack of performance on a back problem than on a lack of ability. One survey found that 20 per cent of horses said to have a back problem didn't have anything demonstrably wrong with their back at all.

Muscle Spasm and Back Problems

I want to discuss back-muscle spasm in some detail, partly because muscle problems are a common source of back pain, and partly because they are a problem the owner can recognise. Most of these back problems are recognised indirectly. In other words the rider is dissatisfied with some aspect of the horse's performance and looks for a cause, rather than the owner finding a painful area on the horse's back. Despite this it should be obvious that if a problem is serious enough to cause a noticeable effect on performance, then there must be significant pain somewhere.

We can test the lateral flexibility of the horse's back by taking something such as a ballpoint pen and, pressing lightly, drawing it along the side of the horse's chest and abdomen. The horse should bend slightly towards the pen. If there is pain it will either hold itself rigid or over-react when the muscles of the affected area come into play. Another test is to hold a bucket of feed against the horse's chest wall and see how near the horse's mouth can get to it.

There are five distinct places along the horse's back where the majority of muscle pain can be detected. Interestingly most of these correspond to acupuncture points as well, which has some relevance to treatment. Using one finger, press on the muscles about 4cm (1.5in) out from the midline and move the finger right along the back on each side. Then imagine where the back of the saddle ends and come forwards 10cm (4in) and press (still 4cm/1.5in out from the midline). You may need to try a couple of centimetres on either side of the spot to reassure yourself that you have tested the right area. Then move about 10cm (4in) towards the tail and press again. Then move a further 10cm and press again. Next, press around the upper border of the tuber coxae, the bony prominence that marks the front of the wing of the pelvis. Finally, imagine a line across the horse's back at 45° from the tuber coxae, and press halfway along this line (Fig 70).

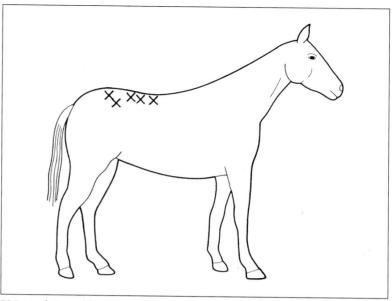

70 Lateral view of horse showing pain pressure points on its back

■ The Normal Horse and the Cold-Backed Horse

Normal horses show no reaction at all when you press on these spots, but horses with muscle spasm will show a reaction at one or more spots on one or both sides. That reaction may take the form of a sudden sinking of the back when the pressure is applied, or it may just show as a visible twitching of the muscle around this point. If a horse gives a reaction consistently when the pressure is applied then it has a problem. It may not be a serious problem, and it may not be a problem that requires treatment, but it is abnormal. It is appropriate at this point to consider 'cold-backed' horses, which sink towards the ground (sometimes by an alarming amount) when the saddle or a heavy object is put on their back. They recover quickly and show no further symptoms, in reaction even to the weight of the rider. I do not like the term 'cold-backed' because it obscures the fact that this is a *pain* reaction – the horse reacts to the pressure in a reflex way and then quickly tightens up all the muscles of the back so that if you lifted up the saddle and immediately replaced it, the horse would not respond any further. In possibly the majority of cases, cold-backed horses will give a significant reaction to one or more of the pressure points described earlier, confirming that back pain is involved rather than it just being a harmless habit.

■ The Vicious Circle of Back Pain

When a horse develops a localised muscle spasm it can become self-perpetuating, and long after the initial cause of the spasm has gone, the spasm itself remains. It may then require relief of the spasm to break what is basically a vicious circle between pain caused by the muscle fibres in spasm sending messages to the spinal cord that something is wrong and so triggering off a reflex localised muscle contraction that reinforces the spasm. Manipulation of the horse's back does not reposition any out-of-place bones, but it can relieve muscle spasm. One effect of this may be that the back muscles look symmetrical again: *ie* there is a visible change. There are various forms of manipulation, but the basic principle is that a sudden movement causes all the muscle fibres in the area to contract in reflex, and when they subsequently relax the fibres which were previously in spasm relax as well. If pressure is then applied to the previously painful area it will hopefully no longer stimulate any reaction. It does not require a degree in veterinary science to see that an area of muscle reacts to pressure, to carry out a simple manoeuvre and then to prove that you have done some good by showing that the muscle no longer reacts abnormally. The reason why manipulation is frowned on by so many vets is that the back manipulators have insisted on building up the mumbo-jumbo about replacing dislocated bones and suchlike, and have not admitted that they are simply applying a pain- and spasm-relieving technique.

Secondary Muscle Spasm

It is important, for instance, to realise that the muscle spasm may be secondary to some other problem, and in this case the spasm will probably return, despite its temporary relief. Indeed it may return within minutes if the horse is just walked around and then re-examined. Commonly a horse will develop an area of muscle spasm as a result of attempting to reposition its weight in order to reduce the effects of lameness. Unless that original lameness is treated at the same time as the manipulation, then the muscle spasm will return. Vets sometimes find that a horse has received repeated visits from the 'back man', each of which probably relieved the muscle spasm temporarily, before the owner eventually called the vet out and a chronic lameness problem such as spavin was diagnosed. Even where there is no underlying problem, there will be some horses where the spasm reforms because the muscle fibres are still over-reactive. Manipulation has no preventive effect to stop this – once the procedure is over, the muscles are on their own, either to recover or to go into spasm again.

■ Manipulative Treatment

Manipulation is a skill. It can, however, be carried out by unskilled people, although it is less likely to be successful in their hands. As you cannot do any harm to the horse using the simple technique I am about to describe, it might be considered a skill worth acquiring: place the fleshy part of the hand at the base of the thumb on the horse's back at the point of back muscle pain. Move the hand until it is lodged against the top of the bony dorsal process of the horse's vertebra. Then with downward pressure, push your hand *suddenly* away from you. You will feel your hand slip over the top of the dorsal process and the horse will dip its back for a second. The first time that you perform the manipulation will probably stimulate the most obvious reaction from the horse because it will not have been expecting the sudden tweak to its back. Now reassess the amount of muscle spasm. It may well have disappeared from that local area. If it hasn't, repeat the manoeuvre once or twice.

It is very satisfying to locate an area of muscle pain, manipulate it, and then confirm that the horse no longer shows any discomfort to pressure over that area. It is usual to box rest the horse for a couple of days after manipulation; as mentioned earlier, this is necessary whilst the muscle settles down. It can be even more dramatic to relieve muscle spasm by cold laser therapy. Holding the emission head $1/2$cm ($1/4$in) above the horse's skin over the affected point for 5–10 minutes can abolish the pain response without even touching the horse. This also provides visible proof that laser therapy does work, because no amount of standing and looking at a horse's back on its own will abolish the abnormal response to pressure.

Kissing Spines

The major bony problem involving the vertebrae is a condition known picturesquely as 'kissing

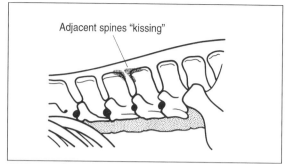

Adjacent spines "kissing"

71 The condition known as 'kissing spines'

spines'. New bone forming on the dorsal processes of two adjacent vertebrae drastically narrows the gap between the tops of the vertebrae until they can touch (hence 'kissing') and rub (Fig 71). It is important to realise that the mere fact that the two dorsal processes are in contact does not necessarily mean that the horse will have a problem. X-rays have shown many trouble-free horses with this abnormality. Undoubtedly, though, on some occasions the condition does cause pain temporarily or even permanently. If a vet suspects that there are kissing spines causing pain, he may inject a small quantity of local anaesthetic down between the vertebrae. If the symptoms then disappear, the kissing spines are likely to be significant. Increasing use is also being made of nuclear scintigraphy to show whether the bone is abnormally active or not.

■ Treatment

When the diagnosis has been made, there are two possible treatments. This sort of problem in many horses will settle down with six months' box rest – not always an easy thing to persuade an owner to consider, but a cheap form of treatment. If this is not successful and scintigraphy shows that the bone is still active, surgery may be considered. This consists of literally cutting off the tops of the affected spinal process (or processes); it is major surgery requiring further convalescence afterwards.

Spinal Cord Problems

Horses do not suffer from 'slipped-disc' problems in the way that people, or indeed dogs, do. There is, however, one condition which produces similar symptoms. Pressure on the horse's spinal cord in the upper neck region results in ataxia and the

loss of the horse's ability to control standing and walking properly. Eventually the horse either becomes paralysed and cannot stand at all, or it suffers serious injuries such as broken bones as it staggers around. Such a horse is said to be a wobbler, for obvious reasons. Classically wobblers are young, growing horses. In this situation the pressure is caused by abnormal growth and maturation of the vertebrae in the upper neck. However, older horses can develop similar symptoms due to new bone laid down during degenerative joint disease of the joints in the upper neck.

Especially when the symptoms develop gradually, it is relatively easy to diagnose the wobbler syndrome just on clinical grounds. Endoscopy of the horse's larynx may help to confirm the diagnosis because the recurrent laryngeal nerve, which when damaged produces laryngeal paralysis, originates further down the spine, and if there is severe damage to the spinal cord in the neck then the so-called slap test will not be positive. In other words, when the horse's withers are slapped with the flat of the hand, the larynx will not be observed to close and open again in reflex. Radiography of the neck to investigate the situation requires a very powerful x-ray machine, but it has the advantage that under general anaesthetic a liquid which shows up on x-rays can be injected into the horse's spinal canal. This technique is called a myelogram. An obstruction to the passage along the canal of the liquid when it reaches the precise area where the canal is narrowed is the ultimate confirmation of the condition.

■ Treatment

In many cases euthanasia is the only choice if a horse becomes a wobbler. Where nutritional factors alone are responsible for abnormal bone development, it may be possible to correct these and hope that with normal growth the spinal canal will no longer press on the spinal cord. Surgery has also been carried out to relieve the pressure but it is unlikely to resolve the condition sufficiently to allow the horse to take part in competitions.

Sacro-Iliac Problems

Sprain of the sacro-iliac ligament is a serious problem for the competition horse. There is no direct treatment apart from rest, and the majority of affected horses fail to respond even after 6–12 months of box rest. The ligament is responsible for holding the pelvis (and so the hind legs) in contact with the spine. Any movement therefore puts tension on the ligament and causes pain if it has been damaged. In addition the contact areas, or facets, between the spine and the pelvis may develop DJD, causing further pain.

The main effect of sacro-iliac problems is a loss of flexibility or control at the hind quarters. Affected horses usually hold their back muscles rigid (which in turn often results in muscle spasm) in order to reduce tension and movement. One common result of this is that the horse prefers to canter rather than to trot because it is easier for it to hold the area rigid at the canter or gallop than at the more relaxed gait. Indeed it may be difficult to persuade the horse to make a smooth transition from the walk to the trot, but easy to go direct to the canter. Affected horses can jump cross-country-style fences but may have difficulty around a show-jumping course. They can race, but may have difficulty doing dressage or basic flatwork.

It has been suggested that far from being an advantage, a well developed 'jumper's bump' on a horse's spine is a sign that the horse will be more susceptible to sacro-iliac problems, both because of conformation and because of lack of muscular support. Affected horses may carry their tails to one side when trotting. When standing squarely and viewed from behind, the gluteal muscles on the affected side will be flat or even concave due to lack of normal usage rather than their normal convex outline.

As mentioned earlier, box rest is the treatment for sacro-iliac problems, initially with the use of anti-inflammatory drugs. Exercise is limited to 10–15 minutes' walking in hand twice a day. Unfortunately many horses appear to recover, only to relapse as their subsequent training peaks before a major competition. The more flexible the horse needs to be for its work, the more likely it is to relapse. The history of a horse with obvious ability which loses that ability every time in the run-up to the big competition is well known. Such horses may be able to perform whilst on painkillers, but of course this usually precludes their participation in competitions.

The Saddle on the Horse's Back

Most back problems stem from our insistence on riding horses, and the introduction of a saddle between the rider and the horse only makes matters worse. The saddle is designed to spread the rider's weight over the horse's rib cage, which is obviously well sprung and so can absorb the jolts from the rider, and to protect the vertebrae. If the saddle is not fitted properly there will be contact between it and the bony spinal processes, as well as pressure on the *longissimus dorsi* muscle as it runs the length of the back and is pinched against those processes. It is surprising how many competition riders use a saddle for their own comfort or stability during the competition, and never spare a thought for the horse. If there is any doubt as to whether the saddle fits properly then the common response is to put a numnah or pad between the saddle and the horse, thus introducing yet another possible cause of friction against the horse's skin. In my opinion a

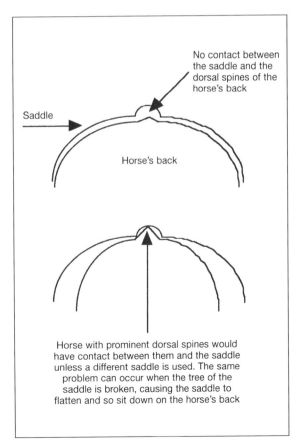

No contact between the saddle and the dorsal spines of the horse's back

Saddle

Horse's back

Horse with prominent dorsal spines would have contact between them and the saddle unless a different saddle is used. The same problem can occur when the tree of the saddle is broken, causing the saddle to flatten and so sit down on the horse's back

72 The Effect of a badly-fitting saddle on the spine

competition horse ridden with a numnah indicates a rider with a wrong set of priorities. The horse would undoubtedly perform better in a properly fitted saddle.

One way to assess how well a saddle fits is to ride a short distance without a girth. Then put French chalk or talcum powder on the under surface of the saddle and put the saddle on the horse. This will produce a white image of the areas of contact on the horse when the saddle is removed. There should, of course, be a clear band down the withers and centre of the back where no contact occurs. Discomfort from an ill-fitting saddle doesn't necessarily result in muscle spasm in the saddle area; often a spasm will be in the lumbar region immediately behind the saddle, so it may be missed unless the whole back area is examined.

■ Saddle Sores

Areas of localised friction between saddle and skin produce saddle sores. As an added complication, dirt rubbed into the broken skin may result in secondary infection. We cannot expect a saddle sore to heal whilst the friction continues, so the horse should be rested. And of course there is little point in leaving the back without a saddle for a few days until healing is underway, and then putting the same ill-fitting saddle back, because the problem will only recur.

■ Treatment

The application of malic, benzoic and salycilic acid preparations to saddle sores helps to encourage speedy healing. If the horse has to be ridden, then a non-stick mellolin dressing should be placed over the saddle sore. A gel weight displacement pad should then be placed between the dressing and the saddle; these pads help to ensure an even distribution of pressure over their whole area, limiting the amount of pressure and movement over the saddle sore. Even so, healing will proceed more quickly if the horse isn't ridden at all, even with a pad.

73 Dirty, ill-fitting tack is a major predisposing cause of girth galls

Repeated saddle sores, often followed by the appearance of patches of white hair when the skin heals over, are not evidence that the horse has a sensitive skin; they indicate that its owner is still using a badly fitting saddle, and should seek expert help. Even when the skin surface isn't broken, localised pressure can produce the equivalent of a corn, namely a localised area of fibrous tissue which extends down into the underlying muscles. Pressure on this saddle or girth gall produces pain just as much as if there was something trapped between the saddle and the skin. Although rest from riding with the saddle may produce an improvement, severe cases may require surgery to resolve the condition.

When a Girth Gall is not a Girth Gall

The saddle area is also a common site of collagen necrosis, or nodular skin disease. This appears as nodules in the skin that may rupture at their point, revealing what feels like (and indeed is) a tiny piece of chalk-like material. The condition appears under the microscope to be some kind of allergic skin disease, but no cause of the allergy is usually found.

Treatment

Most cases of nodular skin disease require no treatment because they do not affect the horse's performance at all. Corticosteroids will usually cause the disappearance of the lumps temporarily, but they may also come and go without any treatment. If a large nodule rubs raw under the saddle, surgery may be necessary to remove it.

The Rider's Responsibility

It would be wrong to conclude a section on back problems without drawing attention to the role of the rider in their cause and effect. Very few riders sit exactly symmetrically, and quite a number thump down into the saddle at the trot and canter. Some riders are also overweight for the type of horse they are riding. All these factors predispose to back problems, not least by encouraging the horse to stiffen up its back to withstand the strain. This in turn often triggers off muscle spasm or saddle problems.

LAMENESS: THE FUTURE

We have tended to take for granted the great advances that have been made over recent years in the treatment of musculo-skeletal problems. There are still large holes in our ability to return horses to full work after major lameness problems. One of the best known of these is our inability to repair fractures of the major long bones of the legs, by which I mean the humerus, radius and ulna of the front leg and the femur, tibia and fibula of the hind leg. Even non-horsey people know that we have to shoot horses with broken legs.

The problem is that the athletic horse has relatively fine legs, with small bones compared with the overall weight of the horse's head, neck and body. As a result great leverage is exerted on the bones of the leg when the horse gets to its feet from lying down. When the horse is still suffering the effects of an anaesthetic that leverage is even less controlled; indeed, fracture of a long bone is one of the known complications of general anaesthesia in horses. So we *can* repair fractures of the long bones, but so far recovery all too often breaks whatever implant we have used in the process. Even when the horse is safely on its feet after the surgery there is still a tremendous amount of force on the repair. Sometimes this loosens the screws used to anchor the stainless-steel plates used, and sometimes the plate or plates just give way as a result of metal fatigue.

One of the problems I foresee when eventually we do manage to repair these upper limb fractures is that because all the muscles of the leg are concentrated in this region, it will be difficult to achieve repair without damaging the muscles. In other words, the horse will still not become sound enough to return to work.

There are two important conditions where we stll need to discover a way to significantly increase the blood flow through small blood vessels. Although navicular disease is undoubtedly a wear-and-tear problem; many horses become sound if, either naturally or by the use of drugs, the blood flow to the navicular bone is increased. The success of warfarin and now isoxsuprine in returning affected horses to competition proves this. Equally the significant percentage of navicular disease cases that either do not go sound, or who go sound only to become lame again later, shows the need for more effective peripheral vasodilators, in other words drugs that open the blood vessels at the extremities such as the foot.

Laminitis is another condition where we have achieved success by using vasodilators, this time to make it easier for blood to circulate through the laminae of the foot. By giving the horse a small dose of radio-active material and measuring how much of the radioactivity gets into the foot of a horse with laminitis compared with a normal horse's foot, we have proved that laminitis is all about blood flow. It looks as if the majority of the pain associated with laminitis is due to oxygen lack because of lack of blood flow. If enough oxygen reaches the foot then the horse will quickly (ie one to two days) become sound. The difficulty lies in finding how to ensure that oxygen supply.

Because the owners of competition horses are very impatient, they are not prepared to let nature heal things; they need a magic cure-all which will speed up the general repair process. By using a drug called bapten we can influence the quality of tendon repair, but we still can't speed up the repair itself. As a result horses are sometimes turned out to pasture too early because the leg looks and feels alright, but in fact is not yet back to normal. If we could discover a way to increase the rate at which new collagen is laid down in tendon repair then this would have a great effect on all spheres of competition.

Many researchers feel that the therapeutic breakthroughs of the next few decades will be metabolic modifiers, drugs which act to alter how the horse heals itself rather than drugs which are solutions in their own right. Indeed bapten is such a drug. It stops one process occurring, namely cross-linking between collagen fibres, without stopping the rest of the healing process. If only we could also speed up the rest of the process then we might have a healed tendon without the adhesions which form with time during slow natural healing. So far we have not got a drug which can either prevent adhesions forming or 'dissolve' them when they have already formed. However, the process of adhesion formation is not too dissimilar to the cross-linking during tendon healing, so there must be hope that one day we will find such a drug.

At one time we could rely on a steady stream of drugs developed for the human field coming across to the veterinary pharmacy. The stringent licensing requirements now in force in most parts of the world for veterinary products mean that the cost of licensing drugs for horse use, where the number of doses used per year will inevitably be low, is not justified by the potential sales. So fewer equine drugs come onto the market now in the developed countries than would have done fifteen to twenty years ago.

INDEX

Page numbers printed in *italics* indicate illustrations